THE CAMBRIDGE BIBLE COMMENTARY
NEW ENGLISH BIBLE

R17

GENERAL EDITORS
P. R. ACKROYD, A. R. C. LEANEY, J. W. PACKER

1 AND 2 ESDRAS

THE FIRST AND
SECOND BOOKS OF
ESDRAS

COMMENTARY ON I ESDRAS BY
R. J. COGGINS
AND
COMMENTARY ON 2 ESDRAS BY
M. A. KNIBB
Lecturers in Old Testament Studies, King's College, London

CAMBRIDGE UNIVERSITY PRESS

CAMBRIDGE

LONDON · NEW YORK · MELBOURNE

Published by the Syndics of the Cambridge University Press
The Pitt Building, Trumpington Street, Cambridge CB2 IRP
Bentley House, 200 Euston Road, London NW1 2DB
32 East 57th Street, New York, NY 10022, USA
296 Beaconsfield Parade, Middle Park, Melbourne 3206, Australia

First published 1979

Printed in Great Britain at the
University Press, Cambridge

Library of Congress cataloguing in publication data

Bible. O.T. Apocrypha. 1 Edras. English. New English. 1978. The first
and second books of Esdras.
(The Cambridge Bible commentary, New English Bible)
Includes index.
1. Bible. O.T. Apocrypha. 1 Esdras – Commentaries. 2. Bible. O.T.
Apocrypha. 2 Esdras – Commentaries. I. Bible. O.T. Apocrypha.
2 Esdras. English. New English. 1978. II. Coggins, R. J., 1929–. III.
Knibb, M. A., 1938–. IV. Series.

BS1713 1978 229'.1'077 78-16420
ISBN 0 521 08656 6 hard covers
ISBN 0 521 09757 6 paperback

GENERAL EDITORS' PREFACE

The aim of this series is to provide the text of the New English Bible closely linked to a commentary in which the results of modern scholarship are made available to the general reader. Teachers and young people have been especially kept in mind. The commentators have been asked to assume no specialized theological knowledge, and no knowledge of Greek, Latin and Hebrew. Bare references to other literature and multiple references to other parts of the Bible have been avoided. Actual quotations have been given as often as possible.

The completion of the New Testament part of the series in 1967 provided the basis upon which the production of the much larger Old Testament and Apocrypha series could be undertaken. With the publication of this volume and its companion (*Genesis 12–50*), the whole series is complete. The welcome accorded to the series in its earlier stages was an encouragement to the editors to follow the same general pattern throughout, and an attempt has been made to take account of criticisms which have been offered. The Old Testament and Apocrypha volumes have included the full footnotes provided by the translators, since these are essential for the understanding of the text.

Within the severe limits imposed by the size and scope of the series, each commentator has attempted to set out the main findings of recent biblical scholarship and to describe the historical background to the text.

The main theological issues have also been critically discussed.

Much attention has been given to the form of the volumes. The aim is to produce books each of which will be read consecutively from first to last page. The introductory material leads naturally into the text, which itself leads into the alternating sections of the commentary.

The series is accompanied by three volumes of a more general character. *Understanding the Old Testament* sets out to provide the larger historical and archaeological background, to say something about the life and thought of the people of the Old Testament, and to answer the question 'Why should we study the Old Testament?' *The Making of the Old Testament* is concerned with the formation of the books of the Old Testament and Apocrypha in the context of the ancient Near Eastern world, and with the ways in which these books have come down to us in the life of the Jewish and Christian communities. *Old Testament Illustrations* contains maps, diagrams and photographs with an explanatory text. These three volumes are designed to provide material helpful to the understanding of the individual books and their commentaries, but they are also prepared so as to be of use quite independently.

With the completion of this project, there are many whom the General Editors wish to thank. The contributors who have produced their manuscripts and co-operated willingly in revisions suggested to them must clearly be mentioned first. With them we thank the succession of members of the staff of the Cambridge University Press, but above all Mr Michael H. Black, now Publisher at the Press, who has joined so fully in the planning and development of the series and who has been present at all the editorial meetings from the initiation of the project to its conclusion.

P.R.A.
A.R.C.L.
J.W.P.

CONTENTS

CONTENTS

THE FOOTNOTES TO THE
N.E.B. TEXT

The footnotes to the N.E.B. text are designed to help the reader either to understand particular points of detail – the meaning of a name, the presence of a play upon words – or to give information about the actual text. Where the Hebrew (Greek or Latin) text appears to be erroneous, or there is doubt about its precise meaning, it may be necessary to turn to manuscripts which offer a different wording, or to ancient translations of the text which may suggest a better reading, or to offer a new explanation based upon conjecture. In such cases, the footnotes supply very briefly an indication of the evidence, and whether the solution proposed is one that is regarded as possible or as probable. Various abbreviations are used in the footnotes:

(1) Some abbreviations are simply of terms used in explaining a point: *ch(s).*, chapter(s); *cp.*, compare; *lit.*, literally; *mng.*, meaning; *MS(S).*, manuscript(s), i.e. Hebrew manuscript(s), unless otherwise stated; *om.*, omit(s); *or*, indicating an alternative interpretation; *poss.*, possible; *prob.*, probable; *rdg.*, reading; *Vs(s).*, Version(s).

(2) Other abbreviations indicate sources of information from which better interpretations or readings may be obtained.

Aq. Aquila, a Greek translator of the Old Testament (perhaps about A.D. 130) characterized by great literalness.

Aram. Aramaic – may refer to the text in this language (used in parts of Ezra and Daniel), or to the meaning of an Aramaic word. Aramaic belongs to the same language family as Hebrew, and is known from about 1000 B.C. over a wide area of the Middle East, including Palestine.

Heb. Hebrew – may refer to the Hebrew text or may indicate the literal meaning of the Hebrew word.

Josephus Flavius Josephus (A.D. 37/8–about 100), author of the *Jewish Antiquities*, a survey of the whole history of his people, directed partly at least to a non-Jewish audience, and of various other works, notably one on the *Jewish War* (that of A.D. 66–73) and a defence of Judaism (*Against Apion*).

Luc. Sept. Lucian's recension of the Septuagint, an important edition made in Antioch in Syria about the end of the third century A.D.

Pesh. Peshitta or Peshitto, the Syriac version of the Old Testament. Syriac is the name given chiefly to a form of Eastern Aramaic used by the Christian community. The translation varies in quality, and is at many points influenced by the Septuagint or the Targums.

Sam. Samaritan Pentateuch – the form of the first five books of the Old Testament as used by the Samaritan community. It is written in Hebrew in a special form of the Old Hebrew script, and preserves an important form of the text, somewhat influenced by Samaritan ideas.

Scroll(s) Scroll(s), commonly called the Dead Sea Scrolls, found at or near Qumran from 1947 onwards. These important manuscripts shed light on the state of the Hebrew text as it was developing in the last centuries B.C. and the first century A.D.

Sept. Septuagint (meaning 'seventy'; often abbreviated as the Roman numeral LXX), the name given to the main Greek version of the Old Testament. According to tradition, the Pentateuch was translated in Egypt in the third century B.C. by 70 (or 72) translators, six from each tribe, but the precise nature of its origin and development is not fully known. It was intended to provide Greek-speaking Jews with a convenient translation. Subsequently it came to be much revered by the Christian community.

Symm. Symmachus, another Greek translator of the Old Testament (beginning of the third century A.D.), who tried to combine literalness with good style. Both Lucian and Jerome viewed his version with favour.

Targ. Targum, a name given to various Aramaic versions of the Old Testament, produced over a long period and eventually standardized, for the use of Aramaic-speaking Jews.

Theod. Theodotion, the author of a revision of the Septuagint (probably second century A.D.), very dependent on the Hebrew text.

Vulg. Vulgate, the most important Latin version of the Old Testament, produced by Jerome about A.D. 400, and the text most used throughout the Middle Ages in western Christianity.

[...] In the text itself square brackets are used to indicate probably late additions to the Hebrew text.

(Fuller discussion of a number of these points may be found in *The Making of the Old Testament* in this series.)

THE FIRST AND SECOND BOOKS OF

ESDRAS

✶ ✶ ✶ ✶ ✶ ✶ ✶ ✶ ✶ ✶ ✶ ✶ ✶

THE EZRA WRITINGS

To the modern reader, one of the most perplexing pheno-
mena which confront him when he begins any study of the
Bible concerns the authorship of books. There are two basic
difficulties which affect many parts of the Old and New
Testaments, and a third which is more characteristic of,
though not peculiar to, the Apocrypha. The two more
general problems are, first, the fact that many biblical books –
prophetic collections, wisdom writings, gospels – have gone
through a long stage of oral transmission, with resultant
modifications, before being set down in writing; and secondly,
the ancient world differed from modern ideas of authenticity
or 'copyright'. Additions might be made to existing collections in the belief that if the 'founding father' of such a
collection were still alive, the addition now being made
would have been his message for a new situation. The later
chapters of the book of Isaiah, especially chs. 40–66, or some
of the letters attributed to Paul but probably written by a
later writer (for example, Ephesians) can best be explained
in this way.

In the last centuries B.C., however, another custom became common, and this represents the third point to which
reference has been made. New writings were issued under a
pseudonym, usually some famous figure from Israel's past.
Many suggestions have been put forward to explain this
custom, ranging from a fear of being punished by authority
if the writer's real identity was discovered, to a simple
desire for secrecy and mystification. Perhaps the established

I

custom that existing writings might be added to and up-dated provides at least part of the explanation. In any case, it should be borne in mind that the book of Daniel is usually held to be an example of such pseudonymous writing, and that there are several examples of this practice in the Apocrypha, including the two books of Esdras.

Though many figures from Israel's past – Adam, Abraham, Moses, the prophets – were associated with these pseudonymous writings, certain individuals became particularly prominent in this connection. Among them was Ezra. He lived in the fifth or fourth century B.C., and played a leading part in establishing the Jerusalem community of his time (see Ezra 7–10; Neh. 8). Later tradition came to regard him as the second founder of Judaism, after Moses, and so it is not surprising that he should have given his name to various pseudonymous writings.

Both the books dealt with in this volume are linked with Ezra in this way. ('Esdras' is simply the Greek form of the Hebrew name.) That is, however, virtually all that they have in common. Even the most cursory reading will show that they represent very different kinds of writing. It is essential to remember that 1 and 2 Esdras cannot be regarded in the same way as 1 and 2 Kings, for example, where the second book is simply a continuation of the first. The first and second books of Esdras stand quite apart. Before examining each book separately, however, it is useful to set out in a table the various names which have been given in different traditions to some of the writings associated with Ezra, since they are very liable to cause confusion. From this point on, the two books are treated quite separately.

The titles of the Ezra literature

Title in the N.E.B. (and other English versions)	Title in the Septuagint (Greek Bible)	Title in the Vulgate (Latin Bible)	Original language
Ezra	} Esdras b	I Esdras	Hebrew and Aramaic
Nehemiah		II Esdras	Hebrew
1 Esdras	Esdras a	III Esdras	Greek (? – see p. 6)
2 Esdras	No equivalent	IV Esdras*	Hebrew (lost; the work is known only from Latin and other translations)

* The custom is also found of dividing this book still further, '4 Ezra' being applied to chs. 3–14, with chs. 1–2 being called '5 Ezra' and chs. 15–16 '6 Ezra': see the commentary on these sections (pp. 76–7, 283–4).

THE FIRST BOOK OF

ESDRAS

✳ ✳ ✳ ✳ ✳ ✳ ✳ ✳ ✳ ✳ ✳ ✳ ✳ ✳

THE LITERARY PROBLEMS

Biblical scholars have sometimes been accused by general readers of creating problems where none existed. Such a charge could never be justified in regard to 1 Esdras, where the problems are all too obvious. No clear consensus of opinion has emerged concerning the date, the purpose, or the language of the book, nor as to its relation to earlier writings dealing with the same events.

The last difficulty may provide the most convenient starting-point. The period of history dealt with is from the seventh to the fifth or early fourth centuries B.C., from the reign of Josiah, king of Judah, to the time of Ezra. Most of the book bears a close relationship to 2 Chron. 35–6, the book of Ezra, and that part of the book of Nehemiah which deals with the activity of Ezra (7: 73*b* – 8: 13). But three points are at once noteworthy: (1) the material in Ezra 4: 7–24, which is there arranged on a thematic rather than a chrono-logical basis, is here placed in a different context, in ch. 2; (2) 1 Esdras 3 and 4, entitled in the N.E.B. *A debate at the Persian court*, have no parallel in Ezra; (3) the book apparently breaks off in mid-sentence at 9: 55 (see the N.E.B. footnote at the end of the book). It is noteworthy, however, that at this point in the Old Testament books of Ezra and Nehemiah we have reached the last reference to the work of Ezra (Neh. 8: 13), as the later references (Neh. 12: 26 and 36) are probably later additions to the text. It is therefore not impossible that the conclusion has in fact been reached. It appears that no reference is made to Nehemiah, though the attempt has

4

sometimes been made to find allusions to him (in particular see 5: 40 and the commentary at that point).

Enough has been said to show that 1 Esdras represents a free rendering in Greek of a selected part of the work of the Chronicler. As the table on p. 3 has indicated, it existed alongside another, more literal translation of the books of Ezra and Nehemiah (Esdras b) in the Greek Bible. Broadly speaking, two main views have been held about the relation of 1 Esdras to the corresponding parts of the Old Testament books. One values 1 Esdras highly as providing an ancient and reliable tradition, giving us a better chronology of the events described in so confusing a way in Ezra 4, and avoiding entirely the overlap of the ministries of Ezra and Nehemiah which presents difficulties for the understanding of the Old Testament books. The other view is more sceptical of the independent value of 1 Esdras, on the grounds that a more credible historical presentation is just as likely to come from a late revision as from early and reliable tradition.

It is not possible here to enter into this argument in detail, but, despite a number of recent attempts to establish the re-liability of the historical traditions underlying 1 Esdras, it seems more likely that we are here presented with a late attempt, probably from the very last centuries B.C., to set out a less confused account of the traditions relating to Ezra. Thus, the omission of all references to Nehemiah may be due to an early tradition which recognized that his mission was quite separate from that of Ezra, but it may also be due to the fact that the traditions relating to Ezra and Nehemiah developed quite distinctly within Judaism. Thus in 2 Macc. 1: 18 – 2: 13 and Ecclus. 49: 13 Nehemiah is mentioned without reference to Ezra, whereas in the chronicles of the Samaritan community as well as in 1 Esdras, it is Ezra who is the focus of attention without mention of Nehemiah. Ezra was a controversial figure in the Judaism of the last centuries B.C., and the beginning of the Christian era, and part at least of the purpose of 1 Esdras was probably to magnify his achievement in establishing the law as the basis of true Judaism. He is claimed to be the last of those great formative figures in Judaism: Josiah, Zerubbabel and Ezra.

Such a claim might be felt to be especially necessary for Jews who did not speak Hebrew and who lived away from Palestine. As with almost everything else connected with 1 Esdras, there is dispute about the original language of the book. It has come down to us in Greek, and it is usually held that this was its original language. The suggestion has also been made, however, that underlying our present work is a now lost original in either Hebrew or Aramaic. Again, certainty is impossible, but it seems unnecessary to envisage any Semitic original other than our books of Ezra and Nehemiah, perhaps with some textual variations from the form familiar to us. It is also disputed whether the section found only in 1 Esdras, *A debate at the Persian court* (chs. 3–4), was first written in Greek, or is a translation from Aramaic.

As for the date of 1 Esdras, general reference has already been made to the last centuries B.C., and it is hardly possible to be more specific than this. It is virtually certain that it was available to the Jewish historian Josephus, writing in the last third of the first century A.D., so it is possible that it was not written until the beginning of the Christian era; linguistic similarities with books written at a slightly earlier date have, however, persuaded many scholars that the most probable date is the late second or early first century B.C.

In the commentary which follows, special attention will be paid to those sections of 1 Esdras which either have no parallel in the earlier writings, or differ significantly from them. Though it is hoped that sufficient background information is provided to make the work intelligible as it stands, any fuller exposition of passages paralleled in Chronicles, Ezra or Nehemiah should be sought in the volumes in this series that comment on those books.

✳   ✳   ✳   ✳   ✳   ✳   ✳   ✳   ✳   ✳   ✳   ✳   ✳

Parallels between Chronicles–Ezra–Nehemiah and 1 Esdras

1 Esdras	Chronicles–Ezra–Nehemiah
1: 1–33	2 Chron. 35
1: 34–58	2 Chron. 36
2: 1–15	Ezra 1
2: 16–30	Ezra 4: 7–24a
3: 1 – 5: 6	*No parallel*
5: 7–46	Ezra 2 (and Neh. 7: 6–73a)
5: 47–65	Ezra 3
5: 66–73	Ezra 4: 1–5
6: 1–22	Ezra 4: 24b – 5: 17
6: 23–34	Ezra 6: 1–12
7	Ezra 6: 13–22
8: 1–27	Ezra 7
8: 28–67	Ezra 8
8: 68–90	Ezra 9
8: 91–6	Ezra 10: 1–5
9: 1–36	Ezra 10: 6–44
9: 37–55	Neh. 7: 73b – 8: 13

As is explained in the commentary, 1 Esdras is not simply a translation of parts of certain Old Testament books, so that the equivalences noted above are not always exact. Some of the events described are also referred to in other Old Testament books (notably 2 Kings, Jeremiah, Haggai and Zechariah).

Exile and return

* The historical period covered by 1 Esdras is from 622 B.C., (Josiah's Passover) to a date in the fifth or early fourth century which cannot be precisely determined (Ezra's mission). Since these events are described partly in 2 Chronicles and partly in Ezra, and since they include the time of exile, our natural inclination is to think of two different 'ages'

being involved. But any such division of history into clearly
defined periods is always a dangerous and somewhat subjective
exercise, and it is in itself perfectly legitimate both to stress
the continuity of Israel's history despite the exile of some of
her leading citizens to Babylon, and also to see a measure of
correspondence between the reforms carried out by Josiah
and those of Ezra. To a later age, this was one of the great
formative periods of Judaism, and we need not be surprised
that special attention was paid to it.

From the point of view of world history, the period covered
was a time of very great changes. Josiah ruled at the time of
the break-up of the Assyrian Empire, which had dominated
Judah and the neighbouring states for a century. After a brief
Egyptian domination, the Babylonian Empire of Nebuchadnezzar became supreme, and overran Judah, destroying
Jerusalem and its temple, and taking many of the leading
citizens into exile. All these events took place in little more
than a generation (609–587 B.C.). Then, in the years between
550 and 539, the rise of Cyrus led to the Persians replacing
Babylon as the dominant power, and under Persian rule, the
fortunes of Judah greatly improved. At Jerusalem, the city
itself and its temple were restored; some exiles may have been
allowed to return; and the work of restoration was brought
to a climax by the work of Ezra. At the very least, the period
between Cyrus and Ezra was one of nearly a century, and it
may have been a good deal more, but from the later viewpoint
of the writer of I Esdras, as already in the book of Ezra
itself, the perspective is shortened, and Ezra's work is seen
as part of the one great task of restoration.✶

JOSIAH

1 JOSIAH KEPT the Passover at Jerusalem in honour of
his Lord and sacrificed the Passover victims on the
2 fourteenth day of the first month. The priests, duly robed
in their vestments, he stationed in the temple of the Lord

according to the order of daily service. He commanded 3
the Levites, who served the temple in Israel, to purify
themselves for the Lord, in order to place the holy Ark
of the Lord in the house which was built by King Solomon, son of David. Josiah said to them, 'You are no 4
longer to carry it on your shoulders. Make yourselves
ready now, family by family and clan by clan, to do
service to the Lord your God and to minister to his
people Israel in the manner prescribed by King David 5
and provided for so magnificently by his son Solomon.
Take your places in the temple as Levites in the prescribed order of your families in the presence of your
brother Israelites; sacrifice the Passover victims, and pre- 6
pare the sacrifices for your brothers. Observe the Passover
according to the ordinance of the Lord which was given
to Moses.'

To those who were present Josiah made a gift of thirty 7
thousand lambs and kids and three thousand calves. These
he gave from the royal estates in fulfilment of his promise
to the people and to the priests and Levites. The temple- 8
wardens, Chelkias, Zacharias, and Esyelus, gave the
priests two thousand six hundred sheep and three hundred calves for the Passover. Jechonias, Samaeas, his 9
brother Nathanael, Sabias, Ozielus, and Joram, army
officers of high rank, gave the Levites five thousand sheep
and seven hundred calves for the Passover.

This was the procedure. The priests and the Levites, 10
bearing the unleavened bread, stood in all their splendour
before the people, in the order of their clans and families,
to make offerings to the Lord as is laid down in the book 11
of Moses. This took place in the morning. They roasted 12

the Passover victims over the fire in the prescribed way
and boiled the sacrifices in the vessels and cauldrons, and
13 a pleasant smell went up; then they carried portions
round to the whole assembly. After this they made preparations both for themselves and for their brothers the
14 priests, the sons of Aaron. The priests went on offering
the fat until nightfall, while the Levites made the preparations both for themselves and for their brothers the
15-16 priests, the sons of Aaron. The sons of Asaph, the temple
singers, with Asaph, Zacharias, and Eddinous of the royal
court, and the door-keepers at each gateway remained at
their station according to the ordinances of David, which
prescribe that no one may lawfully default in his daily
duty; their brothers the Levites made the preparations for
17 them. All that pertained to the Lord's sacrifice was com-
18 pleted that day: the keeping of the Passover and the
offering of the sacrifices on the altar of the Lord according
19 to the command of King Josiah. The Israelites who were
present on this occasion kept the Passover and the Feast
20 of Unleavened Bread for seven days. Such a Passover had
not been kept in Israel since the time of the prophet
21 Samuel; none of the kings of Israel had kept such a Passover as was kept by Josiah, the priests and the Levites,
the men of Judah, and those Israelites who happened to
22 be resident in Jerusalem. It was in the eighteenth year of
Josiah's reign that this Passover was celebrated.

23 All that Josiah did he did rightly and in whole-hearted
24 devotion to his Lord. The events of his reign are to be
found in ancient records which tell a story of sin and
rebellion against the Lord graver than that of any other

nation or kingdom, and of offences against him which
brought down his judgement upon Israel.

After all these doings of Josiah's it happened that 25
Pharaoh king of Egypt was advancing to attack Car-
chemish on the Euphrates, and Josiah took the field
against him. The king of Egypt sent him this message: 26
'What is your business with me, king of Judah? It is not 27
against you that the Lord God has sent me to fight; my
campaign is on the Euphrates. The Lord is with me, the
Lord, I say, is with me, driving me on. Withdraw, and
do not oppose the Lord.' Josiah did not turn his chariot 28
but went forward to the attack. He disregarded what the
Lord had said through the prophet Jeremiah and joined 29
battle with Pharaoh in the plain of Megiddo. Pharaoh's
captains swept down upon King Josiah. The king said to 30
his servants, 'Take me out of the battle, for I am badly
hurt.' At once his servants took him out of the line and
lifted him into his second chariot. He was brought back 31
to Jerusalem, and there he died and was buried in his
ancestral tomb.

All Judah mourned Josiah, and the prophet Jeremiah 32
lamented him. The lamentation for Josiah has been observed by the chief men and their wives from that day
to this; it was proclaimed that it should be a custom for
ever for the whole people of Israel. These things are 33
recorded in the book of the histories of the kings of
Judah; every deed that Josiah did which won him fame
and showed his understanding of the law of the Lord,
both what he did earlier and what is told of him here,
is related in the book of the kings of Israel and Judah.

✳ The account of Josiah's reign is parallel to that in 2 Chron. 35, and the impression created is similar. Though we commonly regard Josiah's reign (640–609 B.C.) as the last flicker of life before the final collapse of Judah, coming as it did shortly before the Babylonian invasion, it is also possible to see the appropriateness of taking this period as a beginning. Josiah's religious reform meant a return to the standard of earlier times (verses 20–1), and thus the pattern to be followed by the Jerusalem community was laid down. Exile might disrupt, but could not finally destroy, the continuity between Josiah and the writer's own day.

1. The beginning seems abrupt, but is not necessarily an indication of a lost earlier section. Some Old Testament books start in almost as direct a fashion (cp. Ezra 1: 1).

5. *so magnificently:* this addition, one of several minor changes from the Chronicles' text which is the author's source, is aimed at stressing the importance of the temple.

7. The *gift* was to enable *those who were present* to offer sacrifice, not, as the text might be thought to imply, for their own use.

8. *Chelkias, Zacharias and Esyelus:* Greek proper names were very different from the forms usual in Hebrew. In 2 Chron. 35: 8 these names are found as 'Hilkiah, Zechariah, and Jehiel'. The last in particular would scarcely be recognizable from the Greek form.

10. *in all their splendour:* 2 Chron. 35: 10 has simply 'in their places'. The change may be due to a misunderstanding, or, perhaps more likely, to a deliberate emphasis on the glory of the ministers.

11. *in the morning:* this is unexpected, since the Law required victims to be sacrificed in the evening (Deut. 16: 6). It is doubtful if a variant in liturgical practice is implied here; more probably the translators misunderstood the Hebrew original.

15. *Zacharias and Eddinous:* the latter name is the Greek version of 'Jeduthun' (2 Chron. 35: 15), but *Zacharias* appears

to be an error, perhaps influenced by verse 8, for the original 'Heman'. The remainder of this verse and verse 16 go beyond the source in 2 Chronicles in stressing the correct carrying out of the ritual by all concerned.

23–4. The death of Josiah in humiliating circumstances after his great religious reform presented a theological problem for later interpreters. The Chronicler had eased this by representing Josiah as falling away at the last and failing to recognize God's hand in the campaign waged by Pharaoh Necho; this section follows 2 Kings 23: 24–7, in the view that even Josiah's piety could not turn away the punishment made inevitable by the nation's sin.

27. This verse goes even further than 2 Chron. 35: 21, its probable source, in identifying Necho as the messenger of Israel's own God.

28. *through the prophet Jeremiah:* this is not found in 2 Chronicles, and it is not clear that any specific passage of Jeremiah is here in mind. It is an elaboration of the reference to Jeremiah in verse 32, which is already found in 2 Chronicles, and shows how that prophet and the book named after him were associated with the whole complex of events leading up to the fall of the kingdom of Judah.✲

THE FALL OF JERUSALEM

His compatriots took Joachaz the son of Josiah and 34 made him king in succession to his father. He was twenty- 35 three years old, and he reigned over Judah and Jerusalem for three months. Then the king of Egypt deposed him, fined the nation a hundred talents of silver and one talent 36 of gold, and appointed his brother Joakim king of Judah 37 and Jerusalem. Joakim imprisoned the leading men and 38 had his brother Zarius arrested and brought back from Egypt.

Joakim was twenty-five years old when he became 39

king of Judah and Jerusalem; he did what was wrong in
40 the eyes of the Lord. Nebuchadnezzar king of Babylon
marched against him; he put him in chains of bronze and
41 took him to Babylon. Nebuchadnezzar also took some
of the sacred vessels of the Lord, carried them off, and
42 put them in his temple in Babylon. The stories about
Joakim, his sacrilegious and godless conduct, are recorded
in the chronicles of the kings.

43 Joakim was succeeded on the throne by his eighteen-
44 year-old son Joakim. He reigned in Jerusalem for three
months and ten days, and did what was wrong in the eyes
of the Lord.

45 A year later Nebuchadnezzar had him deported to
46 Babylon together with the sacred vessels of the Lord. He
made Zedekiah king of Judah and Jerusalem. Zedekiah
47 was twenty-one years old and reigned eleven years. He
did what was wrong in the eyes of the Lord and disregarded what the Lord had said through the prophet
48 Jeremiah. King Nebuchadnezzar had made him take an
oath of allegiance by the Lord, but he broke it and re-
volted. He was stubborn and defiant, and transgressed the
commandments of the Lord, the God of Israel.

49 The leaders of the people and the chief priests committed many wicked and lawless acts, outdoing even the
heathen in sacrilege, and they defiled the holy temple of
50 the Lord in Jerusalem. The God of their fathers sent his
messenger to reclaim them, because he wished to spare
51 them and his dwelling-place. But they derided his messengers, and on the very day when the Lord spoke they
52 were scoffing at his prophets. At last he was roused to
fury against his people for their impieties, and ordained
53 that the kings of the Chaldaeans should attack them. These

put their young men to the sword all round the holy temple, sparing neither old nor young, neither boy nor girl; the Lord handed them all over to their enemies. All the sacred vessels of the Lord, large and small, the 54 furnishings of the Ark of the Lord, and the royal treasures were carried off to Babylon. The house of the Lord was 55 set on fire, the walls of Jerusalem destroyed, its towers burnt, and all its splendours ruined. Nebuchadnezzar 56 carried off to Babylon the survivors from the slaughter, and they remained slaves to him and his sons until the 57 Persians took his empire. This fulfilled the word of the Lord spoken by Jeremiah: 'Until the land has run the full 58 term of its sabbaths, it shall keep sabbath all the time of its desolation till the end of the seventy years.'

✻ These verses cover the years from 609 to 587/6 B.C. in outline, with a brief concluding reference to the period of the exile. A variety of biblical accounts, together with the presentation of these years in the collection of contemporary clay tablet known as the Babylonian Chronicle, has enabled us to reconstruct the events perhaps more fully than those of any other Old Testament period; it does not seem likely that I Esdras preserves any independent sources of information. For the most part it is clearly based on 2 Chron. 36, and conveys a vivid sense of the desperate measures that had to be taken as the political situation steadily worsened for Judah.

34. *His compatriots:* 2 Chron. 36: 1 has 'The people of the land', but by the last pre-Christian centuries this term had come to be one of abuse, denoting the lowest stratum of society, and this may explain the avoidance of it here.

35. *Judah and Jerusalem:* this description, common in the prophets (cp. Isa. 1: 1), brings out the point that Judah was the main body of the land, while Jerusalem stood somewhat apart as the royal city.

38. If these events are correctly described, we have no

other record of them. More probably this is a confused account of the exile of Joachaz to Egypt by Necho (2 Chron. 36: 4). The name *Zarius* is found in various forms in different manuscripts, but it is not easy to identify him with any figure known from other sources.

39-42. The account in 2 Chronicles is followed, both in the otherwise unknown assertion that Joakim was exiled to Babylon, and in its condemnation of his character.

43. *eighteen-year-old:* 2 Chron. 36: 9 has 'eight', and this is followed by some manuscripts of 1 Esdras, but *eighteen* is undoubtedly correct. Some confusion is caused at this point because two very similar Hebrew names, 'Jehoiakim' and 'Jehoiachin' are both rendered *Joakim* in Greek.

45. The actual capture of Jerusalem in 597 B.C. is passed over in silence; it seems as if the author of 1 Esdras envisaged the main damage as having occurred during the time of the first Joakim.

49-58. This sermonic passage, drawing out the moral of the people's wickedness and the inevitability of the fall of Jerusalem, follows the account in 2 Chronicles very closely. At times the emphasis is heightened, as by the reference to a particular 'messenger' (verse 50) and the theme of rejection lasting till 'the very day when the Lord spoke' (verse 51).

54. *the furnishings of the Ark of the Lord:* the N.E.B. translation here is unexpected, and may give too precise an impression; the Greek refers simply to 'treasure-chests'. The fate of the Ark is in fact unknown.

58. The words attributed here to Jeremiah are in fact based partly on Jer. 25: 11 and 29: 10, partly on Lev. 26: 34-5. It is not an exact quotation as we should nowadays understand it. *

THE RESTORATION UNDER CYRUS

During the first year of Cyrus king of Persia, the Lord, 1-2 2 in order to fulfil his word spoken through Jeremiah, moved Cyrus king of Persia to make a proclamation throughout his empire, which he also put in writing: 'This is the decree of Cyrus king of Persia: The Lord of 3 Israel, the most high Lord, has made me king of the world and has directed me to build him a house at Jeru- 4 salem in Judaea. Whoever among you belongs to his 5 people, may his Lord be with him; let him go up to Jerusalem in Judaea and build the house of the Lord of Israel, the Lord who dwells in Jerusalem. Wherever each 6 man lives let his neighbours help him with gold and 7 silver and other gifts, with horses and pack-animals, to- gether with other things set aside as votive offerings for the Lord's temple in Jerusalem.'

Then the chiefs of the clans of the tribe of Judah and of 8 Benjamin, the priests, the Levites, came forward, and all whose spirit the Lord had moved to go up to build the Lord's temple in Jerusalem. Their neighbours helped with 9 everything, with silver and gold, horses and pack-animals; and many were also moved to help with votive offerings in great quantity. King Cyrus brought out the sacred 10 vessels of the Lord which Nebuchadnezzar had taken away from Jerusalem and set up in his idolatrous temple. Cyrus king of Persia brought them out and delivered 11 them to Mithradates his treasurer, by whom they were 12 delivered to Sanabassar, the governor of Judaea. This is 13 the inventory: a thousand gold cups, a thousand silver cups, twenty-nine silver censers, thirty gold bowls, two

thousand four hundred and ten silver bowls, and a thou-
14 sand other articles. In all, five thousand four hundred and
15 sixty-nine gold and silver vessels were returned, and taken
from Babylon to Jerusalem by Sanabassar together with
the exiles.

✻ As in 2 Chronicles, the period between the destruction of
Jerusalem and the rise of Cyrus is passed over without
reference to any historical events; as the last verse of the
previous chapter showed, a theological explanation was
regarded as more appropriate. A greater impression of continuity is given here than in the earlier sources, because 1
Esdras bridges the gap between 2 Chronicles and Ezra. The
events described in these verses correspond to Ezra 1 and took
place around 539 B.C.

1–7. These verses follow the general sense of Ezra 1: 1–4
very closely. In particular the double stress in Cyrus' decree
found there is repeated – the permission for the return of
exiles as well as the permission to rebuild the temple, which
is the point stressed in the other forms of the decree (1 Esdras
6: 24–6; cp. Ezra 6: 3–5).

9. *Their neighbours helped with everything:* as originally described in Ezra 1: 6, this was probably an allusion to a theme
in the book of Exodus; what has sometimes been called 'the
spoiling of the Egyptians', that is, the way in which the
Israelites plundered the Egyptians' jewellery and clothing
when they escaped from Pharaoh (Exod. 12: 36). Here it is
treated as the way in which those Jews unable or unwilling to
return to Jerusalem played their part in the enterprise.

12. *Sanabassar, the governor of Judaea:* the role of this figure
is enigmatic. In Ezra he is called 'Sheshbazzar' and his function is not easily distinguished from that of Zerubbabel;
here the difficulties are compounded by the further variation
in his name, and by the more precise description as *governor
of Judaea*. There is no other evidence that he had so specific a
role.

13–14. The total here equals the sum of the parts, which

18

is not the case in Ezra 1: 9–11. It is more likely that corrections have been made to bring about this correspondence, than that this list is original. There are in any case problems of a historical kind, since according to 2 Kings 24: 13 many of the vessels of the first temple had been destroyed. ✷

OPPOSITION TO THE REBUILDING

In the time of Artaxerxes king of Persia, Belemus, Mithra- 16 dates, Tabellius, Rathymus, Beeltethmus, Semellius the secretary, and their colleagues in office in Samaria and other places, wrote him a letter denouncing the inhabitants of Judaea and Jerusalem in the following terms:

To our Sovereign Lord Artaxerxes your servants 17 Rathymus the recorder, Semellius the secretary, the other members of their council, and the magistrates in Coele-syria and Phoenicia:

This is to inform Your Majesty that the Jews who 18 left you to come here have arrived in Jerusalem and are rebuilding that wicked and rebellious city. They are repairing its streets and walls and laying the foundation of the temple. If this city is rebuilt and the walls com- 19 pleted, they will cease paying tribute and will rebel against the royal house. Since work on the temple is 20 in hand, we have thought it well not to neglect this important matter but to bring it to Your Majesty's 21 notice, in order that, if it is Your Majesty's pleasure, search may be made in the records left by your pre- decessors. You will find in the archives evidence about 22 these matters and will learn that this is a city that has resisted authority and given trouble to kings and to other states, and has been a centre of armed rebellion 23 by the Jews from the earliest times. That is why it was

24 laid in ruins. Now we submit to Your Majesty that, if this city be rebuilt and its walls rise again, you will no longer have access to Coele-syria and Phoenicia.

25 Then the king wrote to Rathymus the recorder, Beel-tethmus, Semellius the secretary, and their colleagues in office in Samaria, Syria, and Phoenicia this reply:

26 I have read your letter. I ordered search to be made and it was discovered that this city has always been opposed to its overlords, and its inhabitants have raised

27 rebellions and made wars. There were kings in Jeru-salem, powerful and ruthless men, who in their time controlled Coele-syria and Phoenicia and exacted

28 tribute from them. I therefore command that the men you mention be prevented from rebuilding the city,

29 and that measures be taken to enforce this order and to check the spread of an evil likely to be a nuisance to the royal house.

30 When the letter from King Artaxerxes had been read, Rathymus, Semellius the secretary, and their colleagues set out at once for Jerusalem with cavalry and a large body of other troops and stopped the builders. The building of the temple was broken off until the second year of the reign of Darius king of Persia.

* Thus far the order and the details of 2 Chronicles and Ezra have been followed closely; at this point occurs the first major rearrangement, as these verses correspond to Ezra 4: 7–24. It is not difficult to see why such a change was considered necessary, since their placing in Ezra is thematic rather than historical, and if the sequence is understood as historical major problems arise. In Ezra, the passage was relevant to the compiler's theme, but the events recorded are from a different period. The rearrangement here made does not in fact solve the historical problem, since 'Artaxerxes king of Persia' did not become king until 465 B.C., but it is probable that the author of 1 Esdras failed to realize this and took Artaxerxes to be a ruler who reigned between the death of Cyrus (530 B.C.) and the accession of Darius I (522). Further evidence of an attempt at harmonization is found in the references to the temple (verses 18–20), where the passage in Ezra mentions only the rebuilding of the city walls. Here again it seems likely that this reference has been inserted to make it more appropriate to the known circumstances of the sixth century B.C. It is noteworthy that the reconstruction found here is followed very closely by the Jewish historian Josephus, writing in the first century A.D., but for the reasons just given it cannot be regarded as throwing any valuable light on the actual course of events.

16. *In the time of Artaxerxes king of Persia:* assuming, as is likely, that Artaxerxes I is intended, this gives the period 465–424 B.C. *Belemus ... and their colleagues:* harmonization of what were originally different sources has also taken place here. Ezra 4: 7 mentions a letter sent 'with the agreement of Mithredath, Tabeel and all his colleagues', while 4: 8 introduces a further letter, subsequently set out in full, from 'Rehum the high commissioner and Shimshai the secretary'. Originally these pieces of correspondence appear to have been unrelated, but 1 Esdras has combined the two strands. There are significant changes in the names: the word which the N.E.B. has translated 'with the agreement of' (Ezra 4: 7) was taken as a proper name, *Belemus*; and the Aramaic word translated 'high commissioner' in Ezra 4: 8 is misunderstood as if it were a proper name, *Beeltethmus*. *in Samaria and other places:* it is not known what the original circumstances underlying the opposition may have been, but as represented here they are set out in terms of the rivalry between Jerusalem and her religious and political rivals.

17. The elaborate introduction to the letter in the Aramaic

of Ezra 4: 9–10 is drastically reduced, probable because the various place-names there mentioned were no longer intelligible. The expression *Coele-syria and Phoenicia* is an explanation rather than a translation, denoting the designation of the land in Roman times as against the expression 'the province of Beyond-Euphrates' (Ezra 4: 10), which was the Persian usage.

18. *laying the foundation of the temple:* there is nothing corresponding to this in the original, and it appears to be part of the attempt to give a more plausible historical development. Throughout the letter, the translation is freer than in the narrative passages, possibly in order to make the contents more readily intelligible to readers in very different circumstances from the time when the letter was first written.

26–9. The royal reply is to an even more marked extent a summary of the original rather than a true translation.

30. *Darius king of Persia:* both Ezra 4: 24 (the original of this passage) and this verse illustrate what appears to have been a widespread confusion among the Jews concerning the order in which the Persian kings had ruled. (A comparable confusion seems to underlie part of the book of Daniel, the author of which seems to have thought that the order of rulers at this period was Belshazzar, Darius, Cyrus (Dan. 5 : 30; 6 : 28).) The reference here must be to Darius I (522–486 B.C.), that is, to a king who reigned long betore Artaxerxes I (465–424), to whom the previous section has referred. *

A debate at the Persian court

✻ There now follows, in chs. 3–4, the one extensive section of this book which is without a close parallel in Chronicles–Ezra–Nehemiah. Indeed there is nothing in the first part of the story which is told here to connect it with the context of this book at all. This link only occurs with the quite unexpected announcement in 4: 13 that one of the three young men is the Jewish leader associated with the temple rebuilding, Zerubbabel. Nor should we be led to expect such an identification by the form of the story up to that point. In the discussion as to the strongest power, it might be expected that the one who would be identified as a Jewish hero would suggest a religious answer to the conundrum. Instead all three answers are thoroughly secular: asked who is the strongest, the three youths reply, respectively, wine, the king and women. It seems likely that we have here a popular story, only later elaborated to fit its present context, by identifying the third youth as Zerubbabel and developing his answer to allow a place for truth as well as for women. Various parallels to the story are known to exist in different cultures, but none that can be regarded as a source of this form of it; nor is it certain whether the Greek form in which it has come down to us represents its original language or whether it is a translation from Aramaic. ✻

DARIUS' BANQUET AND THE WAGER

KING DARIUS held a great feast for all those under **3** him, his household, the chief men of Media and Persia, and the satraps and commanders and governors of **2** his empire in the hundred and twenty-seven satrapies from India to Ethiopia. When they had eaten and drunk their **3** fill, they went away, and King Darius withdrew to his

23

4 bedchamber; he went to sleep but woke up again. Then the three young men of the king's personal bodyguard
5 said to each other: 'Let each one of us name the thing which he judges the strongest; and to the one whose opinion seems wisest King Darius will give rich gifts and
6 prizes: he shall be clothed in purple, drink from gold vessels, and sleep on a golden bed; and he shall have a chariot with gold-studded bridles, and a fine linen turban,
7 and a chain about his neck. His wisdom shall give him the right to sit next to Darius and to be given the title Kins-
8 man of Darius.' Then each wrote down his own state-
9 ment, sealed it, and put it under the king's pillow. 'When the king wakes again,' they said, 'the writing will be given him. The king and the three chief men of Persia shall judge whose statement is wisest, and the award will be made on the merits of the written statement.'

10, 11 One wrote, 'Wine is strongest', the second wrote 'The
12 king is strongest', and the third wrote 'Women are
13 strongest, but truth conquers all'. When the king got up
14 he was presented with what they had written. He read it, and summoned all the chief men of Persia and Media,
15 satraps, commanders, governors, and chief officers. Then he took his seat in the council chamber, and what they
16 had written was read out before them. He said, 'Call the young men and let them expound their statements.' They
17 were called and came in. They were asked, 'Tell us about what you have written.'

* The general background here is reminiscent of parts of Esther and Daniel; the great feast is comparable to Xerxes' (Ahasuerus') banquet (Esther 1), as is also the detail about the wakefulness of the king (cp. Esther 6: 1). The three young

24

men in the royal service remind us of the status of Daniel and his three friends under Nebuchadnezzar (Dan. 1). It is possible that these links with other Old Testament books have been added to the present form of the story to give a distinctively Jewish link to a story which was otherwise a traditional Greek theme: what is strongest?

2. *the hundred and twenty-seven satrapies from India to Ethiopia:* this appears to be based on Esther 1: 1, where already historical problems are raised, since there was never anything approaching this number of satrapies (provinces) in the Persian Empire.

5. The theme of the king at a banquet making extravagant promises to those who gain his favour is a well-known one (cp. Herod in Mark 6: 22–3), but it is remarkable to find this generosity being proposed by the aspiring recipients. The Jewish historian Josephus, in his version of the story, also found this improbable, and modified the story so that Darius himself made the promise of rich rewards.

10–12. It seems probable that in the original form of the story, the three contestants each wrote one answer: *Wine, The king, Women*, but in view of the unexpected dénouement regarding the third young man, his answer has been elaborated with its reference to truth. In the end this proves decisive (see 4: 34–42). ✻

THE FIRST TWO CONTESTANTS

The first, who spoke about the strength of wine, began. 18 'Sirs,' he said, 'how true it is that wine is strongest! It sends astray the wits of all who drink it; king and orphan, 19 slave and free, rich and poor, it has the same effect on them all. It turns all thoughts to revelry and mirth; it brings forgetfulness of grief and debt. It makes all feel 21 rich, cares nothing for king or satrap, and makes men always talk in millions. When they are in their cups, they 22

forget to be friendly to friends and relations, and are
23 quick to draw their swords; when they have recovered
from their wine, they cannot remember what they have
24 done. Sirs, is not wine the strongest, seeing that it forces
men to behave in this way?' With this he ended.

4 Then the second, the one who spoke of the strength of
2 the king, began his speech: 'Sirs, is not man the strongest,
man who masters the earth and the sea and all that is in
3 them? But the strongest of men is the king; he is their
4 lord and master, and they obey all his commands. If he
bids them make war upon one another they do it; if he
dispatches them against his enemies, they march and level
5 mountains and walls and towers. They kill and are killed;
they do not disobey the king's order. If they are victorious they bring everything to the king, their spoils and
6 everything else. Or take those who do not serve as
soldiers or go to war, but work the land: they sow and
reap, and bring their produce to the king. They compel
7 each other to bring him their tribute. Though he is no
more than one man, if he orders them to kill, they kill;
8 if he orders them to release, they release; he orders them
to attack and they attack, to lay waste and they lay waste,
9 to build and they build, to cut down and they cut down,
10 to plant and they plant. So all his people and his troops
obey him. Besides this, while he himself sits at table, eats
and drinks, and goes to sleep, they stand in attendance
11 round about him and none can leave and see to his own
12 affairs; they never disobey him in anything. Sirs, of
course the king must be strongest when he commands
such obedience!' So he stopped speaking.

* There are links throughout this section of the book with the traditions of Jewish wisdom literature. In its earlier stages that had been essentially down-to-earth and practical, concerned with the ability to perform one's allotted task successfully; but in the later Old Testament period, possibly under Greek influence, a more speculative note emerged such as is evidenced here.

18–24. There is an ambiguity in the speech praising *wine* which at times has a remarkably modern ring. In part it is praised for itself and for the release from anxiety and care which it provides; in part, the speech is a warning against the danger of succumbing to the strength inherent in wine. There are many descriptions of wine and its effects in the Old Testament which seem to be quite free of any note of condemnation (cp. Ps. 104: 15*a*) and the tradition is carried on in the New Testament (cp. John 2: 1–11), but the dangers of wine and of drunkenness were also fully recognized and warnings against over-indulgence are found in the wisdom literature (cp. Prov. 23: 29–35 for a particularly vivid picture of the dangers of drunkenness). The references in verses 19 and 21 to wine as overcoming even kings suggest the possibility that at one stage this speech followed the one praising the power of kings.

4: 1–12. If the speech on wine has many modern associations, that on the power of *the king* portrays an order of society which is much less familiar. The Persian rulers are often praised, directly or by implication, in the Old Testament, because of their humaneness in comparison with the Assyrians and Babylonians of an earlier period; but all the evidence available shows that they were still absolute rulers whose word was law. The power of the king as here portrayed depends on the unquestioning acceptance of a strictly hierarchical order of society. *

THE SPEECH IN PRAISE OF WOMEN

13 The third, who spoke about women and truth – and
14 this was Zerubbabel – said: 'Sirs, it is true the king is
great, men are many, and wine is strong, but who rules
15 over them? Who is the sovereign power? Women,
surely! The king and all his people who rule land and
sea were born of women, and from them they came.
16 Women brought up the men who planted the vineyards
17 which yield the wine. They make clothes for men and
they bring honour to men; men cannot do without
18 women. If they have amassed gold and silver and all kinds
of beautiful things, and then see a woman with a lovely
19 face and figure, they leave all these things to gape and
stare at her with open mouth, and all choose her in pre-
20 ference to gold or silver or beautiful things. A man will
desert his father who brought him up, desert even his
21 country, and become one with his wife. He forgets father,
mother, and country, and stays with his wife to the end
22 of his days. Here is the proof that women are your
masters: do you not toil and sweat and then bring all you
23 earn and give it to your wives? A man will take his sword
and sally forth to plunder and rob, to sail on sea and
24 river; he faces lions, he travels in the dark; and when he
has robbed and plundered he brings the spoil home to
his beloved.

25 'A man loves his wife more than his father or mother.
26 For women's sakes many men have been driven out of
27 their minds, many have been sold into slavery, many
28 have died or come to grief or ruined their lives. Do you
believe me now? Certainly the king wields great autho-

28

rity; no country dare lift a finger against him. Yet I　29
watched him with Apame, his favourite concubine,
daughter of the famous Bartacus. She was sitting on the　30
king's right; she took the diadem off his head and put it
on her own, and slapped his face with her left hand; and
the king only gazed at her open-mouthed. When she　31
laughed at him he laughed; when she was cross with him
he coaxed her to make it up. Sirs, if women do as well　32
as this, how can their strength be denied?' The king and　33
the chief men looked at one another.

* It is probable that in the original form of the debate this
speech, like the first two, was anonymous, and was complete
in itself without the elaboration concerning truth which now
follows. The themes here developed are more characteristic of
classical antiquity than of the Old Testament. The Old
Testament has a number of heroines, but the picture given
here of the female as the power behind the throne is not
specially characteristic. (Elijah's opponent, Jezebel (see 1 Kings
19: 1–2; 21: 5–15) may provide an exception.) To some
extent, this speech, like that on wine, brings out the ambiguous
nature of the power it describes (cp. verses 25–6), and this is
reminiscent of the warnings in Proverbs against the seductive
power of women (cp. Prov. 7: 6–23). A similar tension
between the power of the king and that of women is illustrated
by the story in Esther 1 (cp. especially verses 18–20). It is
clear that the themes here discussed were matters for popular
debate in the ancient world.

13. *this was Zerubbabel:* the awkward and unexpected
introduction of the name here has led almost all scholars to
agree that this phrase is a gloss, but it is less clear whether it
was introduced when the rest of the story had already taken
its present form, by way of preparing the reader for the
dénouement, or whether this was part of the basic adaptation
of the story. Only one Zerubbabel is found in the Old

Testament, the figure mentioned in the work of the Chronicler and in the sixth-century prophets Haggai and Zechariah as the leader of the restored community in Jerusalem. The phrase would give the attentive reader his first clue to the significance of the account of the debate.

14–16. These verses take their point from the context. This is a genuine debate, in which the third speaker shows the inadequacies of the views put forward by the first two.

20. There is an obvious comparison with Gen. 2: 24, but whereas there (and in its New Testament citations such as Mark 10: 7) the context is the custom of marriage, as something regarded as desirable, here the stress is on rejection of one's own family and country.

29. *Apame, his favourite concubine, daughter of the famous Bartacus:* presumably the reference is to a concubine of Darius, but there is no other evidence which would enable us to make an identification. *Apame* was certainly a Persian name, and there were at least two prominent women so called in the fourth century B.C. This would scarcely lead us to regard the tale as historical, but it might afford some clue as to a likely date for the original form of the story.

33. It is probable that the original form of the story is here broken off; we should expect this reaction of *The king and the chief men* to lead to their decision, probably the awarding of the prize to the third speaker. Instead, a further speech follows.   *

IN PRAISE OF TRUTH

34   He then went on to speak about truth: 'Sirs, we have seen that women are strong. The earth is vast, the sky is lofty, the sun swift in his course, for he moves through the
35 circle of the sky and speeds home in a single day. How great is he who does all this! But truth too is great and
36 stronger than all else. The whole earth calls on truth; the sky praises her. All created things shake and tremble; with

her there is no injustice. There is injustice in wine, in 37
kings, in women, in all men, and in all their works, and
so forth. There is no truth in them; they shall perish in
their injustice. But truth abides and is strong for ever; 38
she lives and rules for ever and ever. With her there is 39
no favouritism or partiality; she chooses to do justice
rather than what is unjust and evil. All approve her 40
works; in her judgements there is no injustice. Hers are
strength and royalty, the authority and majesty of all
ages. Praise be to the God of truth!'

So he ended his speech, and all the people shouted and 41
said, 'Great is truth: truth is strongest!' Then the king 42
said to him, 'Ask what you will, even beyond what is
in the writing, and I will grant it you. For you have been
proved the wisest; and you shall sit by me and be called
my Kinsman.'

* No explicitly religious themes have been present in the
first three speeches, and they are not prominent here, but at
least this speech is much closer to the kinds of religious belief
familiar to Jewish readers and those sympathetic to Judaism,
and it will have been inserted at this point to make a more
satisfactory introduction to the triumph of Zerubbabel and
the beneficence of the Persian king.

35–40. There are no close parallels to this speech in the Old
Testament, though a comparison might be made with the
speech in honour of wisdom in Prov. 8: 4–36. Truth is here
not simply the avoidance of error or lying; as in many Old
Testament passages it is closely associated with justice (verse
40). This is similar to such a passage as Ps. 85: 10–11 with its
linking of truth (N.E.B. 'fidelity') and justice. This speech
is therefore susceptible of an orthodox Jewish interpretation,
but some scholars have conjectured that it may once have

been part of a lost hymn in praise of Asha, the Persian god responsible for the right ordering of the universe.

42. The story reverts to the earlier theme of the extravagant generosity of the great king (cp. 3: 5–7). The title of royal *Kinsman* was a regular mark of favour under the Persian and later the Seleucid kings. ✶

THE REWARD

43 Then he said to the king: 'Remember the vow you made on the day when you came to the throne. You
44 promised to rebuild Jerusalem and to send back all the vessels taken from it which Cyrus set aside. When he vowed to destroy Babylon he also vowed to restore these
45 vessels; and you too made a vow to rebuild the temple which the Edomites burnt when Judaea was ravaged by the Chaldaeans. This is the favour that I now beg of you,
46 my lord king, this is the magnanimity I request: that you should perform the vow which you made to the King of heaven.'

47 King Darius stood up and kissed him, and wrote letters for him to all the treasurers, governors, commanders, and satraps instructing them to give safe conduct to him and to all those who were going up with him to rebuild
48 Jerusalem. To all the governors in Coele-syria and Phoenicia and in Lebanon he wrote letters ordering them to transport cedar-wood from Lebanon to Jerusalem and
49 join with Zerubbabel in building the city. He gave all Jews going up from the kingdom to Judaea letters assuring their liberties; that no officer, satrap, governor, or
50 treasurer should interfere with them, that all land which they should acquire should be immune from taxation, and that the Edomites should surrender the villages they
51 had seized from the Jews. Each year twenty talents were

to be contributed to the building of the temple until it
was finished, and a further ten talents annually for[a] burnt-   52
offerings to be sacrificed daily upon the altar in accordance
with their law. All those who were going from Baby-   53-54
lonia to build the city were to enjoy freedom, and their
descendants after them. He gave written orders that all
the priests going there should also receive maintenance
and the vestments in which they would officiate; that the   55
Levites too should receive maintenance, until the day
when the building of the temple and Jerusalem was completed; and that all who guarded the city should be given   56
land and pay. He sent back all the vessels from Babylon   57
which Cyrus had set aside. All that Cyrus had commanded, he reaffirmed, ordering everything to be restored to Jerusalem.

When the young man, Zerubbabel, went out, he   58
turned his face toward Jerusalem, looked up to heaven,
and praised the King of heaven. 'From thee comes vic-   59
tory,' he said, 'from thee comes wisdom; thine is the
glory and I am thy servant. All praise to thee who hast   60
given me wisdom; to thee I give thanks, O Lord of our
fathers.'

He took the letters and set off for Babylon, where he   61
told his fellow-Jews. They praised the God of their   62
fathers because he had given them full freedom to go and   63
rebuild Jerusalem and the temple called by his name, and
they feasted for a week with music and rejoicing.

*   The relevance of this episode to the condition of the Jews
is now spelt out. There are details here which do not correspond with other accounts of the restoration, even with what
is said elsewhere in this book. But a concern for exact histo-

[a] *Some witnesses add* seventeen.

rical accuracy is never a major feature of the Chronicler's work, and so it is likely that here the main point is the reward of God for his faithful community. The role of Zerubbabel is here greatly emphasized, and the suggestion has been made that 1 Esdras originated from a group which understood the important parts in the restoration as having been played by Zerubbabel and Ezra, deliberately omitting Nehemiah, whereas other traditions in Judaism emphasized Nehemiah's part over against that of other leaders. There is not really enough evidence for us to be certain about this kind of reconstruction.

43–6. The allusions in these verses present a number of points which are unattested in any other account of the period. None of the vows mentioned here is known from elsewhere, and to some extent they contradict the picture of the return of the *vessels* 'taken from Babylon to Jerusalem by Sana-bassar' (2: 15). *the temple which the Edomites burnt:* again this statement is unsubstantiated, and can be interpreted in two ways. It may be taken as an actual historical event, unrecorded elsewhere, which provides the explanation for the hostility toward Edom shown in the book of Obadiah or in Ps. 137: 7. Alternatively, it may be taken as a comment inspired by those passages and without historical foundation.

47. The problem concerning historicity here becomes even more acute. In the book of Ezra no indication is given of the date of Zerubbabel's arrival in Jerusalem, and in view of his importance and the confusion between his role and that of Sheshbazzar, the issue has been much discussed. Once again, two views are possible for this verse; either that it retains a genuine historical memory and supplies an answer to the problem, or that it is a recognition of the difficulty and an attempt to provide a solution, but does not in fact have any historical worth. If the view that Zerubbabel's role is being deliberately magnified is accepted, then the comparison between this account and the very similar one concerning Nehemiah's return in Neh. 2: 7–9 is noteworthy.

50. Again the reference to the Edomites is without earlier support, and may reflect contemporary rivalries when this book was written. There was great bitterness between the Jews and the Idumaeans, as the later inhabitants of Edom were called, during the last two centuries B.C. The Herod family were Idumaeans, and their power was much resented by many Jews.

51–7. These verses read like a summary of the various decrees by Persian kings mentioned in Ezra and Nehemiah, where great stress is laid on the generosity of the Persian rulers in helping to re-establish the community (cp. Ezra 1: 2–4; 6: 3–12; Neh. 2: 8–9).

59–60. Zerubbabel's prayer is really a psalm, and might have been set out in poetic form. It is characteristic of the literature of the latest Old Testament period to emphasize the importance of prayer.

61. *set off for Babylon:* no indication has been given of where these events are supposed to have taken place. The Persian Empire did not have one fixed capital.

63. This episode ends, as it had begun, with a feast.   *

The temple rebuilt

* After the unparalleled episode described in chs. 3–4, the greater part of the remainder of the book follows its source – mainly the book of Ezra, with a short extract from Nehemiah – very closely. The beginning of this section, however, is without any such close parallel, and appears to be intended as a link between the episode of the three youths and the account of those who returned to Jerusalem.   *

THE RETURN TO JERUSALEM

5 AFTER THIS the heads of families, tribe by tribe, were chosen to go to Jerusalem, with their wives, their sons and daughters, their male and female slaves, and
2 their pack-animals. Darius sent a thousand horsemen to accompany them until they had brought them safely back
3 to Jerusalem, with a band of drums and flutes, and all their brothers dancing. So he sent them off with their escort.

4 These are the names of the men who went to Jerusalem,
5 according to their families, tribes, and allotted duties. The priests, the sons of Phineas son of Aaron, with Jeshua son of Josedek son of Saraeas, and Joakim his son; and*a*
Zerubbabel son of Salathiel of the house of David of the
6 line of Phares of the tribe of Judah, who spoke wise words before Darius king of Persia. They went in the second year of his reign, in Nisan the first month.

✳ These verses serve both to round off the story of the contest and to introduce the list of returning exiles, based on Ezra 2, which follows. Some scholars have regarded this section as a translation of part of the original text of the book of Ezra which has now been lost; but it seems more likely that it was deliberately composed for its present position.

2–3. The picture is of a religious procession rather than of a journey of some 600 miles (965 km).

5. Although the 'hero' of this whole section is Zerubbabel, the dominance of the priesthood in late Judaism is illustrated by the fact that *The priests* are mentioned first. Related to this view of the priesthood was a great concern for the

[a] his son; and: *probable reading (compare Neh. 12: 10).*

proper descent of the priestly line, and so we find here the
stress on *the sons of Phineas son of Aaron*. Phineas' zeal had been
the subject of a story in Num. 25: 6–15, and another book
from the Apocrypha, Ecclesiasticus, provides evidence of the
esteem with which he and his descendants were regarded
(Ecclus. 45: 23–6). *Jeshua*'s name is so spelt in Ezra (3: 2 and
elsewhere), whereas the books of Haggai and Zechariah have
the form 'Joshua'. The Greek describes Joakim as 'son of
Zerubbabel', but the N.E.B. emendation is likely – the
reference to Zerubbabel's sons at 1 Chron. 3: 19 does not
mention 'Joakim'. *Phares* is the Greek form of 'Perez', from
whom David's genealogy is traced in Ruth 4: 18.

6. This very precise dating (March 520 B.C.) has been
taken at its face value by some scholars. It is, however, more
likely that this is modelled on the detailed dating characteristic
of the books of Haggai and Zechariah, which showed that
those prophets were active at that time and that Jeshua and
Zerubbabel were then in Jerusalem. The parallel with Neh.
2: 1 may also be significant, if part of the purpose of our
author is to stress the achievement of Zerubbabel over against
that of Nehemiah. ✳

THE RETURNING EXILES

Now these are the men of Judah who came up from 7
amongst the captive exiles, those whom Nebuchadnezzar
king of Babylon had transported to Babylon. They re- 8
turned to Jerusalem and the rest of Judaea, each to his
own city: they came with Zerubbabel and Jeshua,
Nehemiah, Zaraeas, Resaeas, Enenius, Mardochaeus,
Beelsarus, Aspharasus, Reelias, Romelius, and Baana,
their leaders. The numbers of those from the nation who 9
returned with their leaders were: the line of Phoros two
thousand one hundred and seventy-two; the line of 10
Saphat four hundred and seventy-two; the line of Ares

11 seven hundred and fifty-six; the line of Phaath-moab, deriving from the line of Jeshua and Joab, two thousand
12 eight hundred and twelve; the line of Elam one thousand two hundred and fifty-four; the line of Zathui nine hundred and forty-five; the line of Chorbe seven hundred and five; the line of Banei six hundred and forty-eight;
13 the line of Bebae six hundred and twenty-three; the line of Astaa one thousand three hundred and twenty-two.
14 The line of Adonikam six hundred and sixty-seven; the line of Bagoi two thousand and sixty-six; the line of
15 Adinus four hundred and fifty-four; the line of Ater son of Hezekias ninety-two; the line of Keilan and Azetas sixty-seven; the line of Azurus four hundred and thirty-
16 two; the line of Annias one hundred and one; the line of Arom and the line of Bassa three hundred and twenty-three; the line of Arsiphurith one hundred and twelve;
17 the line of Baeterus three thousand and five. The line of
18 Bethlomon one hundred and twenty-three; the men of Netophae fifty-five; the men of Anathoth one hundred
19 and fifty-eight; the men of Bethasmoth forty-two; the men of Cariathiarius twenty-five; the men of Caphira
20 and Beroth seven hundred and forty-three; the Chadasians and Ammidaeans four hundred and twenty-two; the men of Kirama and Gabbes six hundred and twenty-
21 one; the men of Macalon one hundred and twenty-two; the men of Betolio fifty-two; the line of Phinis one hun-
22 dred and fifty-six; the line of Calamolalus and Onus seven hundred and twenty-five; the line of Jerechus three
23 hundred and forty-five; the line of Sanaas three thousand three hundred and thirty.
24 The priests: the line of Jeddu son of Jeshua, deriving

from the line of Anasib, nine hundred and seventy-two. The line of Emmeruth one thousand and fifty-two. The 25 line of Phassurus one thousand two hundred and forty-seven. The line of Charme one thousand and seventeen.

The Levites: the line of Jesue, Cadmielus, Bannus, and 26 Sudius seventy-four. The temple singers: the line of 27 Asaph one hundred and twenty-eight.

The door-keepers: the line of Salum, of Atar, of 28 Tolman, of Dacubi, of Ateta, of Sabi, in all one hundred and thirty-nine.

The temple-servitors: the line of Esau, of Asipha, of 29 Taboth, of Keras, of Susa, of Phaleas, of Labana, of 30 Aggaba, of Acud, of Uta, of Ketab, of Gaba, of Subai, of Anan, of Cathua, of Geddur, of Jairus, of Desan, of 31 Noeba, of Chaseba, of Gazera, of Ozius, of Phinoe, of Asara, of Basthae, of Asana, of Maani, of Naphisi, of Acum, of Achipha, of Asur, of Pharakim, of Baaloth, 32 of Meedda, of Coutha, of Charea, of Barchue, of Serar, of Thomi, of Nasith, of Atepha. The descendants of 33 Solomon's servants: the line of Asapphioth, of Pharida, 34 of Jeeli, of Lozon, of Isdael, of Saphythi, of Hagia, of Phacareth, of Sabie, of Sarothie, of Masias, of Gas, of Addus, of Subas, of Apherra, of Barodis, of Saphat, of 35 Adlon. All the temple-servitors and the descendants of Solomon's servants numbered three hundred and seventy-two.

The following came from Thermeleth and Thelsas 36 with their leaders Charaathalar and Alar, and could not 37 prove by their families and genealogies that they were Israelites: the line of Dalan, the line of Ban, and the line of Necodan six hundred and fifty-two.

38 From among the priests the claimants to the priesthood whose record could not be traced: the line of Obdia, of Accos, of Joddus, who married Augia one of the daughters
39 of Zorzelleas, and took his name; when search was made for their family record in the register it could not be traced, and so they were excluded from priestly service.
40 Nehemiah the governor[a] told them that they should not participate in the sacred offerings until a high priest arose wearing the breastpiece of Revelation and Truth.

41 They were in all: Israelites from twelve years old, not counting slaves male and female, forty-two thousand
42 three hundred and sixty; their slaves seven thousand three hundred and thirty-seven; musicians and singers two
43 hundred and forty-five; camels four hundred and thirty-five, horses seven thousand and thirty-six, mules two hundred and forty-five, donkeys five thousand five hundred and twenty-five.

44 Some of the heads of families, when they arrived at the temple of God in Jerusalem, made a vow to erect the
45 house again on its site as best they could, and to give to the sacred treasury for the fabric fund one thousand minas of gold and five thousand minas of silver and one hundred vestments.

46 The priests, the Levites, and some of the people settled in Jerusalem and the neighbourhood, with the temple musicians and the door-keepers; and all Israel settled in their villages.

* There follows a list of returning exiles substantially similar to those found in Ezra 2 and Neh. 7. There are some differences in the names, mostly to be accounted for by the

[a] the governor: *probable meaning; Gk.* and Attharias.

translation into Greek, and frequent disparities in the numbers, which are particularly liable to be altered in the course of transmission. A greater difference arises from the fact that the picture of restoration given here places this mass return in the reign of Darius, rather than that of Cyrus as in Ezra 2. This is probably best understood as part of the overall stress on the role of Zerubbabel, whose work is, as we have seen, associated with the time of Darius and the rebuilding of the temple.

8. Twelve leaders are listed here, as in Neh. 7: 7, whereas Ezra 2: 2 has eleven. Some names have been altered out of all recognition, but it is likely that they are to be pictured as leaders of the twelve tribes.

9-39. The categories of those who returned are set out in the same order as in the earlier lists; the details follow Ezra 2 more closely than Neh. 7.

40. *Nehemiah the governor:* as the N.E.B. footnote shows, it appears as if the Greek translator understood this reference as being to two individuals 'Nehemiah and Attharias'. The latter is based on the unusual word *tirshatha*, translated 'governor' in the N.E.B. at Ezra 2: 63, and applied elsewhere only to Nehemiah (Neh. 8: 9; 10: 1). Over and above this misunderstanding our confusion is increased by the fact that Zerubbabel and Nehemiah are taken as contemporaries, whereas it is virtually certain that nearly a hundred years separated them. There is much evidence that later Jews, looking back from a later period at the restoration, fore-shortened the perspective very drastically and treated the leading figures as contemporaries and the main events as virtually simultaneous. Ezra 7: 1 is perhaps the first example of this tendency, which is carried further here and in 2 Maccabees. *the breastpiece of Revelation and Truth:* this repre-sents the Hebrew 'The Urim and the Thummim', words which had once designated some kind of sacred lot. That meaning had been forgotten, but the words are paraphrased here in appropriate Greek forms.

41. The total of those returning is the same as the figure given in Ezra 2 and Neh. 7 despite the many differences in its detailed composition.

45. *one thousand minas of gold:* the 'sixty-one thousand drachmas' of Ezra 2: 69, the exact nature and value of which are unknown to us and may already have been so in the time of the Greek translation, are set out in more familiar terms. The *mina* was worth 50 or 60 shekels, that is, a weight of approximately 20 oz (600 grammes) or a little more.

46. This verse might seem to imply that Jerusalem had already been rebuilt, but we should probably not see too precise a reference in the terms here used. ✶

WORSHIP RESTORED

47 When the seventh month came and the Israelites were in their homes they gathered as one man in the broad square 48 of the first gateway toward the east. Jeshua son of Josedek and his brother priests and Zerubbabel son of Salathiel and his colleagues came forward and made ready the 49 altar of the God of Israel, to offer on it whole burnt-offerings according to the directions in the book of Moses 50 the man of God. They were joined[a] by men from the other peoples of the land and they set up the altar on its site (for the peoples in the land as a whole were hostile to them and were too strong for them); and they offered sacrifices to the Lord at the proper time, and whole burnt-51 offerings morning and evening. They observed the Feast of Tabernacles as enjoined in the law, and the proper 52 sacrifices day by day; and thereafter the continual offer-ings, and sacrifices on sabbaths, at new moons, and on all 53 solemn feasts. All who had made a vow to God offered sacrifices to God from the new moon of the seventh

[a] *Or* attacked; *the clauses are perhaps in a confused order.*

month, although the temple of God was not yet built. Money was paid to the stonemasons and carpenters; the 54-55 Sidonians and Tyrians were supplied with food and drink, and with carts to bring cedar-trees from Lebanon, floating them down as rafts to the anchorage at Joppa, as decreed by Cyrus king of Persia.

* These verses follow Ezra 3: 1-7 in an idealistic description of the way in which the first act of the returning exiles was to establish the altar and resume the correct round of sacrifices. No attempt is made to avoid the basic inconsistency, that according to Ezra 3 these events took place in the reign of Cyrus, presumably in 538/7 B.C., whereas here they are placed under Darius.

47. *in their homes:* this appears to present a contrast with Ezra 3: 1, 'in their towns', but in fact the Greek is very vague – it refers simply to 'their own places'. The reference to *the broad square of the first gateway* which follows is an elaboration; our knowledge of the topography is insufficient for a precise identification to be possible.

49. *the book of Moses:* in Ezra's time the Hebrew word *torah* could appropriately be translated 'law' (Ezra 3: 2); by the time of 1 Esdras 'the torah' had become a technical description of the first five books of the Hebrew Bible, and so the translation *book* is now the natural one. By this time, too, the tradition that Moses was the author had become a well-established one (cp. Mark 12: 26).

50. As the N.E.B. footnote indicates, there may be some confusion in the text at this point. The reference in Ezra 3 corresponding to *the other peoples of the land* speaks only of the dread they caused, whereas there appear to be two traditions woven together here – one of joining together in worship with others, the other of mutual hostility. Neither in Ezra nor here is it entirely clear what the connection was between these relationships and the establishment of *the altar*.

51. *They observed the Feast of Tabernacles as enjoined in the*

law: the structure of 1 Esdras gives special emphasis to the observance of festivals according to the law: it begins with Josiah's Passover and ends with the festival following Ezra's reading of the law, and the emphasis on the role of Zerubbabel makes this a third high point, similarly marked by a festival. ✳

THE FOUNDATIONS OF THE TEMPLE LAID

56 In the second month of the second year, Zerubbabel son of Salathiel came to the temple of God in Jerusalem and started the work. There were with him Jeshua son of
57 Josedek, their kinsmen, the levitical priests, and all who had come to Jerusalem from the exile; and they laid the foundation of the temple of God. This was at the new moon, in the second month of the second year after they
58 had returned to Judaea and Jerusalem. The Levites from the age of twenty and upwards were set over the works of the Lord. Jeshua, his sons, his brothers, his brother Cadoel, the sons of Jeshua Emadabun, and the sons of Joda son of Iliadun with their sons and brothers, all the Levites, supervisors of the work, were active as one man on the works in the house of God. While the builders
59 built the temple of the Lord, the priests in their vestments with musical instruments and trumpets, and the Levites the sons of Asaph with their cymbals, stood singing to the
60 Lord and praising him as David king of Israel had ap-
61 pointed. They sang psalms praising the Lord, 'for his
62 goodness and glory is for ever toward all Israel'. All the people blew their trumpets and gave a loud shout, singing to the Lord as the building rose.

63 The priests, the Levites, and heads of families, the older men who had seen the former house, came to the building

of this one with cries of lamentation; and so, while many 64
were sounding the trumpets loudly for joy – so loudly as
to be heard far away – the people could not hear the 65
trumpets for the noise of lamentation.

✷ These verses are based on Ezra 3: 8–13, and for the most
part follow their source closely, save for the names in verse 58,
where there are changes both in the names themselves and
in the order in which they are listed.

56. *In the second month of the second year:* based on Ezra 3: 8,
where it is placed in the reign of Cyrus. Here we are allegedly
in the reign of Darius, but it seems that this historical difficulty
does not concern our author.

57. *they laid the foundation of the temple of God:* the account
in Ezra appears to be reworded so as to emphasize once again
the importance of the achievement of Zerubbabel. The same
effect is achieved by the addition of details of the date – the
foundation-laying is treated as a solemn ceremony.

60–1. Neither the Greek nor the English translation is free
from ambiguity; it is not clear whether the reference is to
the general worship arrangements laid down by David according to 1 Chron. 15–16, or whether the reference to David is
to his alleged authorship of the Psalms, from one of which a
quotation follows. (The phrase is too generalized for us to be
able to identify a particular psalm with certainty.)

63–5. The weeping may originally have been a formalized
ritual gesture, but here it is presented as being a natural
emotion, on the part of those who remembered the former
temple. Again there is a shortening of historical perspective;
the number of survivors fifty years after the event, in the time
of Cyrus, would have been very few; sixteen years later, in
Darius' reign, as here presented, it seems incredible that there
would have been any sizeable body to make such *cries of
lamentation.* ✷

OPPOSITION

66 The enemies of Judah and Benjamin heard the noise
67 of the trumpets and came to see what it meant. They
found the returned exiles building the temple for the
68 Lord God of Israel; they came to Zerubbabel and Jeshua
69 and the leaders of the families, and said: 'We will build
with you; for like you we obey your Lord and have
sacrificed to him from the time of Asbasareth king of
70 Assyria who transported us here.' But Zerubbabel and
Jeshua and the leaders of the families of Israel replied:
'You can have no share in building the house for the
71 Lord our God; we alone will build for the Lord of Israel,
72 as Cyrus king of Persia decreed.' But the peoples of the
land harassed[a] the men of Judaea, blockaded them, and
73 interrupted the building. Their plots, agitations, and riots
held up the completion of the building all the lifetime of
King Cyrus. They were prevented from building for two
years until Darius became king.

* The theme of opposition, already briefly touched upon
at verse 50, is now elaborated in accordance with Ezra 4.
However, the main part of that chapter (verses 7–24) has
already been used in 1 Esdras 2, and so the account here is
based on verses 1–5 only. Once again there is historical
confusion caused by the taking over of an account dated in
the reign of Cyrus, who is referred to as still being king
(verse 73) despite the earlier stories about Darius.

66. *heard the noise of the trumpets:* this provides a much
closer link between this section and the preceding one than
is found in Ezra 4: 1 where the word 'heard' is used in the
sense of 'hearing about'. This verse pictures the opponents
as other inhabitants of the immediate area of Jerusalem.

[a] *Probable reading; Gk. obscure.*

69. *Asbasareth:* Ezra 4: 2 has 'Esarhaddon' who ruled 681–669 B.C.; Josephus (who normally appears to use 1 Esdras as his source) has Shalmaneser, an earlier Assyrian king. It is not easy to see how the form here can have arisen, as a version of either of these names, or of that of any other foreign ruler known to us.

69–73. Neither here, nor in the source in Ezra, is the exact course of events easy to follow; probably more than one original has been combined, so that one alien group was anxious to help, while another was opposed to the whole venture, rather than, as is pictured here, initial friendliness turning to hostility.

73. This verse is historically very confused. First, we are transported back to the time of *King Cyrus*; secondly, the reference to *two years* appears to arise from a misunderstanding of Ezra 4: 24, which speaks of 'the second year of the reign of Darius'. The interval between the death of Cyrus (530 B.C.) and the accession of Darius (522) was longer than two years. ✣

CAN THE TEMPLE BE REBUILT?

In the second year of the reign of Darius, the prophets **6** Haggai and Zechariah son of Addo prophesied to the Jews in Judaea and Jerusalem in the name of the Lord the God of Israel. Then Zerubbabel son of Salathiel and 2 Jeshua son of Josedek began to rebuild the house of the Lord in Jerusalem. The prophets of the Lord were at their side to help them. At that time Sisinnes, the gover- 3 nor-general of Syria and Phoenicia, with Sathrabuzanes and their colleagues, came to them and said: 'Who has 4 authorized you to put up this building, complete with roof and everything else? Who are the builders carrying out this work?' But, thanks to the Lord who protected 5 the returned exiles, the elders of the Jews were not pre- 6

vented from building during the time that Darius was
being informed and directions issued.

7　　Here is a copy of the letter written to Darius, and sent
by Sisinnes, the governor-general of Syria and Phoenicia,
with Sathrabuzanes and their colleagues the authorities in
Syria and Phoenicia:

8　　　To King Darius our humble duty. Be it known to
our lord the king: we visited the district of Judaea and
entered the city of Jerusalem, and there we found the
9　elders of the Jews returned from exile building a great
new house for the Lord with costly hewn stone and
10　with beams set in the walls. This work was being done
with all speed and the undertaking was making good
progress; it was being executed in great splendour and
11　with the utmost care. We then inquired of these elders
by whose authority they were building this house and
12　laying such foundations. We questioned them so that
we could inform you in writing who their leaders
13　were, and asked for a list of their names. They answered
as follows: 'We are servants of the Lord who made
14　heaven and earth. This house was built and completed
many years ago by a great and powerful king of Israel.
15　When our fathers sinned against the heavenly Lord of
Israel and provoked him, he delivered them over to
Nebuchadnezzar, king of Babylon, king of the Chal-
16　daeans; and they pulled down the house, set it on fire,
17　and took the people into exile in Babylon. In the first
year of the reign of King Cyrus over Babylonia, the
18　king decreed that this house should be rebuilt. The
sacred vessels of gold and silver which Nebuchadnezzar
had taken from the house in Jerusalem, and set up in

his own temple, he brought back out of the temple in
Babylon and delivered to Zerubbabel and Sanabassar
the governor, with orders to take all these vessels and 19
to put them in the temple at Jerusalem, and to rebuild
this temple of the Lord on the same site as before. Then 20
Sanabassar came and laid the foundations of the house
of the Lord in Jerusalem. From then till now the
building has continued and is still unfinished.' There- 21
fore, if it is Your Majesty's pleasure, let search be made
in the royal archives in Babylon, and if it is found that 22
the building of the house of the Lord in Jerusalem took
place with the approval of King Cyrus, and if our lord
the king so decide, let directions be issued to us on this
subject.

* This section follows its source (Ezra 4: 24*b* – 5: 17) closely,
though the overall effect is different, because in Ezra this
passage is presented as part of a series of accounts describing
opposition; as we have seen, the earlier part of this Ezra
material has been placed elsewhere by the author of 1 Esdras.
The confusion concerning dates and the appropriate Persian
ruler is now at an end; this section is clearly anchored in
the reign of Darius and can be dated about 520 B.C.

1. *Haggai and Zechariah . . . prophesied to the Jews:* the
ministry of these prophets is in all traditions closely linked with
the rebuilding of the temple. In Ezra 5: 1 they are said to
have 'upbraided' the people, in accordance with the traditions
in the prophetic books themselves about the negligence of
the community. A different impression is created here, as if
this was the first signal to begin the work.

3. *Sisinnes, the governor-general of Syria and Phoenicia, with
Sathrabuzanes:* the names and title here well illustrate the
translation problem. The original names 'Tattenai' and

'Shethar-bozenai' of Ezra 5: 3 are almost unrecognizable in their Greek form; while the description of the province is changed from the Persian 'Beyond-Euphrates' to a description which made more sense in the political situation of a later age.

6. None of the accounts of opposition described in 1 Esdras leads to any extended breakdown in the process of restoration; that mentioned in 5: 73 is very brief (since 'two years' need only imply short parts of two successive years), and here no interruption of the work is involved.

8–22. The translation of the official letter is in places a very free rendering of Ezra 5: 8–17, but the sense is identical – the local officials are anxious to ensure that all is being carried out on proper authority. Only at one point is an addition made which may give a significant pointer to the concern of 1 Esdras: the addition of the name of *Zerubbabel* in verse 18 (where the original, Ezra 5: 14, only mentions 'Sheshbazzar' (*Sanabassar*)) is a further indication of the importance attributed to him in the whole enterprise.   *

OFFICIAL PERMISSION GRANTED

23 Then King Darius ordered the archives in Babylon to be searched, and a scroll was found in the castle at Ecbatana in the province of Media which contained the following record:

24   In the first year of his reign King Cyrus ordered that the house of the Lord in Jerusalem, where they sacrifice
25 with fire continually, should be rebuilt. Its height should be sixty cubits and its breadth sixty cubits, with three courses of hewn stone to one of new local timber; the
26 expenses to be met from the royal treasury. The sacred gold and silver vessels of the house of the Lord which Nebuchadnezzar removed from the house in Jeru-

salem, and took to Babylon, should be restored to the house in Jerusalem and replaced where they formerly were.

Darius therefore instructed Sisinnes, the governor-general of Syria and Phoenicia, with Sathrabuzanes, their colleagues, and the governors in office in Syria and Phoenicia, to be careful not to interfere with the place, but to allow the servant of the Lord, Zerubbabel, governor of Judaea, and the elders of the Jews to build the house of the Lord on its old site. 'I have also given instructions', he continued, 'that it should be completely rebuilt, and that they should not fail to co-operate with the returned exiles in Judaea until the house of the Lord is finished. From the tribute of Coele-syria and Phoenicia let a contribution be duly given to these men for sacrifices to the Lord, payable to Zerubbabel the governor, for bulls, rams, and lambs; and similarly wheat, salt, wine, and oil are to be provided regularly each year without question, as the priests in Jerusalem may require day by day. Let all this be expended in order that sacrifices and libations may be offered to the Most High God for the king and his children, and that intercession may be made on their behalf.' He also gave these orders: 'If anyone disobeys or neglects any of these orders written above or here set down, let a beam be taken from his own house and let him be hanged on it and his estate forfeited to the king. May the Lord himself, therefore, to whom this temple is dedicated, destroy any king or people who shall lift a finger to delay or damage the Lord's house in Jerusalem. I, Darius the king, decree that these orders be obeyed to the letter.'

✻ The source here is Ezra 6: 1–12, which is followed closely with a few distinctive traces of the characteristic features of I Esdras. As in the original, the beneficent attitude of the Persian imperial power is stressed.

23. Ezra 6: 1–2 had emphasized the fact that the search for 'the scroll' at Babylon was fruitless, and that the relevant document was in fact found in another royal residence, far away to the east, at Ecbatana; here the geographical knowledge of these distant areas seems very hazy, and it seems as if the author thought that Ecbatana was part of Babylon.

24–6. These verses represent the Aramaic form of Cyrus' decree, which is commonly held to be an authentic rendering of the original form, whereas the genuineness of the Hebrew form underlying 2: 3–7 has been widely questioned.

27. *the servant of the Lord, Zerubbabel:* both the specific mention of Zerubbabel by name here and in verse 29, and the use of the exalted title *servant of the Lord* to describe him provide further evidence of the important role given to him by our author.

32. It seems likely that a Roman form of punishment is here substituted for the Persian form found in Ezra 6: 11. ✻

THE TEMPLE REBUILT

7 Then, in accordance with the orders of King Darius, Sisinnes, governor-general of Coele-syria and Phoenicia, 2 with Sathrabuzanes and their colleagues, carefully supervised the sacred works, co-operating with the elders of 3 the Jews and the temple officers. With the encouragement of the prophets Haggai and Zechariah, good progress was 4 made with the sacred works, and they were finished by the ordinance of the Lord God of Israel and with the approval of Cyrus, Darius, and Artaxerxes, kings of 5 Persia. It was on the twenty-third of Adar in the sixth

year of King Darius that the house was completed. The 6
Israelites, the priests, the Levites, and the rest of the former
exiles who had joined them carried out the directions in
the book of Moses. For the dedication of the temple of 7
the Lord they offered a hundred bulls, two hundred rams,
four hundred lambs, and twelve goats for the sin of all 8
Israel corresponding to the twelve patriarchs of Israel.
The priests and the Levites in their vestments stood 9
family by family to preside over the services of the Lord
God of Israel according to the book of Moses. The door-
keepers took their stand at every gateway.

The Israelites who had returned from exile kept the 10
Passover on the fourteenth day of the first month. The
priests and the Levites were purified together; not all the 11
returned exiles were purified with the priests, but[a] the
Levites were. They slaughtered the Passover victims for 12
all the returned exiles and for their brother priests and for
themselves. All those Israelites participated who had re- 13
turned from exile and had segregated themselves from
the abominations of the peoples of the land to seek the
Lord. They kept the Feast of Unleavened Bread for 14
seven days, rejoicing before the Lord; for he had changed 15
the policy of the Assyrian king towards them and
strengthened them for the service of the Lord the God
of Israel.

* The climax of this middle section of the book is reached
with the successful completion of the rebuilding of the
temple, and the solemn celebration of the Passover which

[a] not all .... but: *probable meaning; Gk. obscure; some witnesses*
omit not.

53

follows. The original events took place in 516/15 B.C.; the account here follows closely its source in Ezra 6: 13–22.

2. The co-operation between the imperial authorities and the Jews is stressed even more strongly here than in the original. It is possible that one aim of this book is to emphasize the close and fruitful collaboration that took place between the Jewish leaders and the civil authorities of different periods, perhaps at a time when the Jews were held in suspicion by the contemporary authorities.

4. *Artaxerxes:* this reference is anachronistic, since he did not become Persian Emperor until the following century (465–424 B.C.). Curiously the N.E.B. has relegated the word to a footnote at Ezra 6: 14, but has left it in the text here.

5. The probable date of completion was February/March 515 B.C. The day of the month given here differs from that in Ezra, though the N.E.B. has emended the Ezra text to correspond with this.

6. By the time of the composition of 1 Esdras, *the book of Moses*, the Pentateuch, will have been recognized as the guiding principle of the Jewish community's life, and the loyalty of the leaders to its requirements is here emphasized (cp. 5: 49 and the comment there).

11. The text here is very obscure; the N.E.B. may be right, but certainty is impossible. A parallel may be intended with Hezekiah's Passover in 2 Chron. 30 where the participants from the northern tribes 'had not kept themselves ritually clean, and therefore kept the Passover irregularly' (2 Chron. 30: 18). In a similar way *the returned exiles* here (and the northerners of 2 Chronicles were in a sense returned exiles also) had acted in good faith (verse 13), even though they were not ritually *purified*.

12–15. The last verses follow their source very closely, including the stress on separatism and the curious and unexplained reference to *the Assyrian king*. ✳

Ezra in Jerusalem

٭ The account in 1 Esdras follows that in the book of Ezra
at this point in passing over a considerable intervening period
so as to deal with the mission of Ezra himself, and in that
sense the introduction here of a new heading by the N.E.B.
is entirely justified. It must, however, be borne in mind that
it is our superior knowledge of the chronology of the period,
together with our developed historical sense, which leads us
to stress the gap between the events so far described and the
work of Ezra. Probably neither the original writer of Ezra
nor our present authors realized the length of the gap at this
point; it is furthermore likely that, if they had been aware of
it, it would have been of little consequence to them. Both
regarded the restoration of Israel as a unified process, of the
people's guidance by their God, so that once again they became
his truly dedicated community worshipping in the holy city.

It is universally agreed that there is a long gap between
Zerubbabel and Ezra; it is much less generally agreed exactly
how long that gap was, for we cannot be certain whether
the 'Artaxerxes' referred to in this section is Artaxerxes I
(465–424 B.C.) or Artaxerxes II (404–358). (For some discussion of the chronological problem, see the commentary on
Ezra and Nehemiah in this series, especially pp. 6–8.) For the
reader of 1 Esdras, however, confusion is less likely to arise,
since it is created largely by the uncertainties of the relation
between Ezra and Nehemiah, and that problem does not
arise here, since Nehemiah is ignored altogether. For 1 Esdras,
Zerubbabel and Ezra are the key figures, and the remainder
of the book describes Ezra's accomplishment.

Ezra is sometimes called the 'father of Judaism', and the
implications of this description are important for our understanding of the way he is presented here. In the last pre-
Christian centuries Judaism came to be heavily dependent

upon the law and other written traditions handed down in the community, as it reflected upon and interpreted the way God had dealt with his people in the past. This is the pattern which underlies both post-biblical Jewish writings and the New Testament, and it has been widely held among Jews that Ezra played a major role in establishing this pattern – hence the appropriateness of calling him the 'father of Judaism'. In the traditional view, the religion held to have been founded by Moses has now been codified and structured afresh. ✻

EZRA GOES TO JERUSALEM

8 AFTER THESE EVENTS, in the reign of Artaxerxes king of Persia, came Ezra, son of Saraeas, son of Ezerias,
2 son of Chelkias, son of Salemus, son of Zadok, son of Ahitub, son of Amarias, son of Ezias, son of Mareroth, son of Zaraeas, son of Savia, son of Bocca, son of Abishua, son of Phineas, son of Eleazar, son of Aaron the chief
3 priest. This Ezra came from Babylon as a talented scholar in the law of Moses which had been given by the God of
4 Israel. The king held him in high regard and looked with favour upon all the requests he made. He was accom-
5 panied to Jerusalem by some Israelites, priests, Levites,
6 temple singers, door-keepers, and temple-servitors, in the fifth month of the seventh year of Artaxerxes' reign.[a] They left Babylon at the new moon in the first month and reached Jerusalem at the new moon in the fifth
7 month; for the Lord gave them a safe journey. Ezra's knowledge of the law of the Lord and the command-ments was exact in every detail, so that he could teach all Israel the ordinances and judgements.

[a] *Probable reading; one witness adds* this was the king's second year.

* These verses are based on Ezra 7: 1–10. In that passage there is some ambiguity between the presentation of Ezra as part of the Persian imperial service and his essentially religious role within Judaism; here, as we should expect, all the emphasis is on the latter.

1. Though, as we have seen, an interval of at least fifty-eight years (and perhaps much longer) passed before the arrival of Ezra, it seems likely that the author of 1 Esdras thought of Artaxerxes as approximately contemporary with Cyrus and Darius. He has already referred to him in 2: 16–30 and 7: 4 as if this were so.

1–2. In the last centuries before Christ it was regarded as important for all Jews, and especially for the priestly line, to be able to establish their genealogy. Ezra's family tree is given in various places, each with minor differences. As given in the N.E.B. this list corresponds exactly with Ezra 7: 1–5 save for the Greek form of some of the names, but most Greek manuscripts have a shorter form, omitting the names between *Ezias* and *Bocca*. It is surprising that there is no footnote to indicate this.

3. *a talented scholar in the law of Moses:* in Ezra 7: 6 the description of Ezra as 'a scribe' left open the possibility that this might describe his position in the Persian imperial service; here it is without doubt a religious title, corresponding to the 'scribes' who are frequently mentioned in the gospels.

7. The stress on Ezra's *knowledge of the law of the Lord* fits better in its context here, where the climax of his work will be the proclamation of the law, than in Ezra, where that proclamation is dealt with quite separately. *

THE KING'S MANDATE

The following is a copy of the mandate from King 8 Artaxerxes to Ezra the priest, doctor of the law of the Lord:

9   King Artaxerxes to Ezra the priest, doctor of the law
     of the Lord, greeting.

10   I have graciously decided, and now command, that
     those of the Jewish nation and of the priests and Levites,
     in our kingdom, who so choose, shall go with you to
11   Jerusalem. I and my council of seven Friends have
     decided that all who so desire may accompany you.
12   Let them look to the affairs of Judaea and Jerusalem in
13   pursuance of the law of the Lord, and bring to Jeru-
     salem for the Lord of Israel the gifts which I and my
     Friends have vowed, all the gold and silver in Baby-
     lonia that may be found to belong to the Lord in
14   Jerusalem, together with what has been given by the
     nation for the temple of the Lord their God in Jeru-
     salem. Let the gold and silver be expended upon[a] bulls,
15   rams, lambs, and so forth, so that sacrifices may be
     offered upon the altar of the Lord their God in Jeru-
16   salem. Make use of the gold and silver in whatever ways
     you and your colleagues desire, according to the will of
17   your God, and deliver the sacred vessels of the Lord
     which have been given you for the use of the temple
     of your God in Jerusalem.

18   Any other expenses that you may incur for the needs
     of the temple of your God you shall defray from the
19   royal treasury. I, Artaxerxes the king, direct the trea-
     surers of Syria and Phoenicia to give without fail to
     Ezra the priest, doctor of the law of the Most High
20   God, whatever he may request up to a hundred talents
     of silver, and similarly up to a hundred sacks of wheat
     and a hundred casks of wine, and salt without limit.

[a] *Or* collected for.

58

Let him diligently fulfil in honour of the Most High   21
God all the requirements of God's law, so that divine
displeasure may not befall the kingdom of the king and
of his descendants. You are also informed that no tax   22
or other impost is to be laid on the priests, the Levites,
the temple singers, the door-keepers, the temple-
servitors, and the lay officers of this temple; no one is
permitted to impose any burden on them. You, Ezra,   23
under God's guidance, are to appoint judges and magistrates to judge all who know the law of your God in all
Syria and Phoenicia; you yourself shall see to the instruction of those who do not know it. All who trans-   24
gress the law of your God and of the king shall be
duly punished with death, degradation, fine, or exile.

Then Ezra said: All praise to the Lord alone, who put   25
this into the king's mind, to glorify his house in Jerusalem. He singled me out for honour before the king,   26
his counsellors, and all his Friends and dignitaries. I took   27
courage from the help of the Lord my God and gathered
men of Israel to go up with me.

✻   This section follows its source, Ezra 7: 11–28, very closely;
in the original the royal decree is in Aramaic, the language
used by the Persian court for official decrees in its western
provinces.

8. *doctor of the law:* the phrase reminds us once again of the
similarity between the usage in 1 Esdras and that of the New
Testament (cp. the Authorized Version of Luke 2: 46).

10–24. The decree itself follows its source very closely,
with the occasional modifications necessary in translation
(e.g. the details of the measures in verse 20). The impression
that this is treated as part of the original return of Jews from

Babylon is strengthened by the references to provisions for the temple and its vessels; taken by itself this decree would certainly most naturally be read as the start of an entirely new venture.

23. If the N.E.B. translation is right, this arrangement is different from that laid down in Ezra 7: 25, where Ezra and those appointed by him are to join together in instructing those ignorant of the law. But it is possible to interpret the Greek text as bearing the same meaning as the Aramaic of Ezra 7: 25.

25–7. This psalm-like interjection of praise follows its source (Ezra 7: 27–8) in its switch to the first person.   ✳

THE LEADERS OF THE COMMUNITY

28 These are the leaders according to clans and divisions who went with me from Babylon to Jerusalem in the reign of King Artaxerxes: from the line of Phineas,
29 Gershom; from the line of Ithamar, Gamael; from the
30 line of David, Attus son of Sechenias; from the line of Phoros, Zacharias and a hundred and fifty men with him
31 according to the register; from the line of Phaath-moab, Eliaonias son of Zaraeas and with him two hundred men;
32 from the line of Zathoe, Sechenias son of Jezelus and with him three hundred men; from the line of Adin, Obeth son of Jonathan and with him two hundred and
33 fifty men; from the line of Elam, Jessias son of Gotholias
34 and with him seventy men; from the line of Sophotias,
35 Zaraeas son of Michael and with him seventy men; from the line of Joab, Abadias son of Jezelus and with him
36 two hundred and twelve men; from the line of Bani, Assalimoth son of Josaphias and with him a hundred and
37 sixty men; from the line of Babi, Zacharias son of Bebae

and with him twenty-eight men; from the line of Astath, 38
Joannes son of Hacatan and with him a hundred and ten
men; last came those from the line of Adonikam, by 39
name Eliphalatus, Jeuel, and Samaeas, and with them
seventy men; from the line of Bago, Uthi son of Istal- 40
curus and with him seventy men.

I assembled them at the river called Theras, where we 41
encamped for three days, and I inspected them. As I 42
found no one there who was of priestly or levitical
descent, I sent to Eleazar, Iduelus, Maasmas, Elnathan, 43
Samaeas, Joribus, Nathan, Ennatas, Zacharias, and Mosol- 44
lamus, who were prominent and discerning men. I told 45
them to go to Doldaeus the chief man at the treasury.
I instructed them to speak with Doldaeus, his colleagues, 46
and the treasurers there, and ask them to send us priests
to officiate in the house of our Lord. Under the provi- 47
dence of God they brought us discerning men from the
line of Mooli son of Levi son of Israel, Asebebias and his
sons and brothers, eighteen men in all, also Asebias and 48
Annunus and Hosaeas his brother. Those of the line of
Chanunaeus and their sons amounted to twenty men; and 49
those of the temple-servitors whom David and the leading
men appointed for the service of the Levites amounted
to two hundred and twenty. A register of all these names
was compiled.

✻ These verses – based on Ezra 8: 1–20 – show a characteristic concern to identify the leaders of the true community,
setting out their genealogy as the appropriate credentials
by which they might be judged. Though there are minor
changes the source is followed closely.

28–40. The only significant change in this list (which is related to that given in ch. 5) concerns some of the numbers of kinsmen listed.

41. *the river called Theras:* the name is given in only one manuscript of the Greek text, and is not in Ezra 8; its whereabouts is unknown.

42. *no one . . . of priestly or levitical descent:* Ezra 8: 15 speaks only of the lack of Levites. The text here may be softening the implied criticism, or it may be a misunderstanding of the original. In any case it scarcely makes sense, since the families of Phineas and Ithamar, mentioned in verse 29, were certainly priestly, as being of Aaronic descent (1 Chron. 6: 3–4).

43–4. Only ten names are listed here, as against the eleven of Ezra 8: 16, and there are several differences in detail.

45. *at the treasury:* this is a good instance of the hazards of translation. In Ezra 8: 17 a place, perhaps a sanctuary, ('Casiphia') is mentioned; here the place-name has been interpreted as a common noun meaning *treasury*.

46. *to send us priests:* as in verse 42, there is a discrepancy with the Ezra text, which refers only to 'servitors' – a menial office by comparison with the priests mentioned here. ✡

THE SOLEMN PROCESSION

50 There I made a vow that the young men should fast
before our Lord to beg him to give us a safe journey for
ourselves, our children who accompanied us, and our
51 pack-animals. I was ashamed to ask the king for an escort
52 of infantry and cavalry against our enemies; for we had
told the king that the strength of our Lord would ensure
53 success for those who looked to him. So once more we
laid all these things before our Lord in prayer and found
him gracious.

54 I set apart twelve men from among the heads of the

priestly families, and with them Sarabias and Asamias and
ten of their brother priests. I weighed out for them the 55
silver, the gold, and the sacred vessels of the house of our
Lord; these had been presented by the king himself, his
counsellors, the chief men, and all Israel. When I had 56
weighed it all I handed over to them six hundred and
fifty talents of silver, and vessels of silver weighing a
hundred talents, a hundred talents of gold, and twenty 57
pieces of gold plate, and twelve vessels of brass so fine
that it gleamed like gold. I said to them: 'You are conse- 58
crated to the Lord, and so are the vessels; the silver and the
gold are vowed to the Lord, the Lord of our fathers. Be 59
vigilant and keep guard until you hand them over at
Jerusalem, in the priests' rooms in the house of our Lord,
to the heads of the priestly and levitical families and to
the leaders of the clans of Israel.' The priests and the 60
Levites who received the silver, the gold, and the vessels
in Jerusalem brought them to the temple of the Lord.

We left the river Theras on the twelfth day of the first 61
month, and under the powerful protection which our
Lord gave us we reached Jerusalem. He guarded us against
every enemy on our journey, and so we arrived at Jerusalem. Three days passed, and on the fourth the silver and 62
gold were weighed and handed over in the house of our
Lord to the priest Marmathi son of Uri, with whom was 63
Eleazar son of Phineas. With them also were the Levites
Josabdus son of Jeshua and Moeth son of Sabannus. Everything was numbered and weighed and every weight 64
recorded there and then. The returned exiles offered sacri- 65
fices to the Lord the God of Israel, twelve bulls for all
Israel, with ninety-six rams and seventy-two lambs, and 66

also twelve goats for a peace-offering, the whole as a
67 sacrifice to the Lord. They delivered the king's orders to
the royal treasurers and the governors of Coele-syria and
Phoenicia, and so added lustre to the nation and the
temple of the Lord.

✳ This section follows closely its source in Ezra 8: 21–36,
and in each case what may originally have been a journey
carried out as part of the Persian imperial service is described
as if it were essentially a religious procession. Such a formalized mode of description is reminiscent of some of the
accounts of Israel's wandering in the wilderness before the
entry into Canaan (cp. Ps. 105: 43–5).

50–3. Fasting and prayer as preparation for an important
venture were characteristic practices in Judaism.

54–67. This whole section follows its source very closely,
with the minor variants in names and numbers that we have
by now come to expect. Only the last phrase of verse 67
appears to be different, but this is ambiguous in the Greek,
where the subject of the verb translated *added lustre* is not
expressed. ✳

EZRA'S PRAYER

68 When these matters had been settled the leaders came to
69 me and said: 'The nation of Israel, the rulers, the priests,
and the Levites, have not kept themselves apart from the
alien population of the land with all their pollutions, that
is to say the Canaanites, Hittites, Perizzites, Jebusites,
70 Moabites, Egyptians, and Edomites. For they and their
sons have intermarried with the daughters of these
peoples, and the holy race has been mingled with the
alien population of the land; and the leaders and principal
men have shared in this violation of the law from the very
beginning.'

As soon as I heard of this I tore my clothes and sacred 71
vestment, plucked out the hair of my head and my beard,
and sat down perplexed and miserable. Those who at 72
that time were moved by the word of the Lord of Israel
gathered round me, while I grieved over this disregard
of the law, and sat in my misery until the evening sacrifice. Then I rose from my fast with my clothes and sacred 73
vestment torn, and knelt down and, stretching out my
hands to the Lord, said: 74

'O Lord, I am covered with shame and confusion in
thy presence. Our sins tower above our heads; from the 75–76
time of our fathers our offences have reached the sky,
and today we are as deep in sin as ever. Because of our 77
sins and the sins of our fathers, we and our brothers, our
kings and our priests, were given over to the kings of
the earth to be killed, taken prisoner, plundered, and
humiliated down to this very day. And now, Lord, how 78
great is the mercy thou hast shown us! We still have a
root and a name in the place of thy sanctuary, and thou 79
hast rekindled our light in the house of our Lord, and
given us food in the time of our servitude. Even when 80
we were slaves we were not deserted by our Lord; for
he secured for us the favour of the kings of Persia, who 81
have provided our food and added lustre to the temple
of our Lord and restored the ruins of Zion, giving us a
firm foothold in Judaea and Jerusalem. And now, Lord, 82
what are we to say, we who have received all this? For
we have broken thy commandments given us through
thy servants the prophets. Thou didst say: "The land 83
which you are to occupy is a land defiled with the pollution of its heathen peoples; they have filled it with their
impurities. Do not marry your daughters to their sons nor 84

85 take their daughters for your sons; never try to make
peace with them if you want to be strong and enjoy the
good things of the land and take possession of it for your
86 children for ever." All our misfortunes have come upon
us through our evil deeds and our great sins. Although
thou, Lord, hast lightened the burden of our sins and given
87 us so firm a root, yet we have fallen away again and
broken thy law by sharing in the impurities of the heathen
88 peoples of this land. But thou wast not so angry with us,
89 Lord, as to destroy us, root, seed, and name; thou keepest
faith, O Lord of Israel; the root is left, we are here today.
90 Behold us, now before thee in our sins; because of all
we have done we can no longer hold up our heads before
thee.'

91 While Ezra prayed and made confession, weeping prostrate on the ground before the temple, a very large crowd
gathered, men, women, and youths of Jerusalem, and
there was widespread lamentation among the people.
92 Jechonias son of Jeel, one of the Israelites, called out to
Ezra: 'We have sinned against the Lord in taking alien
wives from the heathen population of this land; and yet
93 there is still hope for Israel. Let us take an oath to the
Lord to expel all our wives of alien race with their
94 children, in accordance with your judgement and the
judgement of all who are obedient to the law of the Lord.
95 Come now, set about it, it is in your hands; take strong
96 action and we are with you.' Ezra got up and laid an
oath upon the principal priests and Levites of all Israel
that they would act in this way, and they swore to it.

✻ Ezra's task in Jerusalem is described as twofold: the breaking-up of mixed marriages, and the proclamation of the law. The relation between these two parts of his work is a complex one, but all forms of the tradition are agreed in placing his action in regard to mixed marriages immediately after his arrival in Jerusalem. Here 1 Esdras is following Ezra 9: 1 – 10: 5; the chapter-division between I Esdras 8 and 9 does not correspond with that between Ezra 9 and 10.

68. Both in the book of Ezra and here it is stressed that the initiative came from the community, not from Ezra himself.

69. *Edomites:* at this point it is likely that 1 Esdras has preserved a better text than Ezra, for it is much more natural to find Edomites – against whom many parts of the Old Testament show hostility – than the 'Amorites' (an alternative name for Canaanites) of Ezra 9: 1.

72. In Ezra 9: 4 it is specified that the offence had been committed by those who had been exiled; that point is omitted here.

74–90. Ezra's prayer is also a word of exhortation to the community. As in its source in Ezra 9, the many allusions to earlier biblical passages serve to identify the contemporary community with the Israel of earlier ages. Already in the original a favourable attitude toward the kings of Persia is found, and this is still more emphasized in verse 81.

91–6. This section reverts to a third-person description of Ezra's action, and again emphasizes how his appeal led to an initiative on the part of the community itself. The reaction may not appear attractive to us, but it is motivated by a strong concern to establish the true meaning of being the people of God in the midst of hostile surroundings. This had been important when Ezra was written; it may have been still more important if 1 Esdras came from a Jewish community away from Palestine and surrounded by adherents of other religions who were suspicious of the Jews. ✻

THE EXPULSION OF FOREIGN WIVES

9 Ezra left the court of the temple and entered the room
2 of the priest Joanan son of Eliasibus. There he stayed,
eating no food and drinking no water, while he mourned
over the serious violations of the law by the community.
3 A proclamation was made throughout Judaea and in
Jerusalem to all the returned exiles that they should
4 assemble at Jerusalem; those who failed to arrive within
two or three days, according to the decision of the elders
in office, were to have their cattle confiscated for temple
use and would themselves be excluded from the community of the returned exiles.

5 Three days later all Judah and Benjamin had assembled
in Jerusalem; the date was the twentieth of the ninth
6 month. They all sat together in the open space before the
7 temple, shivering because winter had set in. Ezra stood up
and said to them: 'You have broken the law and married
alien wives, bringing a fresh burden of guilt on Israel.
8, 9 Now make confession to the Lord God of our fathers; do
his will and separate yourselves from the heathen population of this land and from your alien wives.'

10 The whole company answered with a shout: 'We will
11 do as you have said!' 'But', they said, 'our numbers are
great, and we cannot stay here in the open in this wintry
weather. Nor is this the work of a day or two only;
12 the offence is widespread among us. Let the leaders of the
community stay here, and let all members of our settle-
13 ments who have alien wives attend at an appointed time
along with the elders and judges of each place, until we
turn away the Lord's anger at what has been done.'

Jonathan son of Azael and Hezekias son of Thocanus 14 took charge on these terms, and Mosollamus, Levi, and Sabbataeus were their assessors. The returned exiles duly 15 carried all this out.

Ezra the priest selected men by name, all chiefs of their 16 clans, and on the new moon of the tenth month they sat to investigate the matter. This affair of the men who had 17 alien wives was settled by the new moon of the first month.

Among the priests some of those who had come to- 18 gether were found to have alien wives; these were 19 Mathelas, Eleazar, Joribus, and Joadanus of the line of Jeshua son of Josedek and his brothers, who undertook 20 to send away their wives and to offer rams in expiation of their error. Of the line of Emmer: Ananias, Zabdaeus, 21 Manes, Samaeus, Jereel, and Azarias; of the line of 22 Phaesus: Elionas, Massias, Ishmael, Nathanael, Okidelus, and Saloas. Of the Levites: Jozabadus, Semis, Colius (this 23 is Calitas), Phathaeus, Judah, and Jonas. Of the temple 24 singers: Eliasibus, Bacchurus. Of the door-keepers: Sallu- 25 mus and Tolbanes.

Of the people of Israel there were, of the line of 26 Phoros: Jermas, Jeddias, Melchias, Maelus, Eleazar, Asibias, and Bannaeas. Of the line of Ela: Matthanias, 27 Zacharias, Jezrielus, Oabdius, Jeremoth, and Aedias. Of 28 the line of Zamoth: Eliadas, Eliasimus, Othonias, Jari-moth, Sabathus, and Zardaeas. Of the line of Bebae: 29 Joannes, Ananias, Ozabadus, and Emathis. Of the line of 30 Mani: Olamus, Mamuchus, Jedaeus, Jasubus, Asaelus, and Jeremoth. Of the line of Addi: Naathus, Moossias, 31 Laccunus, Naidus, Matthanias, Sesthel, Balnuus, and

32 Manasseas. Of the line of Annas: Elionas, Asaeas, Mel-
33 chias, Sabbaeas, and Simon Chosomaeus. Of the line of
Asom: Altannaeus, Mattathias, Bannaeus, Eliphalat,
34 Manasses, and Semi. Of the line of Baani: Jeremias,
Momdis, Ismaerus, Juel, Mandae, Paedias, Anos, Cara-
basion, Enasibus, Mamnitanaemus, Eliasis, Bannus, Eliali,
Somis, Selemias, and Nathanias. Of the line of Ezora:
35 Sessis, Ezril, Azael, Samatus, Zambris, and Josephus. Of
the line of Nooma: Mazitias, Zabadaeas, Edaes, Juel, and
36 Banaeas. All these had married alien wives; they sent
them away with their children.

☆ The book of Ezra ends with an account of the carrying out of the measures for the purification of the community. In that context it appears to be a peculiarly lame conclusion; here the source is closely followed, but a different impression is created by the fact that an account of the law-reading immediately follows. In the present context we are given an account of the consequences of the action already described.

1. *the priest Joanan son of Eliasibus:* it has often been argued that this priest should be identified with the 'Jonathan' or 'Johanan' of Neh. 12: 11, 22, and that 'grandson' rather than *son* should be read here, as in the N.E.B. of Ezra 10: 6. If both these suggestions were correct, it would point toward a dating of Ezra in the time of Artaxerxes II (about 398 B.C.), but neither can be regarded as established.

4. *cattle confiscated for temple use:* this is more specific than Ezra 10: 8, and may reflect the custom within the religious community of the author's day.

5–15. The outlines of the religious ceremony follow the same pattern as that described in Ezra 10, with one curious variant. In Ezra 10: 15 'Jonathan ... and Jahzeiah' are recorded as being opposed to Ezra's plea; here they are those who *took charge*. It is possible that this is due to misunder-

standing on the part of 1 Esdras; more probably we see here
a tradition which stressed the unanimity of the community in
all its major decisions.

18–36. The names listed show a number of minor variants
from those in Ezra 10; this has been characteristic of all the
lists of names incorporated in the book. ⋆

THE READING OF THE LAW

The priests, the Levites, and such Israelites as were in 37
Jerusalem and its vicinity, settled down there on the new
moon of the seventh month; the other Israelites remained
in their settlements. The entire body assembled as one in 38
the open space before the east gateway of the temple and 39
asked Ezra the high priest and doctor of the law to bring
the law of Moses given by the Lord God of Israel. On the 40
new moon of the seventh month he brought the law to
all the multitude of men and women alike, and to the
priests, for them to hear. He read it in the open space 41
before the temple gateway from daybreak until noon, in
the presence of both men and women, and the whole
body listened intently. Ezra the priest and doctor of the 42
law stood upon the wooden platform which had been
prepared. There stood with him, on his right, Mattathias, 43
Sammus, Ananias, Azarias, Urias, Hezekias, and Baal-
samus, and on his left, Phaldaeus, Misael, Melchias, 44
Lothasubus, Nabarias, and Zacharias. Ezra took up the 45
book of the law; everyone could see him, for he was
seated in a conspicuous place in front of them all, and
when he opened it they all stood up. Ezra praised the 46
Lord God the Most High God of hosts, the Almighty.
All the multitude cried 'Amen, Amen', and lifting up 47

their hands fell to the ground and worshipped the Lord.
48 Jeshua, Annus, Sarabias, Jadinus, Jacubus, Sabbataeas, Autaeas, Maeannas, Calitas, Azarias, Jozabdus, Ananias, and Phiathas, the Levites, taught the law of the Lord; they read the law of the Lord to the whole company, at the same time instilling into their minds what was read.
49 Then the governor[a] said to Ezra the high priest and doctor of the law and to each of the Levites who taught
50 the multitude: 'This day is holy to the Lord.' All were
51 weeping as they heard the law. 'Go then, refresh yourselves with rich food and sweet wine, and send shares to
52 those who have none; for the day is holy to the Lord. Let there be no sadness; for the Lord will give you glory.'
53 The Levites issued the command to all the people: 'This
54 day is holy, do not be sad.' So they all departed to eat and drink and make merry, and to send shares to those
55 who had none, and to hold a great celebration; because the teaching given them had been instilled into their minds.

They gathered together.[b]

* In the book of Ezra the list of names forms the conclusion, save for an obscure note at the end which the N.E.B. has corrected from the text of 1 Esdras. Too much must not be made of the apparently unsatisfactory nature of this conclusion, for the books of Ezra and Nehemiah were treated as a unity until well into the Christian era, but it is still unexpected to find the account of one part of Ezra's work separated from the account of his reading of the law. That problem does not arise here, for our text passes directly to Neh. 7: 73 and follows closely from that point the account of the reading of the law.

[a] *Gk.* Attharates.
[b] *Probably the text originally carried on from this point; compare Neh. 8: 13.*

It is impossible to be certain whether this placing together of the two parts of Ezra's work was a deliberate rearrangement of his material by the compiler of 1 Esdras, or whether he inherited a tradition which did not include the early chapters of Nehemiah, and so presented Ezra's work as a unity. In view of the evidence we have already seen of the creative way in which 1 Esdras develops existing traditions (e.g. with regard to Zerubbabel), the former possibility is more likely.

37. *the new moon of the seventh month:* this date is taken over from Neh. 8: 2, where in turn it appears to be dependent on Ezra 3: 1. Here it is understood as one of the sequence of dates already given in this chapter.

37–8. The N.E.B. translation reads somewhat awkwardly at this point, appearing to state first that some of the community *remained in their settlements*, then that all *assembled as one*. Probably there is no contradiction; the end of verse 37 refers to the fact that various settlements had by now been established.

38. *before the east gateway of the temple:* this differs from its source, and may be a deliberate attempt to link the solemn law-reading ceremony more closely with the temple.

39. *Ezra the high priest:* he is never so described in the books of Ezra and Nehemiah. This is probably one example of the tendency represented by 1 Esdras, to magnify the role of Ezra in establishing the religious community. *the law of Moses:* here, as probably already in Neh. 8, this is understood as being the Pentateuch. Whether the book actually was the Pentateuch as a whole or in part, is much less certain.

43–4. There are thirteen names listed, as in Neh. 8: 4, but there the disposition is six on the right, seven on the left, whereas here the numbers are reversed, and there are changes in detail.

45–8. To an even clearer extent than its source, this passage appears to reflect the pattern of assembly which was normal in the synagogue. This is particularly noteworthy in the piling-up of divine titles in verse 46.

49. *the governor:* in Neh. 8: 9 there is a reference – widely

73

held to be a later gloss – to 'Nehemiah the governor' at this point. It is likely that here, as at 5: 40, the Greek translators understood the rare word 'tirshatha' as a proper name (cp. the N.E.B. footnote). As presented here, his role is to lead a kind of liturgical refrain.

54. No attempt is made here to set out the festival in terms of the main Jewish autumn festival, Tabernacles, or of the Day of Atonement, which became the major observance of that festival.

55. *They gathered together:* both the way in which the N.E.B presents the text, and the accompanying footnote, make its assumption clear that part of the original text has now been lost. This is probably correct, though it is possible that the work could be regarded as complete; the original has no paragraphs, and it might be regarded as quite appropriate to end with a picture of the gathering together of the faithful community. In any case, it is unlikely that a substantial part of the work is missing, since Ezra's achievement has now been described, and there is no further material dealing with him in the original Hebrew. (The Septuagint form of the work (Esdras b in the table on p. 3) attributes the long prayer in Neh. 9 to Ezra and this is followed by some modern translations (not the N.E.B.), but it seems that this was probably a later attribution of an originally anonymous prayer.) The intention of the compiler of 1 Esdras appears to have been to concentrate on the three great moments in the life of the community associated with Josiah, Zerubbabel and Ezra, and his purpose has now been achieved. ✷

✷ ✷ ✷ ✷ ✷ ✷ ✷ ✷ ✷ ✷ ✷ ✷ ✷

✷ 1. Esdras is quite possibly the least-read book in the whole of the Bible and Apocrypha. This is understandable, for so much of it repeats material which has appeared elsewhere, and this is nowadays regarded as a major problem. But the Bible provides plenty of evidence that this was quite acceptable in the ancient world – the inclusion of both Kings and Chronicles in the Old Testament and of the gospels of Matthew, Mark and Luke in the New amply illustrate this. In other words, what is provided here in the way of creative reflection on the events and figures of the past provides an important clue to the self-understanding of the Jewish (and later the Christian) community. We see here a new estimate of the importance of particular individuals, with the role of Zerubbabel emphasized and that of Nehemiah played down. We see a new perspective on history, linking events before and after the Babylonian exile which we often keep separate; other traditions, such as the book of Daniel, elaborated very greatly the importance of the exile, with the idea often being found that the people were still in a sense 'exiled' from their God, but in 1 Esdras the exile is an episode of past history and the continuity of the people's experience is stressed. Above all, therefore, we see a new interpretation, fitted for changing circumstances, of the way in which God had guided his faithful community when they remained loyal to him.   ✳

A NOTE ON FURTHER READING

Very few commentaries have been written on 1 Esdras; much the most useful recent one (which also includes 2 Esdras) is by J. M. Myers, Anchor Bible (Garden City, New York, 1974). An outline of the literary problems of the book is provided by J. A. Soggin, *Introduction to the Old Testament* (S.C.M. Press, 1976) and the historical background of the period dealt with is covered by M. Noth, *A History of Israel*, 2nd ed. (A. & C. Black, 1960) or S. Herrmann, *A History of Israel in Old Testament Times* (S.C.M. Press, 1975).

THE SECOND BOOK OF
ESDRAS

✳   ✳   ✳   ✳   ✳   ✳   ✳   ✳   ✳   ✳   ✳   ✳   ✳

A COMPOSITE BOOK

At the beginning of this volume it was pointed out that it is customary to divide 2 Esdras, and to refer to chs. 1–2 as 5 Ezra, and chs. 15–16 as 6 Ezra (see p. 3). It will be apparent from even a casual reading that chs. 1–2, 3–14, and 15–16 form in fact three quite separate works, and this is confirmed by the evidence of the Latin version, in which language alone the text of 2 Esdras has survived in its entirety. The manuscripts of the Latin version clearly distinguish between the three sections of the composite book, and some even have chs. 1–2 after ch. 16, or place 1 Esdras between 2 Esdras 1–2 and 3–14 + 15–16. Of these three works, the oldest is 2 Esdras 3–14. This is a Jewish apocalypse, probably composed in Hebrew, and dating from towards the end of the reign of the Emperor Domitian (A.D. 81–96). 2 Esdras 1–2 and 15–16 form two quite independent additions to the original Jewish writing. These are Christian works; they were apparently composed in Greek, and date from the second and third centuries respectively. These additions were made when 2 Esdras had been taken over by the Christian Church, but whereas 2 Esdras 15–16 seems to have been written from the outset as an appendix to chs. 3–14 which was intended to make the earlier work relevant to a new situation, chs. 1–2 initially had an independent existence. The fact that these additions were made to 2 Esdras 3–14 is an indication of the high regard in which the name of Ezra was held by Christians as well as Jews (see further pp. 1-2). The practice in the English versions of the Bible of referring to this composite book as

2 Esdras goes back to the Geneva Bible of 1560. The Geneva
Bible took the number 2 Esdras from the Latin translation, but
the Latin manuscripts in fact vary quite considerably in the
numbers which they assign to the Ezra-writings and to the
different sections of 2 Esdras 1–16, and because of this there is
some confusion in the numbering of the various Ezra-books.
In modern publications 2 Esdras 3–14 is often referred to as
4 Ezra, in distinction from 2 Esdras 1–2 (5 Ezra) and 2 Esdras
15–16 (6 Ezra).

✳   ✳   ✳   ✳   ✳   ✳   ✳   ✳   ✳   ✳   ✳   ✳   ✳

2 ESDRAS 1–2

Israel's rejection and glory to come

✳   The main theme of 2 Esdras 1–2, which forms, as we have
seen, a quite independent work, is that the Church has taken
the place of Israel. By content these chapters divide into two
parts, of which the first (1: 1 – 2: 9) is primarily concerned
with Israel, and the reasons for her rejection, and the second
(2: 10–48) with the Church, and the glorious future which
awaits it. As will become apparent, the author was a Jewish
Christian, and his work represents an attempt to resolve the
problem of the relationship of the Church to Israel. In form
2 Esdras 1–2 imitates the style of Old Testament prophecy,
and, as in chs. 15–16, Ezra is presented as a prophet. The Old
Testament traditions about Ezra do not say this at all, but in
later interpretation a number of notable Old Testament
characters are described as speaking prophetically, e.g. Moses
(Deut. 18: 15; 34: 10–11) and David (2 Sam. 23: 2; Acts 2: 30;
see also the commentary on 2 Samuel in this series, p. 219).
Besides this, the author of 2 Esdras 1–2 draws very heavily
on the Old and New Testaments for the language and content
of his work which in places has the appearance of being a

mosaic of biblical quotations.

The date of 2 Esdras 1–2 can only be fixed approximately. The author reveals an acquaintance with several New Testament writings (notably the gospels of Matthew and Luke, and the book of Revelation), and this brings us down to the end of the first century A.D. On the other hand, the fact that the controversy between Judaism and Christianity was still a live issue suggests that we should not come down too far beyond the end of the first century, and we should probably think in terms of a date about the middle of the second century A.D. This dating is supported by a parallel which exists between 2: 43 and the *Shepherd of Hermas*, a Christian work which is likewise to be dated about the middle of the second century. Going beyond this, it has been suggested that 2 Esdras 1–2 was written as a Christian response to the unsuccessful outcome of the Jewish revolt of A.D. 132–5; this is an attractive, but somewhat uncertain, possibility. The place of composition is completely unknown. There are hints that the author was writing in the western part of the Roman Empire (see the comments on 1: 11 and 38), but these are so uncertain that no reliance can be placed upon them.

2 Esdras 1–2 has survived only in a Latin translation, but it is generally believed that the language of composition was Greek. The Latin manuscripts of 2 Esdras divide into two groups, or families, one French and the other Spanish. In 2 Esdras 1–2 there are some significant differences between these two groups of manuscripts, but it has been thought inappropriate to discuss these here, and almost without exception they have been ignored. However, it may be noted that the N.E.B. follows the French family of manuscripts. *

EZRA'S PROPHETIC CALL

1 THE SECOND BOOK of the prophet Ezra, son of Seraiah, son of Azariah, son of Hilkiah, son of
2 Shallum, son of Zadok, son of Ahitub, son of Ahijah,

son of Phinehas, son of Eli, son of Amariah, son of Aziah,
son of Marimoth, son of Arna, son of Uzzi, son of
Borith, son of Abishua, son of Phinehas, son of Eleazar,
son of Aaron, of the tribe of Levi.   3

I, Ezra, was a captive in Media in the reign of Artaxerxes,
king of Persia, when the word of the Lord came to me: 4
'Go to my people and proclaim their crimes; tell their 5
children how they have sinned against me, and let them
tell their children's children. They have sinned even more 6
than their fathers; they have forgotten me and sacrificed
to alien gods. Was it not I who rescued them from Egypt, 7
the country where they were slaves? And yet they have
provoked me to anger and ignored my warnings.

   'Now, Ezra, pluck out your hair and let calamities 8
loose upon these people who have disobeyed my law.
They are beyond correction. How much longer shall I 9
endure them, I who have lavished on them such benefits?
Many are the kings I have overthrown for their sake; 10
I struck down Pharaoh with his court and all his army.
I destroyed every nation that stood in their way, and in 11
the east I routed the peoples of two provinces, Tyre and
Sidon, and killed all the enemies of Israel.

* Ezra is summoned as a prophet to denounce Israel for her
sin.

   1–3*a*. An introduction, lacking in some of the manuscripts,
which gives Ezra's genealogy and establishes his priestly
descent. It is comparable to the genealogies at the beginning
of the account of Ezra's work in the book of Ezra (cp. 7: 1–5)
and in 1 Esdras (cp. 8: 1–2), but differs from these in a number
of respects. *the prophet Ezra:* this description of Ezra (for

which cp. 12: 42) reflects the fact that 2 Esdras 1–2 has the form of a prophecy, but is in striking contrast to Ezra's role in the Old Testament as 'a scribe learned in the law of Moses' (Ezra 7: 6).

3*b. a captive in Media in the reign of Artaxerxes, king of Persia:* cp. Ezra 7: 1. The prophecy is assumed to have been given to the exiles at a time before Ezra made his journey to Jerusalem. *Media:* here used in a very general way to describe the area in which the exiles were living.

4. *the word of the Lord came to me:* the formula which is used frequently in the Old Testament to introduce the revelation of God's word to a prophet; cp. e.g. Jer. 1: 4; 2: 1; Ezek. 7: 1; 12: 1. This formula is not used of Ezra in the Old Testament.

5–11. Despite the many mercies shown to her, Israel has sinned against God to such an extent that her relationship with him has been brought into question. Here and elsewhere in 2 Esdras 1–2 the author draws very heavily on the language and thought of the Old Testament; some examples of this are indicated in the notes.

6. *they have forgotten me and sacrificed to alien gods:* cp. Jer. 2: 32; 5: 19.

7. Cp. Exod. 20: 2.

8. *pluck out your hair:* based on Ezra 9: 3. In the Old Testament tearing the hair was a physical indication of distress; Ezra is commanded to do it here as a sign of God's anger at Israel's sin.

10. *Many are the kings I have overthrown ... I struck down Pharaoh:* cp. Exod. 14: 27–8; Ps. 135: 9–10.

11. *and in the east I routed the people of two provinces, Tyre and Sidon:* an obscure passage, made more so by uncertainties about the text (the Latin manuscripts differ quite considerably). Tyre and Sidon are cities, not provinces, and in any case lie to the west, not the east, of Media (cp. verse 3). This latter point has led to the suggestion that 2 Esdras 1–2 was written in the west, but there are difficulties about the

reading *in the east*, and it is not clear how much should be read into this phrase. It is also not clear to what historical situation the author was referring. It is possible that he had in mind such events as the siege of Tyre by Alexander the Great and the destruction of Sidon by Artaxerxes III, but he may also have been influenced by the prophecies about Tyre and Sidon in Ezek. 26: 1 – 28: 23. ✶

ISRAEL'S DISOBEDIENCE AND REJECTION

'Say to them, "These are the words of the Lord: Was 12, 13 it not I who brought you through the sea, and made safe roads for you where no road had been? I gave you Moses as your leader, and Aaron as your priest; I gave you light 14 from a pillar of fire, and performed great miracles among you. And yet you have forgotten me, says the Lord.

'"These are the words of the Lord Almighty: I gave 15 you the quails as a sign; I gave you a camp for your protection. But all you did there was to grumble and complain – instead of celebrating the victory I had given you 16 when I destroyed your enemies. From that day to this you have never stopped complaining. Have you forgotten 17 what benefits I conferred on you? When you were hungry and thirsty in your journey through the desert, you cried out to me, 'Why have you brought us into this 18 desert to kill us? Better to have remained in Egypt as slaves than to die here in the desert!' I was grieved by 19 your complaints, and gave you manna for food; you ate the bread of angels. When you were thirsty, I split open 20 the rock, and out flowed water in plenty. Against the summer heat I gave you the shelter of leafy trees. I gave 21 you fertile lands to divide among your tribes, expelling

the Canaanites, Perizzites, and Philistines who opposed
you. What more could I do for you? says the Lord.

22 '"These are the words of the Lord Almighty: When
you were in the desert, suffering thirst by the stream of
23 bitter water and cursing me, I did not bring down fire
upon you for your blasphemy; I cast a tree into the stream
24 and made the water sweet. What am I to do with you,
Jacob? Judah, you have refused to obey me. I will turn to
other nations; I will give them my name, and they will
25 keep my statutes. Because you have deserted me, I will
desert you; when you cry for mercy, I will show you
26 none; when you pray to me, I will not listen. You have
stained your hands with blood; you run hot-foot to
27 commit murder. It is not I whom you have deserted, but
yourselves, says the Lord.

* The remainder of the chapter, with the exception of
verses 38–40, consists of a series of prophecies, each introduced
by the formula 'These are the words of the Lord (Almighty)',
which Ezra is to proclaim to the exiles. The theme of the
chapter is that Israel, because of her disobedience, is to lose her
privileged position with God and be replaced by another
people, i.e. by the Christian Church. In verses 12–27 the
author gives an account of God's dealings with his people
from the exodus from Egypt to the entry into the Promised
Land. The account is reminiscent of such Old Testament
passages as Ps. 78 and Ezek. 20, and, as in these passages, the
emphasis falls on Israel's constant ingratitude and sin. The
climax is reached in verse 24 with the rhetorical question,
'What am I to do with you, Jacob?' Israel's sin is such that
God will reject her and turn to others.

12. *These are the words of the Lord:* the common formula
used in the Old Testament to introduce the words which a

prophet, acting as God's messenger, is to speak to the people; cp. e.g. Jer. 2: 1–2*a*, 4–5*a*; Amos 1: 3*a*, 6.

13. Cp. Exod. 14: 21–2, 29.

14. *light from a pillar of fire:* cp. Exod. 13: 21. *And yet you have forgotten me:* cp. Jer. 2: 32.

15. *the Lord Almighty:* cp. 2 Cor. 6: 18 (where the N.E.B. translates the same expression as 'the Lord, the Ruler of all being'); the title is not used in the Old Testament. *the quails:* cp. Exod. 16: 13; Ps. 105: 40. *a camp:* cp. Deut. 1: 32–3. *But all you did there was to grumble and complain:* the complaints of the people in the wilderness form a constant theme of Exod. 15: 22 – 17: 7; Num. 14.

18. Based on Exod. 14: 11–12, but cp. Exod. 16: 3. A more obvious allusion to the latter might have been expected.

19. *and gave you manna for food:* cp. Exod. 16: 14–15, 31. *you ate the bread of angels:* cp. Ps. 78: 25; Wisd. of Sol. 16: 20. The similarity between Ps. 78 and 2 Esdras 1: 12–27 has already been mentioned; the thought of Ps. 78: 15–31 is closely comparable to that of 2 Esdras 1: 15–21.

20. *I split open the rock:* cp. Exod. 17: 6; Num. 20: 11. *I gave you the shelter of leafy trees:* there is no Old Testament tradition to this effect, but the passage is perhaps an elaboration of Exod. 15: 27.

21. *the Canaanites, Perizzites:* cp. Judg. 1: 4–5. *and Philistines:* the mention of the Philistines together with the Canaanites and Perizzites is a little unexpected because there is no Old Testament tradition that the Philistines were defeated at the time of the Israelite settlement in Palestine.

22–3. Cp. Exod. 15: 22–25*a*.

24–7. In the Old Testament Israel is frequently condemned for her sin, and threatened with punishment, but never rejected in such final terms as are used here. This passage, in common with others which refer to the replacement of Israel by another people, is a clear indication that 2 Esdras 1–2 is the work of a Christian, and this view is confirmed by the fact that in a number of places the author appears to make direct use of the New Testament; cp. particularly 2: 42-8 with Rev. 7: 9-17. However, the concern with Israel suggests that the author was a Jewish, not a gentile, Christian.

24. *I will turn to other nations; I will give them my name, and they will keep my statutes:* Israel is to be replaced by the Christian Church; cp. Matt. 21: 43, 'the kingdom of God will be taken away from you, and given to a nation that yields the proper fruit'. The parallel with Matthew is even clearer in a variant reading which is preferable to the text adopted in the N.E.B., 'I will turn to another nation ...' Cp. also Acts 13: 46.

25. *Because you have deserted me, I will desert you:* cp. 2 Chron. 15: 2; 24: 20.

26. *when you pray to me, I will not listen. You have stained your hands with blood:* apparently based on Isa. 1: 15:

> 'When you lift your hands outspread in prayer,
> I will hide my eyes from you.
> Though you offer countless prayers,
>   I will not listen.
> There is blood on your hands'

The reference to blood may, however, have been occasioned by Jewish ill-treatment of Christians. *you run hot-foot to commit murder:* cp. Prov. 1: 16; Isa. 59: 7; Rom. 3: 15. ✳

GOD'S CONCERN FOR ISRAEL

28 '"These are the words of the Lord Almighty: Have I not pleaded with you as a father with his sons, as a mother with her daughters or a nurse with her children?
29 Have I not said, 'Be my people, and I will be your God;
30 be my sons, and I will be your father'? I gathered you as a hen gathers her chickens under her wings. But now
31 what am I to do with you? I will toss you away. When you offer me sacrifice, I will turn from you; I have

rejected your feasts, your new moons, and your circum- cisions. I sent you my servants the prophets, but you took 32 them and killed them, and mutilated their dead bodies. For their murder I will call you to account, says the Lord.

✻ The author develops further the points that have been made in verses 24–7. Here he is concerned to emphasize that Israel's rejection was very far from being God's original intention. God had taken the initiative in seeking Israel, and it was Israel's failure to respond (exemplified in her treatment of the prophets) that made her rejection inevitable. The character of this passage, with its concern for Israel, is a further indication that the author was a Jewish, rather than a gentile, Christian.

28–9. The N.E.B. has slightly obscured the force of the original by inserting *Have I not said* at the beginning of verse 29. The text reads literally, 'Have I not pleaded with you as a father ... , that you should be my people, and I should be your God ... ?' To say that God *pleaded* that Israel should be his people is an exaggeration of the thought of the Old Testament; the purpose is to make clear the ingrati- tude of Israel. '*Be my people, and I will be your God; be my sons, and I will be your father*': not an actual quotation, and not presented as such in the Latin. For the first half cp. Exod. 6: 7; Jer. 7: 23. So far as the second half is concerned, the thought that God is Israel's father is reflected in such passages as Jer. 3: 19; 31: 9, but there is nothing in the Old Testament exactly comparable except the saying addressed to David in 2 Sam. 7: 14. Cp., however, 2 Cor. 6: 16–18.

30. *I gathered you as a hen gathers her chickens under her wings*: based on Matt. 23: 37 (cp. Luke 13: 34), 'How often have I longed to gather your children, as a hen gathers her brood under her wings; but you would not let me.'

31. Based on Isa. 1: 13–14.

32. The theme of the rejection of the prophets occurs

frequently in the Old Testament (cp. e.g. 2 Chron. 36: 15–16), but this verse is based directly on Matt. 23: 34–6, and the parallel, Luke 11: 49–51. *I will call you to account:* the use of this expression points to the particular influence of Luke 11: 49–51, '"I will send them prophets and messengers; and some of these they will persecute and kill"; so that this generation will have to answer for the blood of all the prophets ... this generation will have to answer for it all.' *

THE PEOPLE SOON TO COME

33 '"These are the words of the Lord Almighty: Your house is abandoned. I will toss you away like straw before
34 the wind. Your children shall have no posterity, because like you they have ignored my commandments and done
35 what I have condemned. I will hand over your home to a people soon to come; a people who will trust me, though they have not known me; who will do my
36 bidding, though I gave them no signs; who never saw the prophets, and yet will keep in mind what the prophets
37 taught of old. I vow that this people yet to come shall have my favour. Their little ones shall jump for joy. They have not seen me with their eyes, but they shall perceive by the spirit and believe all that I have said."

38 'Now, father Ezra, look with triumph at the nation
39 coming from the east. The leaders I shall give them are Abraham, Isaac, and Jacob, Hosea and Amos, Micah and
40 Joel, Obadiah and Jonah, Nahum, Habakkuk, and Zephaniah, Haggai and Zechariah, and Malachi, who is also called the Lord's Messenger.

✶ After a further statement of the rejection of Israel the author turns his attention for the first time to the group which is to take Israel's place, i.e. the Christian Church.

33. *Your house is abandoned:* apparently a reference to the temple; cp. Matt. 23: 38; Luke 13: 35*a*. *like straw before the wind:* a common Old Testament simile; cp. e.g. Job 21: 18.

35. *I will hand over your home* (literally 'your houses') *to a people soon to come:* a symbolic statement of the transfer of Israel's privileges to the Christian Church; cp. 2: 10. *a people who will trust me, though they have not known me:* the author is thinking particularly of gentile Christians; cp. Rom. 15: 21.

37. *They have not seen me with their eyes:* cp. John 20: 29; 1 Pet. 1: 8.

38-40. Ezra is told to observe the coming of a nation 'from the east', whose leaders are to be the patriarchs and the twelve minor prophets.

38. *Now, father Ezra:* Ezra is addressed by God as the father of the nation; the title does not occur in the Old Testament, and is used only here and in 2: 5. Perhaps the author's intention was to compare Ezra with Abraham who is more usually called 'father'; cp. Luke 16: 24, 30. *look with triumph at the nation coming from the east:* the Christian Church is meant, but it is not clear why it should be said to come from the east. It is possible that the author has been influenced by Baruch 4: 36-7 ('Jerusalem, look eastwards and see the joy that is coming to you from God. They come, the sons from whom you parted, they come, gathered together at the word of the Holy One from east to west, rejoicing in the glory of God'), and that he has interpreted this text, which pictures the return of the Babylonian exiles to Jerusalem, to refer to the coming of the Church to take the place of Israel. Alternatively, it is possible that the phrase *from the east* reflects the place of composition of 2 Esdras 1-2 (cp. verse 11); on this view the author, writing in the west, describes Jewish Christians coming from Palestine to the west.

39-40. The Church is to take over from Israel her spiritual

leaders, the patriarchs (cp. Matt. 8: 11), and her prophets. The latter are represented here by the twelve minor prophets (arranged in the order in which they occur in the Septuagint). Isaiah and Jeremiah are mentioned in 2: 18. *who is also called the Lord's Messenger:* a play on the name *Malachi* which means 'my messenger'. *

GOD'S JUDGEMENT ON ISRAEL

2 'These are the words of the Lord: I freed this people from slavery, and gave them commandments through my servants the prophets; but they shut their ears to the 2 prophets, and let my precepts become a dead letter. The mother who bore them says to them: "Go, my sons; I am 3 widowed and deserted. Joyfully I brought you up; I have lost you with grief and sorrow, because you have sinned against the Lord God and done what I know to be wrong. 4 What can I do for you now, widowed and deserted as 5 I am? Go, my sons, ask the Lord for mercy." Now I call upon you, father Ezra, to add your testimony to hers, 6 that her children have refused to keep my covenant; and let your words bring confusion on them. May their mother be despoiled, and may they themselves have no 7 posterity. Condemn them to be scattered among the nations, and their name to vanish from the earth, because they have spurned my covenant.

8 'Woe to you, Assyria, for harbouring sinners! Remember, you wicked nation, what I did to Sodom and 9 Gomorrah: their land lies buried under lumps of pitch and heaps of ashes. That is how I will deal with those who have disobeyed me, says the Lord Almighty.

✼ 1–7. In a prophetic saying addressed to Ezra the author takes up once more the theme of ch. 1: Israel's response to God's actions on her behalf has been one of disobedience and ingratitude, and because of this the people are to be scattered and lose their identity as a nation.

1. *I freed this people from slavery:* cp. 1: 7. *and gave them commandments through my servants the prophets:* for the idea that laws were given by the prophets cp. Ezra 9: 10–11; Dan. 9: 10. *but they shut their ears:* cp. 1: 32.

2–4. *The mother who bore them:* i.e. Jerusalem, personified as the mother of the nation. The personification goes back ultimately to Isa. 49: 14–21; 54: 1–8 (cp. Gal. 4: 26–7), but there are also similarities between this passage of 2 Esdras and Baruch 4: 5–29, especially verses 8–12, 17, 19, 21. In Isaiah the Jerusalem of the period of the exile is depicted as a bereaved and barren woman who, through the return of the exiles, will acquire a family larger than the one she had before (cp. 49: 19–21; 54: 1). In 2 Esdras Jerusalem is likewise pictured as a mother who has lost her children. *widowed and deserted*, she accuses her sons (Israel) of having brought their punishment on themselves; she can do nothing for them and tells them to cast themselves on the mercy of God. However, a deliberate contrast seems to be intended between mother Jerusalem (verses 2–4) and the mother addressed in verses 15, 17 and 30, namely the Church. The former has lost her family, the latter is described as the mother of sons and is told to nurture her children carefully. The use of the mother theme is a further illustration of the idea that the Church has taken the place of Israel.

5–7. Ezra is to confirm the truth of the mother's accusation (verse 5) and to proclaim God's judgement on her children (verses 6–7).

5. *father Ezra:* see the comment on 1: 38.

6–7. The punishment is to consist of the destruction of Jerusalem and the dispersion of the Jews from Palestine. These events were already facts of history at the time at which 2

Esdras 1–2 was written, but the pseudonymous author is able to make Ezra 'foretell' them. *May their mother be despoiled:* an allusion either to the fall of Jerusalem in A.D. 70, or to the capture of Jerusalem by the forces of the Emperor Hadrian in the course of the suppression of the Bar Cochba revolt (A.D. 132–135). *and may they themselves have no posterity:* cp. 1: 34. *Condemn ... their name to vanish from the earth:* Israel is to lose even her identity as a nation; contrast Isa. 66: 22. This bitter curse reflects the hostility between the Jewish and Christian communities.

8–9. The judgement on the Jewish people is extended to include the nation which harbours them. The fate of Sodom and Gomorrah ought to serve as an example of the way God deals with those who disobey him. *Assyria:* here a cryptic name for the Roman Empire; a similar usage is found in the Qumran War Scroll. Cp. the use of Babylon as a symbolic name for Rome (see e.g. 15: 43; Rev. 14: 8). *sinners:* the Jewish people. *wicked nation:* Assyria (Rome). *what I did to Sodom and Gomorrah:* cp. Gen. 19: 24. Sodom and Gomorrah are frequently used as examples; cp. Zeph. 2: 8–9. ✳

ISRAEL'S PRIVILEGES GIVEN TO THE CHURCH

10 'These are the words of the Lord to Ezra: Tell my people that I will give to them the kingdom of Jerusalem
11 which once I offered to Israel. I will withdraw the splendour of my presence from Israel, and the home that was
12 to be theirs for ever I will give to my own people. The tree of life shall spread its fragrance over them; they shall
13 not toil or grow weary. Ask, and you shall receive; so pray that your short time of waiting may be made shorter still. The kingdom is ready for you now; be on the
14 watch! Call heaven, call earth, to witness: I have cancelled the evil and brought the good into being; for I am the Living One, says the Lord.

✻ These verses mark a turning-point in 2 Esdras 1–2. So far the author has been primarily concerned to explain why Israel has been rejected. He now turns his attention to the group which is to take Israel's place.

10–11. Ezra is told to announce to God's people that the kingdom of Jerusalem, which should have belonged to Israel, is to be given to them. *my people:* used frequently in the Old Testament to refer to Israel, but here, in deliberate contrast, to refer to the Church. The author was possibly influenced by Hos. 2: 23. *the kingdom of Jerusalem:* the expression is not found in the Old or New Testament, but is comparable to, and conveys much the same idea as, 'the kingdom of God'. The use of the expression emphasizes the idea that the coming of the kingdom will involve the re-establishment of an earthly kingdom based on Jerusalem; cp. Mark 11: 10, 'the coming kingdom of our father David', which in a similar way envisages the re-establishment of the Davidic Empire; cp. also Matt. 21: 5, in which Jesus is depicted as the messianic king coming to Jerusalem, 'Tell the daughter of Zion, "Here is your king, who comes to you in gentleness."' Participation in this kingdom was a privilege that had been intended for Israel, but this privilege has now been transferred to the Church; cp. verses 35, 41. *and the home that was to be theirs for ever:* in a more literal translation 'and the eternal home that was to be theirs'. The phrase 'the eternal home' is possibly taken from Luke 16: 9; cp. verse 37 'the heavenly realms'.

12. *The tree of life:* cp. 8: 52; Rev. 2: 7; 22: 2, 14.

13. In phrases reminiscent of the New Testament the Christians are urged to pray that the kingdom may come as quickly as possible. *Ask, and you shall receive:* cp. Matt. 7: 7; Luke 11: 9. *so pray that your short time of waiting may be made shorter still:* cp. Matt. 24: 22. *The kingdom is ready for you now:* cp. Matt. 25: 34. *be on the watch:* a frequent command in the gospels; cp. Mark 13: 37; Matt. 24: 42; 25: 13 (where the N.E.B. in all three cases translates 'Keep awake').

14. *Call heaven, call earth, to witness:* cp. Deut. 30: 19. *I have cancelled the evil and brought the good into being:* a statement

referring specifically to the replacement of Israel by the Church. ✻

ADVICE TO THE CHURCH

15 'Mother, cherish your sons. Rear them joyfully as a dove rears her nestlings; teach them to walk without
16 stumbling. You are my chosen one, says the Lord. I will raise up the dead from their resting-places, and bring them out of their tombs, for I have acknowledged that
17 they bear my name. Have no fear, mother of many sons; I have chosen you, says the Lord.

18 'I will send my servants Isaiah and Jeremiah to help you. As they prophesied, I have set you apart to be my people. I have made ready for you twelve trees laden
19 with different kinds of fruit, twelve fountains flowing with milk and honey, and seven great mountains covered with roses and lilies. There will I fill your sons with joy.
20 Champion the widow, defend the cause of the fatherless, give to the poor, protect the orphan, clothe the naked.
21 Care for the weak and the helpless, and do not mock at the cripple; watch over the disabled, and bring the blind
22 to the vision of my brightness. Keep safe within your walls both old and young.

23 'When you find the dead unburied, mark them with the sign and commit them to the tomb; and then, when I cause the dead to rise, I will give you the chief place.
24 Be calm, my people; for your time of rest shall come.
25 Care for your children like a good nurse, and train them
26 to walk without falling. Of my servants whom I have given you not one shall be lost; I will demand them back
27 from among your number. Do not be anxious when the

time of trouble and hardship comes; others shall lament
and be sad, but you shall have happiness and plenty. All 28
nations shall envy you, but shall be powerless against
you, says the Lord.

'My power shall protect you, and save your sons from 29
hell. Be joyful, mother, you and your sons, for I will 30
come to your rescue. Remember your children who 31
sleep in the grave; I will bring them up from the depths
of the earth, and show mercy to them; for I am merciful,
says the Lord Almighty. Cherish your children until I 32
come, and proclaim my mercy to them; for my favour
flows abundantly from springs that will never run dry.'

☆ God assures the Church, personified as a mother, of his
continuing care and protection, and exhorts her to practise
good works.

15. *Mother:* probably the Church, personified as the mother
of its members. It has sometimes been held that, as in verses
2-4, the reference is to Jerusalem, thought of here as the
mother of the Church. It is true that the earliest Christian
Church was in Jerusalem, but the exhortation is addressed
directly to the Church as a whole. Indeed, a deliberate
contrast seems to be intended between Jerusalem as mother
and the Church as mother; see the comment on verses 2-4.
my chosen one: it is a commonplace of the Old Testament that
Israel has been chosen by God; here the idea is deliberately
transferred to the Church.

16. *I will raise up the dead from their resting-places:* the promise
of resurrection is a dominant theme of this passage; cp.
verses 23, 29-31. *and bring them out of their tombs:* cp. Ezek.
37: 12-13; Matt. 27: 52-3.

18a. *I will send my servants Isaiah and Jeremiah to help you:*
see the comment on 1: 39-40.

18b-19. A description of the paradise prepared by God for

his people. *twelve trees laden with different kinds of fruit:* the author appears to be dependent on the tree-of-life motif in Rev. 22: 2 (part of the vision of the New Jerusalem, Rev. 21: 1 – 22: 5), 'On either side of the river stood a tree of life, which yields twelve crops of fruit, one for each month of the year; the leaves of the trees serve for the healing of the nations.' However, the twelve trees are possibly intended to symbolize the twelve apostles. *twelve fountains flowing with milk and honey:* the traditional description of the promised land (cp. e.g. Exod. 3: 8) is here applied to the paradise prepared by God for Christians. For the fountains cp. 1 Enoch 48: 1 (the introduction to a passage which describes the naming of the Son of Man in the presence of the Lord of Spirits in heaven), 'And in that place I saw an inexhaustible spring of righteousness, and many springs of wisdom sur-- rounded it, and all the thirsty drank from them and were filled with wisdom.' In traditional interpretation the 'spring of righteousness' is the law and the 'springs of wisdom' the prophets. It is possible that in a similar way the twelve foun- tains in 2 Esdras are meant to symbolize the minor prophets (cp. 1: 40). (On 1 Enoch see below, p. 108.) *and seven great mountains covered with roses and lilies:* the author seems to be drawing on 1 Enoch 24–5, a passage which describes the paradisial region of seven mountains where the throne of God is situated, the throne on which he 'will sit when he comes down to visit the earth for good' (1 Enoch 25: 3). Further links with this passage of Enoch are evident in the fact that around the throne are a number of fragrant trees, amongst which is the tree of life; cp. 24: 4, 'And there was among them a tree such as I have never smelt, and none of them nor any others were like it; it smells more fragrant than any fragrance, and its leaves and its flowers and its wood never wither; its fruit (is) good, and its fruit (is) like the bunches of dates on a palm', and 25: 5, 'From its fruit life will be given to the chosen.'

20–2. An exhortation reflecting some of the basic ethical

demands of the Old and New Testaments and reminiscent in
particular of such passages as Ps. 82: 3-4; Isa. 1: 17; 58: 7;
Matt. 25: 35-6; Jas. 1: 27.

23. *When you find the dead unburied, mark them with the sign
and commit them to the tomb:* this command has apparently
been added under the influence of Tobit 1: 17-19. *the sign:*
probably the sign of the cross; cp. verse 38. *I will give you
the chief place:* cp. Matt. 20: 23.

26. *Of my servants whom I have given you not one shall be lost:*
apparently based on John 17: 12, 'When I was with them, I
protected by the power of thy name those whom thou hast
given me, and kept them safe. Not one of them is lost except
the man who must be lost.'

27. *the time of trouble and hardship:* the troubles that will
immediately precede the end of this age; cp. Mark 13 and
parallels.

29. *hell:* literally 'Gehenna', here the place of final punishment in the next life, cp. 7: [36]; Matt. 5: 22; 18: 9; see
further the comment on 7: [36].

31. *I will bring...the earth:* see the comment on verse 16. ✻

THE REWARDS OF THE KINGDOM

I, Ezra, received on Mount Horeb a commission from 33
the Lord to go to Israel; but when I came, they scorned
me and rejected the Lord's commandment. Therefore I 34
say to you Gentiles, you who hear and understand: 'Look
forward to the coming of your shepherd, and he will give
you everlasting rest; for he who is to come at the end
of the world is close at hand. Be ready to receive the 35
rewards of the kingdom; for light perpetual will shine
upon you for ever and ever. Flee from the shadow of this 36
world, and receive the joy and splendour that await you.
I bear witness openly to my Saviour. It is he whom the 37

Lord has appointed; receive him and be joyful, giving
thanks to the One who has summoned you to the
38 heavenly realms. Rise, stand up, and see the whole company of those who bear the Lord's mark and sit at his
39 table. They have moved out of the shadow of this world
40 and have received shining robes from the Lord. Receive,
O Zion, your full number, and close the roll of those
arrayed in white who have faithfully kept the law of the
41 Lord. The number of your sons whom you so long
desired is now complete. Pray that the Lord's kingdom
may come, so that your people, whom he summoned
when the world began, may be set apart as his own.'

---

* The major part of 2 Esdras 1–2 consists of a speech from
God (1: 5 – 2: 32), but in the final verses (2: 33–48) Ezra
himself speaks. In verses 33–41, as a consequence of Israel's
rejection both of himself and of the Lord's commandment,
he addresses the Gentiles. He urges them to await the imminent
coming of their 'shepherd' and describes the blessings that
lie in store for them.

33. *on Mount Horeb:* like Moses; cp. Exod. 3: 1. Implicit
here is the idea that Ezra was a second Moses, an idea developed at much greater length in ch. 14.

34. *your shepherd:* i.e. Jesus; cp. John 10: 11; Heb. 13: 20;
1 Pet. 2: 25; 5: 4 ('when the Head Shepherd appears, you will
receive for your own the unfading garland of glory').
rest: cp. Matt. 11: 28–9.

35. *the kingdom:* cp. verses 10, 13. *for light perpetual will
shine upon you for ever and ever:* cp. Isa. 60: 19–20; Rev. 21:
23; 22: 5.

36–7. In anticipation of what will only become a complete
reality at the end of this age the Gentiles are exhorted to *Flee
from the shadow of this world,* and to accept thankfully both
their salvation and their coming *Saviour. the shadow of this*

world: cp.Wisd. of Sol. 2: 5, 'A passing shadow – such is our life'; cp. also 1 Chron. 29: 15. *the One who has summoned you to the heavenly realms:* cp. 1 Thess. 2: 12.

38–9. As an encouragement to them, the Gentiles are urged to observe the blessings which are enjoyed by those who have already *moved out of the shadow of this world,* i.e. the Christian dead. *the whole company of those who bear the Lord's mark:* there appears to be a link with Rev. 7: 2–8; cp. also Rev. 9: 4; Ezek. 9: 4–6. The mark is a sign of protection. *and sit at his table:* for the idea of the heavenly banquet cp. Isa. 25: 6; Luke 13: 29; 14: 15; Rev. 19: 9. *and have received shining robes from the Lord:* cp. verse 40, 'those arrayed in white who have faithfully kept the law of the Lord'. The shining or white robes symbolize the glorified state of Christians who have died; cp. Rev. 3: 4–5; 6: 11; 7: 9, 13–14.

40–1. Ezra's speech ends with some words addressed to Zion which here represents the Church. *Receive ... your full number, and close the roll ... The number of your sons ... is now complete:* reflected here is the idea that the number of Christians had been determined in advance, an idea which has a fairly close parallel in Rev. 6: 11, 'Each of them was given a white robe; and they were told to rest a little while longer, until the tally should be complete of all their brothers in Christ's service who were to be killed as they had been'; cp. also 2 Esdras 4: 36–7. The deterministic thought which underlies such passages as these was extremely common in Jewish writings of the intertestamental period (2 Esdras 3–14 is a typical example), and finds expression in these writings in a variety of different ways. For the author to say that the predetermined number of Christians was *complete* is an indication that he believed the end of the world was extremely close; cp. verse 34. *those arrayed in white:* see the comment on verses 38–9. *who have faithfully kept the law of the Lord:* the attitude to the law reflected here is a further indication that the author was a Jewish Christian. *Pray that the Lord's kingdom may come* (literally 'Ask for the Lord's kingdom'): cp. verse 13. But the translation is uncertain because the word rendered 'kingdom' is not *regnum* (as in verses 10, 13, 35), but *imperium*, and it is not quite clear what this means in the context. The passage might mean something like 'Pray to the power of the Lord that . . .' *whom he summoned when the world began:* a further indication of the deterministic thought underlying this passage; cp. Rom. 8: 29–30. ✳

EZRA'S VISION

42 I, Ezra, saw on Mount Zion a crowd too large to
43 count, all singing hymns of praise to the Lord. In the middle stood a very tall young man, taller than all the rest, who was setting a crown on the head of each one of them; he stood out above them all. I was enthralled at
44, 45 the sight, and asked the angel, 'Sir, who are these?' He replied, 'They are those who have laid aside their mortal dress and put on the immortal, those who acknowledged the name of God. Now they are being given crowns and
46 palms.' And I asked again, 'Who is the young man setting crowns on their heads and giving them palms?',
47 and the angel replied, 'He is the Son of God, whom they acknowledged in this mortal life.' I began to praise those
48 who had stood so valiantly for the Lord's name. Then the angel said to me: 'Go and tell my people all the great and wonderful acts of the Lord God that you have seen.'

✳ In the final section of 2 Esdras 1–2 Ezra describes how in a vision he saw a countless number of resurrected Christians being crowned. The vision serves as a confirmation of the reality of the blessings promised to the Church in what has preceded.

42. *I, Ezra, saw on Mount Zion:* cp. Rev. 14: 1, 'Then I

looked, and on Mount Zion stood the Lamb.' *Mount Zion* is the heavenly Jerusalem; cp. Heb. 12: 22–3. *a crowd too large to count, all singing hymns of praise to the Lord:* cp. Rev. 7: 9–10:

> 'After this I looked and saw a vast throng, which no one could count…they shouted together:
> "Victory to our God who sits on the throne, and to the Lamb!"'

In fact the whole vision (2 Esdras 2: 42–8) seems to be based on Rev. 7: 9–17.

43. *a very tall young man:* i.e. Jesus; cp. verse 47. Comparable descriptions of Jesus can be found in a number of early Christian writings; cp. e.g. the *Shepherd of Hermas*, Similitude IX.6.1, 'And lo, after a little time I saw an array of many men coming, and in the middle there was a man so tall, that he overtopped the tower' (Loeb Classical Library translation of the Apostolic Fathers, vol. 2, pp. 231, 233; the *Shepherd of Hermas* dates from the second century A.D.). The description of the crowning also has a parallel in the same work, cp. Similitude VIII.2.1 and 3.6:

> 'And the angel of the Lord commanded crowns to be brought, and crowns were brought, made, as it were, of palm leaves and he crowned the men … "Who then, Sir," said I, "are they who were crowned and went into the tower?" "All those," said he, "who wrestled with the devil and conquered him, have been crowned. These are they who suffered for the law"' (Loeb translation, pp. 193, 197).

a crown: the crowns, like the palms (verse 45), were symbols of victory; cp. Rev. 2: 10.

44. The dialogue with the angel is apparently modelled on Rev. 7: 13–14.

45. Cp. Rev. 7: 14, 'Then he said to me, "These are the men who have passed through the great ordeal; they have

washed their robes and made them white in the blood of the Lamb.'" *laid aside their mortal dress and put on the immortal:* cp. 1 Cor. 15: 53-4. *crowns and palms:* cp. Rev. 2: 10 and 7: 9. Both are symbols of victory, and the implication is that those who were being crowned were martyrs.   *

2 ESDRAS 3–14
THE APOCALYPSE OF EZRA

The main part of 2 Esdras, i.e. chs. 3–14, consists of a Jewish apocalypse which dates from towards the end of the first century A.D. and is quite independent of the additional chapters (1–2, 15–16) which precede and follow it. In modern writings 2 Esdras 3–14 is often referred to as 4 Ezra, or as the Apocalypse of Ezra; for further discussion of the character and relationship of the different parts of 2 Esdras see pp. 76–7.

2 Esdras 3–14 is ostensibly set in Babylon in the sixth century B.C.; it takes as its starting-point the question whether the fate of Israel, with Jerusalem destroyed and her inhabitants taken into captivity, can be reconciled with the promises which God had made to her. But this question, with its purely national concerns, is broadened out (particularly in the section 6: 35 – 9: 25) into a discussion of the much larger problem whether the eternal punishment of sinners can be reconciled with God's love for mankind. This problem remains in the end unresolved, and in the last part of the book the concern is once more primarily national; Ezra experiences a number of visions which provide an assurance that Israel's distress will very shortly be brought to an end.

This summary account of the contents of 2 Esdras 3–14 already gives some indication of the way in which it is divided up. It falls very clearly into seven sections. The first three (3: 1 – 5: 19; 5: 20 – 6: 34; 6: 35 – 9: 25) are dialogues in which the problems that have just been mentioned are discussed. In each of these a characteristic pattern is followed.

Ezra prays to God and attempts to set out the problems which overwhelm him; the angel Uriel comes to him, and the problem is debated between Ezra and Uriel. Sometimes, however, Uriel recedes into the background, and it appears that God himself answers Ezra directly. These dialogues are in some ways similar to (and may have been modelled on) the dialogues in the Book of Job, just as the problems that are discussed in the two books are similar. However, there are also very real differences in the character of the dialogues.

The fourth, fifth and sixth sections of 2 Esdras 3–14 (9: 26 – 10: 59; 11–12; 13) are accounts of visions that are closely similar in form to the visions in Dan. 2, 7, and 8. The characteristic features of these visions are, first, that what is seen is not straightforward but requires to be interpreted by the angel (or, again, God himself), and secondly, that the interpretation is normally given in terms of allegory. As in Daniel, the visions in 2 Esdras 3–14 are used to make clear that the events of history do not occur by chance, but are predetermined by God. More specifically they are used to provide an assurance that the oppression of Israel will shortly be brought to an end, and to give detailed information about how this will happen.

The seventh section of 2 Esdras 3–14 (i.e. ch. 14) is a legend which describes how, just before the end of his life, Ezra was instructed by God to restore the scriptures.

THE HISTORICAL BACKGROUND AND DATE OF 2 ESDRAS 3–14

As we have already seen, the ostensible setting of 2 Esdras 3–14 is the Babylonian exile. According to 3: 1 the book is an account of Ezra's experiences in Babylon in the thirtieth year after the fall of Jerusalem, and this would give a date of 557 B.C. This supposed date is historically inappropriate because Ezra belongs not to the sixth century, but to the fifth or even the beginning of the fourth century B.C. (see further the comment on 3: 1–3). It is worth noticing in passing that a similar historical inaccuracy is to be found already in the Old Testament; according to the priestly genealogy of Ezra 7: 1–5 Ezra was the son and successor of Seraiah, the last chief priest of the pre-exile temple (cp. 2 Kings 25: 18–21; see also the commentary on Ezra in this series, p. 44). However, the important point to notice here is that 2 Esdras 3–14 is written as if it were a response to the fall of Jerusalem in 587 B.C., and the question with which the work apparently begins in ch. 3 is, why did God allow Jerusalem to fall in 587, and why did he allow his chosen people to be carried into captivity in Babylon? This setting is purely fictitious; 2 Esdras 3–14 actually belongs to the first century A.D. and reflects the troubled events of that much later time.

In the first century A.D. affairs in Palestine were controlled by the Romans. The arrangements under which the Jewish population was governed changed a number of times during the early decades of the century, but from the death of Herod Agrippa I in A.D. 44 the territory known as Judaea was a Roman province under the direct control of a governor who resided at Caesarea. Partly as a result of the corrupt and provocative rule of the governors, and partly because the belief was current in certain sections of Jewish society that submission to Rome was an offence against God, a revolt broke out in A.D. 66. The Romans were unable to put the revolt down immediately, and because of some initial success the entire Jewish population was forced to join in, including those who did not support the revolt and would have liked to reach some settlement with Rome.

The short- and long-term consequences of this revolt were very serious indeed for the Jews. The Emperor Nero appointed Vespasian, an experienced general, to deal with the situation, and he began his campaign in 67 by subduing Galilee. In the spring of 68 he brought under control the areas around Jerusalem and was preparing to concentrate his attack on the city when the news reached him of the death of Nero in

June 68. Vespasian paused in his campaign to await the outcome of events in Rome, and there was a further pause in
69 which was occasioned by continuing uncertainty over the
succession to Nero. Three emperors followed in rapid
succession, but eventually Vespasian himself was proclaimed
emperor by his troops in the summer of 69, and it was he
whose cause finally triumphed. Vespasian handed over
control of affairs in Palestine to his son Titus, and the latter
resumed the campaign against the Jews in the spring of 70.
Jerusalem was besieged and taken, the temple burnt and the
city destroyed. This was the effective end of the revolt,
although it was at least three more years before the last of
the rebels was overcome; a group at the fortress of Masada
managed to hold out until 73 (or possibly, as has recently
been argued, until 74), but finally killed themselves when
capture by the Romans became inevitable.

The destruction of Jerusalem, the city chosen by God
(cp. 3 : 24), and the burning of the temple, which meant that
sacrifice could no longer be offered, caused profound anguish
to the Jews, and it is these events – not the events of the sixth
century B.C. – which lie behind the composition of 2 Esdras
3–14. Ezra's lament in ch. 3, although ostensibly directed
towards the circumstances surrounding the fall of Jerusalem
in 587 B.C., is in reality concerned with the events of A.D. 66–
73 and their aftermath. The question is not, how could God
have given his city into the hands of the Babylonians, but
how could he have given it into the hands of the Romans,
and this perspective needs to be borne in mind throughout
2 Esdras 3–14. Some indication of the profound effect which
these events had upon the Jews can be obtained by reading the
very vivid account of them in the work of the Jewish historian
Josephus entitled the *Jewish War*. Josephus composed his
account shortly after the events which he describes, and his
history was in any event published before A.D. 79, the year of
Vespasian's death. For Josephus see the Note on Further
Reading, p. 306.

2 Esdras 3–14 not only has a fictitious setting; it is also pseudonymous in authorship, for it purports to be an auto-biographical account. These facts ought not to cause surprise. A close parallel to the literary procedures which the author has adopted can be found already in the Old Testament Book of Daniel (see the commentary on Daniel in this series, pp. 4–6). This also is set in Babylon in the period of the exile, but in reality it belongs to the second century B.C. and is directed specifically towards the circumstances of the persecution of Antiochus Epiphanes. Furthermore, the authorship of the second half of Daniel (chs. 7–12) is pseudonymous. Both 2 Esdras 3–14 and Daniel are in fact examples of apocalyptic writings the characteristics of which commonly include pseudonymity of authorship and a fictitious setting. Before, however, pursuing this question further it is perhaps useful to say a little about the evidence on which 2 Esdras 3–14 is dated at the end of the first century A.D.

The first point to be made is that 2 Esdras 3–14 is clearly later than the middle of the second century B.C. because it is not merely similar to the Book of Daniel in form, but also draws heavily on Daniel for its content (see e.g. p. 239 and the comments on 11: 1–2). Secondly, the fact that the author takes as his starting-point the fall of Jerusalem in 587 B.C. suggests that we have to think in terms of a comparable situation in the later period, and this points directly to the fall of Jerusalem in A.D. 70. Beyond this, a more precise dating is provided by the vision in chs. 11–12. As we shall see, this vision refers to the events of Roman history in the first century A.D., and although some of the details are obscure, it is clear that the vision reaches its climax in the reigns of Vespasian and his two sons, Titus and Domitian. Of these only Domitian (emperor from 81 to 96) was still alive at the time at which 2 Esdras 3–14 was written, and the author believed that his death would be one of the events of the last days (see the comment on 12: 28). Thus, the composition of 2 Esdras 3–14 is to be placed between A.D. 81 and 96. However, there is one other indication of date which suggests that we should think in terms of the end rather than the beginning of Domitian's reign. According to 3: 1 the events described in the book took place thirty years after the fall of Jerusalem. This date is apparently taken from Ezek. 1: 1 and is hardly to be taken as indicating that 2 Esdras 3–14 was composed exactly thirty years after A.D. 70 (see further the comment on 3: 1–3). But for it to make sense even as a symbolic date a fair interval of time must have elapsed since the fall of Jerusalem, and thus indirectly we are pointed towards the end of the reign of Domitian.

2 ESDRAS 3–14 AS AN APOCALYPSE

2 Esdras 3–14 belongs, as has already been indicated (see p. 100), among the apocalyptic writings, a group which includes such works as 1 Enoch, the Assumption of Moses, 2 Baruch, and the Apocalypse of Abraham, as well as Daniel and the Revelation of John. Few of these writings in the ancient world were actually called apocalypses, and in some respects they form a rather disparate collection. But they have sufficient in common in terms both of literary form and theological outlook to make it helpful, and indeed essential, to consider them together as a group. The adjective applied to them, 'apocalyptic', has not, it must be admitted, always been used in a very precise way. It comes from the Greek verb *apoka-lupto* ('to uncover, reveal'), from which the noun *apokalupsis* ('revelation' – our English word 'apocalypse') is derived. This noun was used, first of all, to refer to a 'revelation' of divine secrets, and it is in this sense that it occurs in Rev. 1: 1 as the title of the Revelation of John. But it was also used to refer to the 'revelation' of Jesus at his second coming at the end of this age; cp. 1 Pet. 1: 7, 13, 'when Jesus Christ is revealed' (literally 'at the revelation of Jesus Christ'). Both these ideas underlie the modern use of the term 'apocalyptic'. To describe the writings listed above as 'apocalyptic' is

primarily an indication that they are to be understood as
works which, like the Revelation of John, provide a revelation of divine secrets. But there is also the implication that
these secrets have to do above all with the end of this age. Both
these ideas are certainly applicable to 2 Esdras 3–14, which
(particularly in 9: 26 – 13: 58, but in a general way throughout the book) is concerned to provide a revelation of the
secret plans of God for the end of this age. There are both
Jewish and Christian apocalypses, but we are here concerned
only with the former. The writings listed above, which date
from the second and first centuries B.C. and the first century
A.D., are all either Jewish or (in the case of Revelation) have
a strong Jewish substratum.

What then are the common features which justify the treatment of these writings as a group? They are, first of all,
united by a common theological attitude. The authors of all
these writings believed that history was nearing its climax,
and that the end of this present age was imminent. They
stress the contrast between this age, which is under the control
of the forces of evil, and the age to come, when evil will have
been swept away and God will rule unchallenged. They were,
furthermore, convinced that God had determined in advance
the whole course of history – including the time of its end.
These ideas are all present in 2 Esdras 3–14, as we shall see.
It has to be said, however, that this kind of theological
emphasis is not unique to the apocalyptic writings, but is
commonplace in Jewish and Christian literature from the
period. What is unique to the apocalyptic writings is that
these theological ideas, with their emphasis on the end of this
age, are presented as if they were revelations that were made –
usually by means of visions or heavenly journeys – to pious
men who lived long before the time at which these writings
were actually composed. The Revelation of John is here the
exception which proves the rule inasmuch as it is not set in
some remote past, but refers explicitly to the circumstances
of the author's own day, and inasmuch as it is quite unlikely

that 'John' is a pseudonym (see the commentary on Revelation in this series, pp. 1–4). The visions which Ezra experiences, as well as the fictitious setting and pseudonymous authorship of 2 Esdras 3–14, are all entirely typical of this genre. It is the combination of distinctive theological emphasis and distinctive literary form which provides the unifying factor for the apocalyptic writings and justifies their treatment as a coherent group.

The use of pseudonymity is not restricted to the apocalyptic writings, and at the beginning of this volume a number of explanations for the occurrence of this phenomenon were mentioned (see pp. 1–2). Apocalyptic pseudonymity has to be seen against the background of the widespread use of pseudonymity in other types of literature. However, it is possible to suggest a particular reason why the authors of the apocalyptic writings should have used this literary device, namely a desire to provide comfort and assurance for their readers. As we have seen, the apocalyptic authors believed that God had predetermined the course of history. Their writings contain a number of what are, in fact, largely historical retrospects (cp. e.g. 2 Esdras 12: 10–34; Dan. 11: 2–12: 4), but by the use of pseudonymity, and of a fictitious setting in the past, they were able to present what had happened in history as if it had been revealed in advance by God. The fact that history had fallen out as it had been 'foretold' provided confirmation that God was indeed the one who determined the course of history, and an assurance that the future would likewise fall out as God had promised. Thus by the device of pseudonymity the authors were able to reassure their readers: even if circumstances seemed black, everything that happened had been determined in advance by God and was part of his plan; he would shortly intervene to put things right.

The names chosen as pseudonyms by the apocalyptic authors seem largely to have been drawn from the early period (e.g. Enoch, Abraham, Moses) or the age of the exile (e.g. Daniel, Baruch, Ezra). It was doubtless the similarity of the circumstances in which Israel found herself after A.D. 70 to those which obtained after 587 B.C. which led to the choice of Ezra as the pseudonymous author of 2 Esdras 3–14.

In the course of the commentary which follows reference will be made to a number of the apocalyptic writings in order to illustrate particular points, and it is perhaps convenient to say a little about them here. Of the writings mentioned in this commentary, the most important and influential is perhaps 1 Enoch; this is a composite work the individual sections of which range in date from the beginning of the second century B.C. to (probably) the first century A.D. The Assumption of Moses, which purports to give an account of the last words of Moses to Joshua, can be dated by means of the events which are referred to in it to shortly after the death of Herod the Great in 4 B.C. Very similar in character and purpose to 2 Esdras 3–14 is 2 Baruch; this apocalypse is in fact generally thought to be modelled on 2 Esdras 3–14, and to have been composed at approximately the same time, i.e. at the end of the first century A.D. It is to this same period that we are to attribute the Apocalypse of Abraham, a work which describes the revelations which Abraham received when he was carried up to heaven. On these works, and on the apocalyptic writings in general, see further the volume in this series entitled *The Making of the Old Testament*, pp. 75–82.

This is perhaps the place to mention that reference is also made in the commentary to the writings of the Rabbis, and particularly to the collection of traditional Jewish law known as the Mishnah (see *The Making of the Old Testament*, pp. 96–7, 167–73). In its present form this collection dates from the latter part of the second century A.D., but it contains older materials.

For English translations of all these writings see the Note on Further Reading, pp. 306–7.

THE UNITY OF 2 ESDRAS 3–14

At the beginning of this century the view was held by some scholars that 2 Esdras 3–14 was not a unity. These scholars drew attention to differences and apparent discrepancies in the various sections of the book, and argued that it was a compilation of several different writings which were put together by an editor. Reference will be made to this view in a number of places throughout the following pages, and here it must suffice to say that the evidence on which it was based now appears unconvincing. It is true that the author has not always worked out his ideas with complete consistency, and a number of minor differences can be observed in the various sections of the book. It is also true that in places he appears to have made use of older traditions. But 2 Esdras 3–14 has an essential dramatic unity, and it is clear that we have to do with an author who has stamped his views and his personality on the entire work; this is not a unity which derives its form merely from an editor or compiler.

Related to the question of unity is the question whether the views which the author himself held are to be found in the speeches of Ezra, or of the angel (and God), or of both. It has been argued that the speeches of Ezra represent a pessimism (about the fate of Israel and of mankind) which the author wished to rebut, and that the speeches of the angel (and God) alone represent the views of the author. It is, however, nowhere made clear that what Ezra says is wrong, and it seems more likely that the dialogue form reflects a tension within the author's own mind. In the first three sections (3: 1 – 9: 25) the author struggles with the problems that overwhelm him, and the two sides of the argument reflect this inner tension. In the fourth section (9: 26 – 10: 59) the author manages to come to terms with the problems that face him, and thereafter Ezra and the angel represent essentially the same viewpoint. Ezra does still question the angel, but his questions are intended merely to elicit information, not to challenge what the angel says.

THE TEXT OF 2 ESDRAS 3–14

It is generally held that 2 Esdras 3–14 was composed in Hebrew, that it was subsequently translated into Greek, and that it was from the Greek version that all the existing translations of this work were made. Neither the Hebrew original nor the Greek translation have survived, but the character of the existing translations points very strongly to the view that the language of composition was Hebrew, while the existence at one time of a Greek translation – which in any case is likely on general grounds – is confirmed by the fact that there are quotations from 2 Esdras 3–14 in Greek in early Christian writings. Of the existing translations, the Latin is undoubtedly the most important, and it was primarily from this version that the N.E.B. translation was made. But 2 Esdras 3–14 was also translated into several oriental languages: complete versions exist in Syriac, Ethiopic, Arabic (in fact there are two Arabic versions), and Armenian, but there are also fragments of Coptic and Georgian translations. Reference is occasionally made to these oriental versions in the N.E.B. footnotes; the most important is the Syriac.

The use of Hebrew for the composition of 2 Esdras 3–14 suggests that the author probably wrote his work in Palestine – but this is by no means certain.

The mystery of human destiny

THE FIRST DIALOGUE (3: 1 – 5: 19)

✻ In the prayers with which each of the first four sections of
2 Esdras 3–14 begin (3: 1–36; 5: 20–30; 6: 35–59; 9: 26–37)
the author attempts to set out the problems with which he is
concerned. His starting-point is the difficulty of understanding
Israel's fate in the light of her choice by God. ✻

EZRA'S PRAYER

IN THE THIRTIETH YEAR after the fall of Jerusalem, I, **3**
Salathiel (who am also Ezra), was in Babylon. As I lay
on my bed I was troubled; my mind was filled with
perplexity, as I considered the desolation of Zion and the 2
prosperity of those who lived in Babylon. My spirit was 3
deeply disturbed; and I uttered my fears to the Most
High. 'My Lord, my Master,' I said, 'was it not you, and 4
you alone, who in the beginning spoke the word that
formed the world? You commanded the dust, and Adam
appeared. His body was lifeless; but yours were the hands 5
that had moulded it, and into it you breathed the breath
of life. So you made him a living person. You led him 6
into paradise, which you yourself had planted before the
earth came into being. You gave him your one com- 7
mandment to obey; he disobeyed it, and thereupon you
made him subject to death, him and his descendants.

'From him were born nations and tribes, peoples and
families, too numerous to count. Each nation went its 8
own way, sinning against you and scorning you; and you

9 did not stop them. But then again, in due time, you brought the flood upon the inhabitants of the earth and
10 destroyed them. The same doom came upon all: death
11 upon Adam, and the flood upon that generation. One man you spared – Noah, with his household, and all his righteous descendants.

12 'The population of the earth increased; families and peoples multiplied, nation upon nation. But then once again they began to sin, more wickedly than those before
13 them. When they sinned, you chose for yourself one of
14 them, whose name was Abraham; him you loved, and to him alone, secretly, at dead of night, you showed how
15 the world would end. You made an everlasting covenant with him and promised never to abandon his descendants.
16 You gave him Isaac, and to Isaac you gave Jacob and Esau; of these you chose Jacob for yourself and rejected Esau; and Jacob grew to be a great nation.

17 'You rescued his descendants from Egypt and brought
18 them to Mount Sinai. There you bent the sky, shook*a* the earth, moved the round world, made the depths
19 shudder, and turned creation upside down. Your glory passed through the four gates of fire and earthquake, wind and frost; and you gave the commandments of the
20 law to the Israelites, the race of Jacob. But you did not take away their wicked heart and enable your law to
21 bear fruit in them. For the first man, Adam, was burdened with a wicked heart; he sinned and was overcome,
22 and not only he but all his descendants. So the weakness became inveterate. Although your law was in your

[a] *So some Vss.; Lat.* fixed.

people's hearts, a rooted wickedness was there too; so
that the good came to nothing, and what was bad
persisted.

'Years went by, and when the time came you raised 23
up a servant for yourself, whose name was David. You 24
told him to build the city that bears your name and there
offer to you in sacrifice what was already your own. This 25
was done for many years; until the inhabitants of the
city went astray, behaving just like Adam and all his line; 26
for they had the same wicked heart. And so you gave 27
your own city over to your enemies.

'I said to myself: "Perhaps those in Babylon lead 28
better lives, and that is why they have conquered Zion."
But when I arrived here, I saw more wickedness than I 29
could reckon, and these thirty years I have seen many
evil-doers with my own eyes. My heart sank, because 30
I saw how you tolerate sinners and spare the godless; how
you have destroyed your own people, but protected
your enemies. You have given no hint whatever to any- 31
one how to understand your ways.[a] Is Babylon more
virtuous than Zion? Has any nation except Israel ever 32
known you? What tribes have put their trust in your
covenants as the tribes of Jacob have? But they have seen 33
no reward, no fruit for their pains. I have travelled up and
down among the nations, and have seen how they pros-
per, heedless though they are of your commandments.
So weigh our sins in the balance against the sins of the 34
rest of the world; and it will be clear which way the scale
tips. Has there ever been a time when the inhabitants of 35

[a] how . . . . ways: *so some Vss.; Lat. obscure.*

the earth did not sin against you? Has any nation ever
36 kept your commandments like Israel? You may find one
man here, one there; but nowhere a whole nation.'

* The recounting of the main events in the history of God's
dealings with his people forms a characteristic feature of a
number of Old Testament passages which have similarities
with Ezra's prayer. Sometimes this occurs within the context
of the praise of God (e.g. Pss. 105; 135), and sometimes
within the context of the reproach of his people (e.g. Ps. 78;
Ezek. 20). By contrast Ezra retells this same history as the
basis of his accusation that God had treated his people unfairly;
his prayer perhaps has its closest parallel in the Old Testament
in Ps. 89, in which the rejection of the Davidic king is the
centre.

In his prayer Ezra acknowledges that God had on numerous
occasions acted graciously on behalf of his people since the
time of creation; he refers to the sparing of Noah, the choice
of Abraham and of the line descended through Isaac and
Jacob, the deliverance from Egypt, the gift of the law, the
covenant with David, and the choice of Jerusalem as the site
of the temple. But at the same time Ezra recognizes that at
each stage in this history the people had failed to respond and
had continued in a state of wickedness, so that in the end God
had handed his own city (Jerusalem) over to his enemies.
So far the presentation is not very different from, e.g., Ps. 78
or Ezek. 20. What is distinctive here is that Ezra blames this
state of affairs on God. It is true that God had given his
people the law which ought to have provided them with the
means of salvation. But he had failed to take their 'wicked
heart' away from them, and this is why the Israelites had
continued in sin and had, in consequence, been punished by
God at the hands of the Babylonians. Ezra had been prepared
to admit that this might be because the Babylonians lived
better lives than the Israelites. But his experiences in Babylon

had shown him that the exact opposite was true. To make matters worse, no other nation had entered into covenant relationship with God or had kept his commandments as well as Israel. The fact that God was punishing his people thus appeared inexplicable to Ezra (verse 30), and implicitly he accuses God of acting unjustly towards his people. Ezra's prayer is directed ostensibly to the situation of the Jews in the sixth century B.C.; in reality, as we have seen (see pp. 102–3), the prayer, like the whole book, reflects the doubt and anguish of the Jews in the period after the war with the Romans in A.D. 66–73.

1–3. Introduction to the prayer. *In the thirtieth year:* the date (cp. verse 29) was perhaps given in order to imitate the opening words of the Book of Ezekiel, which, like 2 Esdras 3–14, is set in the Babylonian exile, and in any event it is unlikely that an exact time-reference is intended. However, a date thirty years after the fall of Jerusalem in 587 B.C. is not out of place for Salathiel (see below), while a date thirty years after A.D. 70 corresponds, at least in very general terms, with the date which on other grounds seems probable for the composition of 2 Esdras 3–14. From the vision recorded in chs. 11–12 it seems clear that this work was composed during the reign of Domitian (A.D. 81–96). Unless the thirty years are totally out of step with reality, the evidence of 3: 1 suggests that we should think in terms of the end, rather than the beginning, of Domitian's reign (see further pp. 104–5). *Salathiel:* the Greek form of the Hebrew name Shealtiel, and not elsewhere mentioned in 2 Esdras 3–14. Shealtiel appears in the Old Testament (1) as the son of Jeconiah (i.e. Jehoiachin) and uncle of Zerubbabel (1 Chron. 3: 17–19) and (2) as the father of Zerubbabel (Ezra 3: 2; Neh. 12: 1). Whether he was the uncle or father of Zerubbabel, Shealtiel is a link between the beginning and the end of the period of the exile, and a date thirty years after 587 B.C. is not inappropriate for him. The rather artificial identification made here between Shealtiel/Salathiel and Ezra was, therefore, perhaps intended to overcome the chronological difficulties involved in making Ezra, who belongs in a much later period, a figure of the exile. *Babylon:* 2 Esdras 3–14 is set in Babylon because that is where the Old Testament places Ezra (cp. Ezra 7). However, it seems clear that in several places in 2 Esdras 3–14, just as in Revelation (cp. e.g. 14: 8), 'Babylon' is meant to be a symbolic name for Rome (see verses 2, 28, 31*b*). But these references do not necessarily mean that 2 Esdras 3–14 was actually composed in Rome, although such a view is not impossible. We do not know where 2 Esdras 3–14 was written, but the use of Hebrew as the language of composition suggests that it may have been in Palestine (cp. p. 110). *As I lay on my bed I was troubled:* the description is reminiscent of that of Daniel (cp. Dan. 7: 1, 15). *the Most High:* this title for God, although found throughout the Old Testament (see e.g. Gen. 14: 18; Num. 24: 16), is used particularly frequently in the writings of the intertestamental period (see also e.g. Dan. 4: 17; Acts 7: 48). It serves to emphasize God's universal sovereignty and his superiority over all other gods.

4–36. The prayer. One of the characteristic features of 2 Esdras 3–14 (as of the apocalyptic literature in general) is the extensive use that is made of Old Testament material. Sometimes this amounts to no more than a general similarity with Old Testament thought and language; in other places the author seems to draw his inspiration from quite specific passages in the Old Testament which he uses as the basis of his own writing. Ezra's prayer is a case in point: verses 3–15 draw heavily on the early chapters of Genesis, and there seems little doubt that these chapters were quite definitely in the mind of the author as he composed the prayer. After verse 15 the account of the history is abbreviated and dependence on the Old Testament text is much less direct.

4–7*b*. The story of Adam. Creation by *the word* (verse 4*a*) recalls Gen. 1, but the account of the creation of Adam (verses 4*b*–5) follows Gen. 2: 4*b*–7 (cp. particularly *and into it you breathed the breath of life. So you made him a living person* with

Gen. 2: 7). Verses 6 and 7*a* draw on Gen. 2: 8, 9, 15–17, while verse 7*b*, death following upon disobedience, summarizes Gen. 3.

7*c*–11. The flood; cp. Gen. 6–9.

12. An allusion to Gen. 10: 32 and the story of the tower of Babel (Gen. 11: 1–9) which follows.

13–15. The choice of Abraham.

14. *to him alone, secretly, at dead of night, you showed how the world would end:* an allusion to Gen. 15, and particularly to verses 12–17. However, the language used (*you showed how the world would end*) suggests that a wider tradition was in mind according to which Abraham was the recipient of apocalyptic mysteries. There does, in fact, exist an Apocalypse of Abraham (cp. p. 108); this work, which dates from the end of the first century A.D., tells how Abraham was carried up to heaven and there received from God revelations concerning heaven, the origins of sin, the fate of Israel, and the coming judgement.

15. *You made an everlasting covenant with him:* cp. Gen. 15: 18–21; 17: 1–8.

16–22. The author passes quickly over the stories of Isaac, Jacob, the period in Egypt and the deliverance from Egypt, but spends some time dealing with the revelation of the law at Sinai because this provided him with an opportunity of dealing with an aspect of the problem with which he was concerned: although God had given his people the law, he had not taken away 'their wicked heart' which caused them to sin; the perplexing result was 'that the good came to nothing, and what was bad persisted'. At the time at which 2 Esdras 3–14 was written there were in Judaism a number of different explanations of why men sin, and two of these have been brought together here. (1) It was believed that each man has an evil and a good inclination, but that the evil inclination is predominant and causes sin. The idea of the evil inclination is comparable to the idea in 2 Esdras 3–14 of the 'wicked heart' (verse 20; cp. 4: 30–2; 7: [48], [92]). This idea has been integrated with (2) the idea that men sin as a result of the fact that Adam sinned (verse 21; cp. 7: [116], [118]; Rom. 5: 12–14).

18–19. According to the Old Testament, disturbances in the world of nature were the regular accompaniment of God's manifestations of himself; for the revelation of Sinai see Exod. 19: 16–18. *four gates:* perhaps the gates of a series of heavens, each containing a different element, through which the glory of God was thought to descend. Three of the elements are mentioned in connection with a self-revelation of God in 1 Kings 19: 11–12.

23–7. In his account of the history of God's dealings with his people the author jumps from the revelation at Sinai to the time of David and the period of the monarchy. He is able now to be very brief because the points he wanted to emphasize (the divine choice of Israel and the gift of the law) have already been made; it only remains for him to refer to the fate which overtook Israel despite the divine choice.

24. The command *to build the city* and to *offer . . . sacrifice* does not as such occur in the Old Testament, but perhaps there is in part an allusion to 2 Sam. 5: 9 and 1 Chron. 11: 8. At the time at which 2 Esdras 3–14 was written sacrifice could not be offered in Jerusalem, and for pious Jews this was one of the worst aspects of their position after A.D. 70.

26. *behaving just like Adam and all his line; for they had the same wicked heart:* as in verses 20–2, the author integrates the ideas of the sin of Adam and of the wicked heart in order to explain why the inhabitants of Jerusalem kept on sinning during the period of the monarchy and so brought about the capture of Jerusalem by the Babylonians (cp. 2 Kings 25: 1–21).

27. The capture of Jerusalem, exactly as in the Old Testament (cp. 2 Kings 24: 20; 2 Chron. 36: 15–17), is interpreted as God's judgement and abandonment of his people.

28–36. The author reflects on what had happened. *Perhaps those in Babylon lead better lives:* but this initial reaction that Israel's punishment had been justified was rapidly shown by experience to be wrong. No *nation except Israel* had *ever known* God, and no *nation* had *ever kept* the *commandments like Israel*. God thus appeared to him to be acting contrary to expectation: to be destroying his own people, and to be protecting and prospering his enemies. The problem was to understand how this could be. ✻

URIEL'S RESPONSE

✻ The angel Uriel now appears for the first time. He is introduced somewhat abruptly, but we are to understand that he is sent to Ezra in response to his prayer in order to answer the difficulties that he had raised. In this first dialogue Uriel essentially makes only two points: (1) it is impossible for a mere man to understand the ways of God (4: 1–11, 12–21); (2) the end will in any case make all things clear (4: 22–32). ✻

MAN CANNOT UNDERSTAND THE WAYS OF GOD

The angel who was sent to me, whose name was Uriel, **4** replied: 'You are at a loss to explain this world; do you 2 then expect to understand the ways of the Most High?' 'Yes, my lord', I replied.   3

'I have been sent to propound to you three of the ways of this world,' he continued, 'to give you three illustrations. If you can explain to me any one of them, then 4 I will answer your question about the way of the Most High, and teach you why the heart is wicked.'

I said, 'Speak, my lord.' 'Come then,' he said, 'weigh 5 me a pound of fire, measure me a bushel*a* of wind, or call back a day that has passed.'

'How can you ask me to do that?' I replied; 'no man 6

[a] *So some Vss.; Lat.* the blast.

7 on earth can do it.' He said: 'Suppose I had asked you,
"How many dwellings are there in the heart of the sea?
or how many streams to feed the deep? or how many
watercourses above the vault of heaven? Where are the
paths out of the grave, and the roads into[a] paradise?",
8 you might then have replied, "I have never been down
into the deep, I have not yet gone down into the grave,
9 I have never gone up into heaven." But, as it is, I have
only asked you about fire, about wind, and about yesterday, things you are bound to have met; and yet you have
failed to tell me the answers.

10 'If then', he went on, 'you cannot understand things
11 you have grown up with, how can your small capacity
comprehend the ways of the Most High? A man corrupted by the corrupt world can never know the way of
the incorruptible.'[b]

✻ Uriel challenges Ezra to do various things and answer
various questions which, although having to do only with
this world, are clearly beyond men's capabilities – as Ezra
himself is forced to admit (verse 6). If Ezra cannot understand
these essentially simple matters, how, Uriel asks, can he hope
to 'comprehend the ways of the Most High' (verses 10–11).

1. The role of Uriel in 2 Esdras 3–14 is similar to his role in
1 Enoch (on which see p. 108); Uriel is one of the seven
archangels and frequently acts as Enoch's guide to explain
to him the significance of what he sees.

2–3a. *You are at a loss to explain this world*: these words
look forward to the point which the angel develops in the
following verses.

[a] the grave . . . into: *so some Vss.; Lat. omits.*
[b] A man . . . incorruptible: *reading based on other Vss.; Lat. obscure.*

120

3*b*. *three . . . ways . . . three illustrations:* those described in verse 5.

4. The main thrust of Ezra's prayer concerned the fate of Israel, the chosen people of God, in comparison with that of the other nations (3: 28–36), but Ezra also touched on the problem of why men sin (3: 20–2). In the light of this it is interesting to observe that the angel interprets Ezra's prayer as being really concerned with the second point, i.e. *why the heart is wicked*. These two questions were in fact interrelated for the author, and at different points in 2 Esdras 3–14 one or other aspect of what was essentially the same problem is emphasized.

5–6. *measure me a bushel of wind:* Job 28: 25 lists the setting of a weight (N.E.B. 'counterpoise') for the wind as one of God's mysterious acts of creation. Although fire, wind and yesterday are all familiar to Ezra (cp. verse 9), the three actions described in verse 5 are ones which only God can carry out, not a mere man.

7–9. The questions which Uriel admits he would expect to be beyond Ezra are strongly reminiscent of the questions put to Job when God answers him out of the tempest; cp. Job 38: 16–18.

7. *paradise:* see the comment on 7: [36].

8. *"I have never been down into the deep . . .I have never gone up into heaven":* cp. John 3: 12–13:

'If you disbelieve me when I talk to you about things on earth, how are you to believe if I should talk about the things of heaven?

'No one ever went up into heaven except the one who came down from heaven, the Son of Man whose home is in heaven.'

Cp. also verse 21.   *

A PARABLE

12 When I heard that, I fell*ᵃ* prostrate and exclaimed:
'Better never to have come into existence than be born
into a world of wickedness and suffering which we cannot
13 explain!' He replied, 'I went out into a wood, and the
14 trees of the forest were making a plan. They said, "Come,
let us make war on the sea, force it to retreat, and win
15 ground for more woods." The waves of the sea made a
similar plan: they said, "Come, let us attack the trees of
16 the forest, conquer them, and annex their territory." The
plan made by the trees came to nothing, for fire came and
17 burnt them down. The plan made by the waves failed
just as badly, for the sand stood its ground and blocked
18 their way. If you had to judge between the two, which
would you pronounce right, and which wrong?'

19 I answered, 'Both were wrong; their plans were impossible, for the land is assigned to the trees, and to the
sea is allotted a place for its waves.'

20 'Yes,' he replied, 'you have judged rightly. Why then
21 have you failed to do so with your own question? Just
as the land belongs to the trees and the sea to the waves,
so men on earth can understand earthly things and nothing
else; only those who live*ᵇ* above the skies can understand
the things above the skies.'

✱ Ezra's inability to understand makes him despair of life
(verse 12), but Uriel, far from sympathizing with him,
reiterates his point by means of a parable (verses 13–17).

[a] When...fell: *so some Vss.; Lat. defective.*
[b] *Or* he who lives.

The question and answer at the end of the story (verses 18–21) emphasizes the moral: 'men on earth can understand earthly things and nothing else' (cp. Isa. 55: 8–9).

13–17. The imagery of the story reminds us in some ways of Jotham's fable (Judges 9: 7–21), and the author of 2 Esdras 3–14 may perhaps have drawn his inspiration from there. But it is also possible that the author has taken over from another source a fable that was already in existence.

19. The idea that a definite place has been assigned to the sea by God occurs more than once in the Old Testament, e.g. Jer. 5: 22, 'who made the shivering sand to bound the sea' (cp. Job 38: 8–11).

21. Cp. John 3: 12–13 (quoted in the comment on verse 8). ✶

THE NEW AGE WILL MAKE ALL THINGS CLEAR

'But tell me, my lord,' I said, 'why then have I been 22 given the faculty of understanding? My question is not 23 about the distant heavens, but about the things which happen every day before our eyes. Why has Israel been made a byword among the Gentiles; why has the people you loved been put at the mercy of godless nations? Why has the law of our fathers been brought to nothing, and the written covenants made a dead letter? We pass like a 24 flight of locusts, our life is but a vapour, and we are not worth the Lord's pity, though we bear his name; what then will he do for us? These are my questions.' 25

He answered: 'If you survive, you will see; if you live 26 long enough, you will marvel.[a] For this present age is quickly passing away; it is full of sorrow and frailties, too 27 full to enjoy what is promised in due time for the godly.

[a] *So one Vs.; Lat.* live, you will often marvel.

28 The evil about which you ask me has been sown, but its
29 reaping has not yet come. Until the crop of evil has been
reaped as well as sown, until the ground where it was
sown has vanished, there will be no room for the field
30 which has been sown with the good. A grain of the evil
seed was sown in the heart of Adam from the first; how
much godlessness has it produced already! How much
31 more will it produce before the harvest! Reckon this
up: if one grain of evil seed has produced so great a crop
32 of godlessness, how vast a harvest will there be when good
seeds beyond number have been sown!'

✳ 22–5. Ezra is not satisfied with Uriel's answer and
reformulates his problem with greater clarity: he is not concerned with things beyond men's experience, but with the
fate that Israel was actually suffering. Why had Israel 'been
put at the mercy of godless nations', and why had the law,
which ought to have provided the means of salvation, 'been
brought to nothing'?

24. Israel's sorry condition is such that their lives appear
completely transient and insignificant; cp. Ps. 109: 23;
Nahum 3: 17; and Pss. 39: 11; 144: 4. To make matters
worse Israel does not seem to be *worth the Lord's pity* (the
thought of unworthiness contrasts to some extent with the
attitude expressed in 3: 28–36). The anguish of the situation
in which the Jews found themselves after the war of A.D. 66–73
here finds vivid expression (see pp. 102–3).

25. The text could also be translated. 'What then will he
do for his name which we bear?'; cp. Josh. 7: 9.

26–32. In his reply the angel now makes a second point:
the new age is coming soon and will make all things clear,
but the evil in the world which began with Adam must first
run its course, and the judgement take place, before the new
age can come. Jews and Christians at the time at which 2

Esdras 3–14 was written commonly made a distinction between the 'present age' (verse 26) and the new age, and in the writings of that period we often find the terms 'this age' and 'the age to come' used in a technical sense to refer to the two ages (sometimes the same words are translated 'this world' and 'the world to come'); see e.g. Matt. 12: 32; Eph. 1: 21; or frequently in the Mishnah (see p. 108). The distinction between the two ages forms a key theme in 2 Esdras 3–14 and is used by the author as a means of trying to solve the problems which burdened him.

27. *full of sorrow and frailties:* one of the characteristics of the present age which mean that it cannot serve as the setting for the enjoyment of the good things promised to *the godly*.

28. Ezra had asked specifically about the fate of Israel (verses 22–5), but the angel deals with the much larger question of the existence of evil in general (for this change of emphasis see the note on 4: 4). *evil* is a further characteristic of the present age; it began with Adam's sin (see verse 30), and the judgement which will bring it to an end has yet to come. In talking of these ideas the author uses for the first time imagery which he subsequently re-uses in different ways on more than one occasion, that of sowing and reaping. This kind of symbolism is familiar both from the Old Testament (cp. Joel 3: 13) and the New (cp. e.g. Matt. 13: 24–30, 36–43; Rev. 14: 14–20).

29. The *evil* in the world must run its course, the judgement take place, and the present age (*the ground*) be brought to an end, before the new age (*the field which has been sown with the good*) can come. The deterministic ideas implicit here are further developed in the remainder of the chapter.

30. The imagery of sowing is used to bring together once more the ideas of the wicked heart and of the sin of Adam and its after-effects; see 3: 20–2 and the note on 3: 16–22.

32. *how vast a harvest will there be when good seeds beyond number have been sown:* the N.E.B., probably correctly, has followed the oriental versions in which the thought is that the

blessings of the new age will be incomparably greater than the troubles of the present. However, the Latin version omits the word 'good'; the contrast would then be between the effect of the sin of one man Adam, and the cumulative effect of the sins of all mankind.   ✳

WHEN WILL THE NEW AGE COME?

33 I asked, 'But when? How long have we to wait? Why
34 are our lives so short and so miserable?' He replied, 'Do not be in a greater hurry than the Most High himself. You are in a hurry for yourself alone; the Most High
35 for many. Are not these the very questions which were asked by the righteous in the storehouse of souls: "How long must we stay here? When will the harvest begin,
36 the time when we get our reward?" And the archangel Jeremiel gave them this answer: "As soon as the number
37 of those like yourselves is complete. For the Lord has weighed the world in a balance, he has measured and numbered the ages; he will move nothing, alter nothing, until the appointed number is achieved."'

38 'But, my lord, my master,' I replied, 'we are all of us
39 sinners through and through. Can it be that because of us, because of the sins of mankind, the harvest and the
40 reward of the just are delayed?' 'Go,' he said, 'ask a pregnant woman whether she can keep the child in her womb
41 any longer after the nine months are complete.' 'No, my lord,' I said, 'she cannot.' He went on: 'The storehouses
42 of souls in the world below are like the womb. As a woman in travail is impatient to see the end of her labour, so they are impatient to give back all the souls com-
43 mitted to them since time began. Then all your questions will be answered.'

I said, 'If it is possible for you to tell and for me to 44
understand, will you be gracious enough to disclose one
thing more: which is the longer – the future still to come, 45
or the past that has gone by? What is past I know, but 46
not what is still to be.' 'Come and stand on my right,' 47
he said; 'you shall see a vision, and I will explain what
it means.'

So I stood and watched, and there passed before my 48
eyes a blazing fire; when the flames had disappeared from
sight, there was still some smoke left. After that a dark 49
rain-cloud passed before me; there was a heavy storm,
and when it had gone over, there were still some raindrops
left. 'Reflect on this,' said the angel. 'The shower of rain 50
filled a far greater space than the drops of water, and the
fire more than the smoke. In the same way, the past far
exceeds the future in length; what remains is but raindrops and smoke.'

* Ezra is by no means satisfied with the answers he has so
far received, but for the time being he gives up his attack and
begins to ask questions which are intended simply to elicit
information, more precisely to find out when the present age
will come to an end and the new age begin. A comparable
change in the character of the dialogue is to be observed also
in the second and third sections of 2 Esdras 3–14 (i.e. 5:
20 – 6: 34; 6: 35 – 9: 25). The answer to Ezra's main question
is developed in three stages: (1) the end will only come at the
time appointed by God, therefore be patient (verses 33–7);
(2) on the other hand the sin of men cannot affect God's
plan and delay the end (verses 38–43); (3) we are nearer the
end of the present age than the beginning (verses 44–50).

33–4. *How long?:* a common formula in psalms of lament
(e.g. Pss. 74: 10; 80: 4). However, Ezra is urged to be patient.

35–6. The souls of the righteous dead had already asked

the same question as Ezra and had been given the answer that *the harvest . . . the time when* they would get their *reward*, would only come when the predetermined number of the righteous was complete; cp. 2: 40-1; Rev. 6: 9-11. *the storehouse of souls:* the fate of the individual after death was a matter of some concern to the author of 2 Esdras 3-14, and his views on this subject are set out at length in 7: [75-115]. For the time being it is enough to observe that a place (here called a *storehouse*) is set apart for the souls of the righteous where they wait until the day of judgement, the day on which they would rise from the dead to enjoy their reward in the life of the new age. There are similar ideas in e.g. 1 Enoch 22; 2 Baruch 21: 23; 30:2 (on these two apocalypses see p. 108). *Jeremiel:* the name is perhaps the same as the Old Testament name Jerahmeel (cp. e.g. Jer. 36: 26), and the archangel is possibly to be identified with the archangel Remiel who is said in 1 Enoch 20: 8 to be 'in charge of those who rise', i.e. from the dead.

37. The same point is made as in verse 36, but in a slightly different way. The idea that God has exactly determined the course of history, including the time of the end, forms an important element in many writings of the intertestamental period, but receives particular emphasis in 2 Esdras 3-14.

38-43. Ezra is concerned that the sins of mankind may be delaying the day of judgement, but is assured that once the moment fixed by God is reached nothing will hinder the resurrection from the dead, the time when the just will receive their reward.

40. *a pregnant woman:* this was an important image for the author which he used more than once in the development of his argument in much the same way as he used and reused the image of sowing and reaping.

42. *to give back all the souls committed to them:* cp. the description of the resurrection in 1 Enoch 51: 1, 'And in those days the earth will return that which has been entrusted to it, and Sheol will return that which has been entrusted to

it, that which it has received, and destruction will return what
it owes.'

43. The new age will solve all Ezra's difficulties, the same
point that is made in verse 26.

44–50. Ezra now asks how much of the history of this
world remains to run its course and is told by means of a
vision that he is much nearer the end of this age than the
beginning; *the past far exceeds the future in length.* Many Jews
in the intertestamental period, like the early Christians, lived
in the expectation that the end of this world would come
very quickly, and in the apocalyptic writings there are sometimes attempts to specify exactly when it would be (cp. e.g.
Dan. 7: 25*b*; 8: 13–14; 12: 7, 11–12). By contrast it is noticeable that the nature of the reply given here leaves open the
question precisely how much time was left before the end.
The attitude of reserve reflected here was perhaps partly
conditioned by a feeling that heightened expectations of the
end were one of the factors which had contributed to the
downfall of the Jewish community. ✳

THE SIGNS OF THE END

'Pray tell me,' I said, 'do you think that I shall live to 51
see those days? Or in whose lifetime will they come?'
'If you ask me what signs will herald them,' he said, 52
'I can tell you in part. But the length of your own life
I am not commissioned to tell you; of that I know
nothing.

'But now to speak of the signs: there will come a time **5**
when the inhabitants of the earth will be seized with
panic.*a* The way of truth will be hidden from sight, and
the land will be barren of faith. There will be a great 2
increase in wickedness, worse than anything you now see

[a] *So some Vss.; Lat. corrupt.*

3 or have ever heard of. The country you now see governing the world will become a trackless desert, laid waste
4 for all to see. After the third period (if the Most High grants you a long enough life) you will see confusion everywhere. The sun will suddenly begin to shine in the middle of the night, and the moon in the day-time.
5 Trees will drip blood, stones will speak, nations will be in confusion, and the courses of the stars will be changed.
6 A king unwelcome to the inhabitants of earth will suc-
7 ceed to the throne; even the birds will all fly away. The Dead Sea will cast up fish, and at night a voice will
8 sound, unknown to the many but heard by all.*a* Chasms*b* will open in many places and spurt out flames incessantly. Wild beasts will range far afield, women will give birth
9 to monsters, fresh springs will run with salt water, and everywhere friends will become enemies. Then understanding will be hidden, and reason withdraw to her
10 secret chamber. Many will seek her, but not find her;
11 the earth will overflow with vice and wickedness. One country will ask another, "Has justice passed your way,
12 or any just man?", and it will answer, "No." In those days men will hope, but hope in vain; they will strive, but never succeed.

13 'These are the signs I am allowed to tell you. But turn again to prayer, continue to weep and fast for seven days; and then you shall hear further signs, even greater than these.'

[a] *Some Vss. read* and at night one whom the many do not know will utter his voice, and all will hear it.

[b] *So one Vs.; Lat.* Chaos.

✻ 51–2. *do you think that I shall live to see those days? Or in whose lifetime will they come?*: Ezra tries to force the angel to be more precise about when the end of this age will come, but the angel refuses to commit himself, and his answer (which no doubt represents the views of the author) is consistent with the attitude of reserve reflected in verses 48–50 (see above on 44–50). The angel does, however, agree to tell Ezra something about the signs that will precede the end. Descriptions of the signs of the end – the New Testament calls them 'the birth-pangs of the new age' (Matt. 24: 8; Mark 13: 8*b*) – were a conventional feature of apocalyptic and related writings, and it is possible to trace many parallels to the signs described here; cp. e.g. Joel 2: 30–1; Mark 13: 3–27 (and parallels); 2 Baruch 70. The character of 2 Baruch 70 is well illustrated by verses 2–3:

> 'Behold! the days come, and it shall be when the time of
>   the age has ripened,
> And the harvest of its evil and good seeds has come,
> That the Mighty One will bring upon the earth and its
>   inhabitants and upon its rulers
> Perturbation of spirit and stupor of heart.
> And they shall hate one another,
> And provoke one another to fight,
> And the mean shall rule over the honourable,
> And those of low degree shall be extolled above the
>   famous'

(Translation from R. H. Charles, *Apocrypha and Pseudepigrapha*, vol. 2, p. 517.) However, in 2 Esdras 4, because verse 52 introduces the signs very abruptly (the N.E.B. has smoothed over the harshness of the Latin, see below), and because the signs (5: 1–12) at first sight appear to be rather out of character with what has gone before, it has sometimes been argued that the passage about the signs is an interpolation (the same view has also been held about three related passages: 6: 11–28; 7: 26–[44]; 8: 63 – 9: 12). But the fact that this material seems slightly out of character is largely a result of the fact that the author has used traditional motifs in order to fill out his picture of what will happen before the end, and it is very unlikely that this passage about the signs is an interpolation.

52. In the Latin the reply of the angel begins literally 'Concerning the signs about which you ask me', but Ezra has not yet mentioned any signs. It is possible that a sentence or so has dropped out of the text, but the awkwardness of the existing text is not a justification for doubting the originality of the following passage.

5: 1–12. The character of the signs – the spread of panic and confusion, the loss of faith and increase in wickedness, the complete reversal of the natural order of things – is entirely typical of such lists; cp. the examples mentioned above.

3. *The country you now see governing the world:* i.e. Rome. The judgement of Rome for arrogance and cruelty forms the theme of chs. 11 and 12.

4a. It is not clear what is meant by *the third period*, but number schemes are a common characteristic of apocalyptic literature; cp. Dan. 7: 17 ('four kingdoms'), Rev. 12: 14 ('three years and a half'). The passage in 2 Esdras may ultimately go back to Dan. 7: 25.

4b–5. 1 Enoch 80: 4–6 describes how in the days of the sinners, i.e. the last days before the end, the sun, moon, and stars will all appear at the wrong time; cp. also Joel 2: 10; Amos 8: 9. 'The very stones will cry out from the wall' (Hab. 2: 11) perhaps provided the inspiration for *stones will speak.*

6. *A king:* Jewish belief about the last days, as expressed in such passages as Assumption of Moses 8: 1 (on this work see p. 108) or 2 Baruch 40: 1, included the expectation of a cruel and despotic ruler, and in Christian writings this has developed into the belief in 'Antichrist' (1 John 2: 18, 22) or 'the Enemy' (2 Thess. 2: 4).

7. *fish:* another reversal of the natural order, since nothing can live in the waters of *The Dead Sea.* There is a similar prophecy in Ezek. 47: 7–10, but there it is one of the blessings of the new era, not one of the terrors of the last days. *a voice:* a similar phenomenon is recorded by Josephus (*Jewish War* 6: 299–300): one of the many portents of the fall of Jerusalem was a mysterious voice speaking in the temple.

8–9a. Further horrors of the last days. *Chasms:* the idea is apparently of a series of earthquakes; cp. Zech. 14: 4. The Latin 'Chaos' (see the footnote) probably derives from a confusion in the Greek text underlying our Latin version. *Wild beasts:* probably mentioned here as one of the dangers that will face men; cp. Ezek. 14: 15. *monsters:* cp. 6: 21. But the word used really conveys the idea that the children born will be signs or portents of what is to come.

9b–10. The withdrawal of wisdom also appears as a characteristic of the last days in 2 Baruch 48: 36:

'And many shall say to many at that time:
"Where hath the multitude of intelligence hidden itself,
And whither hath the multitude of wisdom removed itself?"'

(Translation from R. H. Charles, *Apocrypha and Pseudepigrapha*, vol. 2, p. 506.)

13. The end of the first dialogue with the angel. On the command to pray and fast see the comment on 5: 20–2.   ✳

THE CONCLUSION OF THE FIRST DIALOGUE

I awoke with a start, shuddering; my spirit faltered, and 14 I was near to fainting. But the angel who had come and 15 talked to me gave me support and strength, and set me on my feet.

The next night Phaltiel, the leader of the people, came 16 to me. 'Where have you been?' he asked, 'and why that

17 sad look? Have you forgotten that Israel in exile has been
18 entrusted to your care? Rouse yourself, take nourishment.
Do not abandon us like a shepherd abandoning his flock
19 to savage wolves.' I replied: 'Leave me; for seven days
do not come near me, then you may come again.' When
he heard this, he left me.

* 14–15. Ezra's reaction to what he had experienced as he
lay on his bed (cp. 3: 1) was one of terror and consternation.
This is a traditional feature in apocalyptic writings; cp. Dan.
7: 28; 8: 27.

16–19. The dialogue with Phaltiel provides a certain
relaxation of tension in the development of the argument;
there is a comparable interlude in 12: 40–50.

16. *Phaltiel:* the identification is uncertain because no
person with this name is mentioned in the Old Testament as
living in the time of Ezra. It is true that the name Phaltiel is
related to the name Pelatiah, and that Pelatiah is the name
(1) of a grandson of Zerubbabel (1 Chron. 3: 21), and (2) of
a chief of the people in the time of Nehemiah (Neh. 10: 22);
it is possible that one or other of these passages was in the
mind of the author of 2 Esdras 3–14, but we have no idea
whether this is in fact so.

18. *shepherd:* Ezra is presented to us not only as an apocalyptic seer, but also, in a much more limited way, as the leader
and pastor of the people; cp. 12: 40–50; 14: 23–36. Brief as
these passages are, they are important as reminding us that the
author of 2 Esdras 3–14 did not write his book in isolation,
but in order to meet the needs of a community in a troubled
situation. The shepherd imagery is familiar from the Old
Testament; cp. Ezek. 34; Zech. 11: 4–17. *

THE SECOND DIALOGUE (5: 20 – 6: 34)

* This short dialogue has a similar structure to the first and goes over a good deal of the same ground. However, there is a difference of emphasis in that the first part of the dialogue (5: 20-40) concentrates exclusively on Israel's fate and ignores the problems of sin and the fate of the individual (see the comment on 4: 4). The latter part of the dialogue provides further information about the end of this age. *

EZRA'S SECOND PRAYER

For seven days I fasted, with tears and lamentations, as 20 the angel Uriel had told me to do. By the end of the 21 seven days my mind was again deeply disturbed, but I 22 recovered the power of thought and spoke once more to the Most High.

'My Lord, my Master,' I said, 'out of all the forests 23 of the earth, and all their trees, you have chosen one vine; from all the lands in the whole world you have chosen 24 one plot; and out of all the flowers in the whole world you have chosen one lily. From all the depths of the sea 25 you have filled one stream for yourself, and of all the cities ever built you have set Zion apart as your own. From all the birds that were created you have named one 26 dove, and from all the animals that were fashioned you have taken one sheep. Out of all the countless nations, 27 you have adopted one for your own, and to this chosen people you have given the law which all men have approved. Why then, Lord, have you put this one people 28 at the mercy of so many? Why have you humiliated[a]

[a] *So some Vss.; Lat.* prepared.

this one stock more than all others, and scattered your
29 own people among the hordes of heathen? Those who
reject your promises have trampled on the people who
30 trust your covenants. If you so hate your people, they
should be punished by your own hand.'

✷ 20–2. The preparation for the prayer. In the apocalyptic
writings prayer and fasting were the regular means of
preparation for a divine revelation; cp. Dan. 9: 3 (and the
following prayer, verses 4-14); 2 Baruch 21: 1 (and the
following prayer, verses 2-26).

23–30. The prayer. This prayer differs in character from
the prayer in 3: 4–36, but has a similar function. The author
uses a variety of images drawn from the Old Testament in
order to describe the choice of Israel (verses 23–7), and then
poses the problem which concerned him: if God had really
chosen Israel, why had he put her at the mercy of the nations
(verses 28–30)? Unlike the prayer in the first dialogue there is
no suggestion here that Israel's fate might be justified because
of her sin, and no concern with the problem of why men sin.

23. *vine:* a common Old Testament symbol for Israel;
cp. e.g. Ps. 80: 8, 'Thou didst bring a vine out of Egypt';
Isa. 5: 1–7; Hos. 14: 7.

24. *plot:* the Latin version is obscure, and although the
other versions support the N.E.B. translation, it is not clear
what word was used in the Hebrew original. It is possible
that in the original the reference to the choice of the land of
Palestine was expressed symbolically, like that of the nation
itself. *lily:* cp. Hos. 14: 5; Song of Songs 2: 1–2 (the Song of
Songs was interpreted allegorically by Jewish commentators
to refer to God's dealings with his beloved people, Israel).

25. *stream:* the Old Testament background to this symbol
is not as certain as in some of the other examples, but there
may be an allusion to the 'waters of Shiloah, which run so
softly and gently' (Isa. 8: 6). Water is a frequent symbol of

life and healing (cp. John 4: 14). *Zion:* the divine choice of
Jerusalem is an important theme in the Old Testament and is
mentioned in several psalms which use the ancient name
Zion; see e.g. Ps. 78: 68:

> 'he chose the tribe of Judah
> and Mount Zion which he loved'

26. *dove:* the same symbol for Israel is used in the Hebrew
version of Ps. 74: 19 (see the footnote in the N.E.B.); cp. also
Song of Songs 2: 14. *sheep:* another very common Old
Testament symbol for Israel; cp. e.g. Ps. 80: 1:

> 'Hear us, O shepherd of Israel,
> who leadest Joseph like a flock of sheep.'

This symbol is also used in 1 Enoch 85–90 in an extended
allegory of the history of Israel.

27. This verse summarizes what has been described
symbolically in verses 23–6 and makes a further point: God
had not only chosen Israel, but had also given them *the law*,
the means intended by God to provide blessing and salvation;
see above 3: 19–22.

28. *Why then, Lord, have you put this one people at the mercy
of so many?:* the divine choice of Israel and the gift of the law
made God's punishment of her at the hands of the nations all
the more inexplicable. Although writing ostensibly in the
sixth or fifth centuries B.C., the author again really has in
mind the situation which faced the Jews at the end of the first
century {A.D. {*humiliated:* the Latin 'prepared' (see the N.E.B.
footnote) derives from a corruption in the Greek text on
which the Latin translation is based. *stock:* for the symbolism
cp. Isa. 60: 21; 1 Enoch 93: 8, 'the whole race of the chosen
root will be scattered' (as in 2 Esdras, the reference is to the
exile). *scattered:* at the time at which 2 Esdras 3–14 was
written many Jews lived away from Palestine in the so-called
Dispersion, and there were Jewish communities throughout
the Roman Empire. Although granted certain privileges by

the Romans, these Jewish communities were at times subject
to harassment.

29. This verse repeats in summary form the point made in
3: 28–36.

30. The author believed that if punishment were necessary,
it ought to be carried out by God's *own hand* (i.e. by means of
some natural disaster), and not by human enemies; cp. 2
Sam. 24: 14. ✳

THE MYSTERY OF GOD'S JUDGEMENTS

31 When I had finished speaking, the angel who had
visited me that previous night was sent to me again.
32 'Listen to me,' he said, 'and I will give you instruction.
33 Attend carefully, and I will tell you more.' 'Speak on,
my lord', I replied.

He said to me, 'You are in great sorrow of heart for
Israel's sake. Do you love Israel more than Israel's Maker
34 does?' 'No, my lord,' I said, 'but sorrow has forced me
to speak; my heart is tortured every hour as I try to
understand the ways of the Most High and to fathom
some part of his judgements.'

35 He said to me, 'You cannot.' 'Why not, my lord?'
I asked. 'Why then was I born? Why could not my
mother's womb have been my grave? Then I should
never have seen Jacob's trials and the weariness of the
race of Israel.'

36 He said to me, 'Count me those who are not yet born,
collect the scattered drops of rain, and make the withered
37 flowers bloom again; unlock me the storehouses and let
loose the winds shut up there; or make visible the shape
of a voice. Then I will answer your question about Israel's
trials.'

'My Lord, my master,' I said, 'how can there be any- 38
one with such knowledge except the One whose home
is not among men? I am only a fool; how then can I 39
answer your questions?'

He said to me, 'Just as you cannot do any of the things 40
I have put to you, so you will not be able to find out my
judgements or the ultimate purpose of the love I have
promised to my people.'

---

* In response to the prayer the angel comes to Ezra again
and by means of a series of questions and answers leads Ezra
to accept two points: (1) Ezra does not love Israel more than
God (see verses 33–4); (2) God's judgements and God's love
for Israel are beyond human understanding (see verse 40). It
will be apparent that we have not advanced very far beyond
the first dialogue; cp. 4: 1–21.

32. The reply of the angel is introduced in much the same
way that the instruction of a wisdom teacher is introduced;
cp. e.g. Prov. 4: 1:

'Listen, my sons, to a father's instruction,
    consider attentively how to gain understanding'

A similar stylistic device is used in 2 Esdras 7: [49].

33–4. Ezra readily admits that God's love for Israel is
greater than his own (cp. 8: 47), but the anguish he experiences
as he tries *to understand the ways of the Most High* forces him to
speak.

35. *Why then was I born?*: the angel's blank denial of the
possibility of understanding God's ways evokes a cry of
despair, the language of which is reminiscent of Job 10:
18–19. The same theme is used in Job 3: 11, closely similar
to Jer. 20: 17–18. *Jacob's trials . . . weariness . . . of Israel:* Ezra's
concern at this point is with the nation, not the individual.

36–40. The angel takes up the question posed by Ezra in
verse 35, 'Why not, my lord?', and uses methods similar to

those already used in the first dialogue (cp. 4: 1-21, especially verses 3-11) in order to prove his point: the purposes of God are beyond the powers of human understanding.

36. *collect the scattered drops of rain:* according to Job 36: 26-7, a passage which was very probably in the mind of the author, one of the signs that 'God is so great that we cannot know him' is that

> 'He draws up drops of water from the sea
> and distils rain from the mist he has made'

Ezra is being asked to do things which God does, but which are impossible for a mere man. *withered flowers:* cp. Ezek. 17: 24, God is the one who makes 'the dry tree put forth buds'.

37. *storehouses:* the idea that the wind is kept in a series of storehouses goes back to Job 37: 9 (cp. 38: 22: there is a similar idea in 1 Enoch 41: 4); the wind is thought of as being kept shut up until it is released at the command of God (cp. Job 37: 6).

38. *except the One whose home is not among men:* a comparable idea is expressed in Dan. 2: 11.

40. *so you will not be able to find out my judgements . . . the love I have promised to my people:* the conclusion drawn is the same as in 4: 20-1, but the author temporarily forgets that the angel, not God, is speaking. This kind of transition occurs frequently in 2 Esdras 3-14, possibly because what is said could often quite naturally and appropriately be attributed to God himself. The same kind of transition (from an angel to God) can be found already in the Old Testament: cp. Gen. 18; Judg. 6: 11-24. ✻

WHY GOD'S JUDGEMENT IS DELAYED

41 I said, 'But surely, lord, your promise[a] is to those who are alive at the end. What is to be the fate of those who

[a] *So one Vs.; Lat. obscure.*

lived before us, or of ourselves, or of those who come after us?'

He said to me, 'I will compare the judgement to a 42 circle: the latest will not be too late, nor the earliest too early.'

To this I replied, 'Could you not have made all men, 43 past, present, and future, at one and the same time? Then you could have held your assize with less delay.' But he 44 answered, 'The creation may not go faster than the Creator, nor could the world support at the same time all those created to live on it.'

'But, my lord,' I said, 'you have told me that you will 45 at one and the same time restore to life every creature you have made; how can that be? If it is going to be possible for all of them to be alive at the same time and for the world to support them all, then it could support all of them together now.' 'Put your question in terms 46 of a woman's womb', he replied. 'Say to a woman, "If you give birth to ten children, why do you do so at intervals? Why not give birth to ten at one and the same time?"' 'No, my lord, she cannot do that,' I said, 'the 47 births must take place at intervals.' 'True,' he answered; 48 'and I have made the earth's womb to bring forth at intervals those conceived in it. An infant cannot give 49 birth, nor can a woman who is too old; and I have made the same rule for the world I have created.'

* 41. Ezra refuses to be silenced, but seizes upon the words used by God in order to express his problem in a new way: God's promised love may well be of benefit to those who will be *alive at the end*, but *What is to be the fate* of those who live

before then? Ezra's starting-point remains the same, the difficulty of reconciling God's promises to his people with the situation in which the Jews found themselves after the war of A.D. 66–73, but here the problem is broadened in scope to take account of all the generations who had lived, and would live, before the judgement.

42. God replies by means of the analogy of *a circle* that the judgement will affect all generations; the reason for this, although the point is not made explicit here, is that on the day of judgement all men will rise from the dead; see verse 45; 7: 32, [37].

43–4. Ezra is not satisfied with this and asks why all men could not have been created at the same time, and then it would not have been necessary to wait so long for the judgement. To this the same kind of deterministic answer is given that we have already observed in the first dialogue: God's plan for the world must run its course (cp. 4: 36–7). But the point is also made that *the world* could not *support at the same time all those created to live on it.*

45–9. Ezra argues that there is a contradiction in what God is saying: on the one hand God has stated that he 'will at one and the same time restore to life' all those whom he has created, i.e. so that they can be present at the judgement (cp. verse 42); on the other hand God has argued that the earth could not at the same time support all those who would live on it (cp. verse 44). To Ezra these statements are incompatible: if the first is true, then surely the world 'could support all of them together now'. Underlying this argument is Ezra's concern that the last judgement should not be delayed (cp. verse 43 and 4: 39), but in response a deterministic answer is once more given. Ezra is told, again by means of an analogy, that God has so ordered the earth that the successive generations must live 'at intervals', i.e. in turn, upon it. God's plan for the world cannot be hurried.

46. *Say to a woman:* the analogy of a woman giving birth is already familiar from 4: 40–3 where it is used to make a

different, but not unrelated, point; the author develops the analogy in verses 50–5 in order to discuss once more the question of when the end will come.   ✻

WHEN AND HOW WILL THE END COME?

I continued my questions. 'Since you have opened the 50 way,' I said, 'may I now ask: is our mother that you speak of still young, or is she already growing old?' He 51 replied, 'Ask any mother why the children she has lately 52 borne are not like those born earlier, but smaller. And 53 she will tell you, "Those who were born in the vigour of my youth are very different from those born in my old age, when my womb is beginning to fail." Think of 54 it then like this: if you are smaller than those born before you, and those who follow you are smaller still, the 55 reason is that creation is growing old and losing the strength of youth.'

I said to him, 'If I have won your favour, my lord, 56 show me through whom you will visit your creation.' He said to me, 'Think of the beginning of this earth: the **6** gates of the world had not yet been set up; no winds gathered and blew, no thunder pealed, no lightning 2 flashed; the foundations of paradise were not yet laid, nor were its fair flowers there to see; the powers that 3 move the stars were not established, nor the countless hosts of angels assembled, nor the vast tracts of air set up 4 on high; the divisions of the firmaments had not received their names. Zion had not yet been chosen as God's own footstool; the present age had not been planned; the 5 schemes of its sinners had not yet been outlawed, nor had God's seal yet been set on those who have stored up a

6 treasure of fidelity. Then did I think my thought; and the whole world was created through me and through me alone. In the same way, through me and through me alone the end shall come.'

7 'Tell me', I went on, 'about the interval that divides the ages. When will the first age end and the next age
8 begin?' He said, 'The interval will be no bigger than that between Abraham and Abraham; for Jacob and Esau were his descendants, and Jacob's hand was grasping Esau's heel
9 at the moment of their birth. Esau represents the end of
10 the first age, and Jacob the beginning of the next age. The beginning of a man is his hand, and the end of a man is his heel.[a] Between the heel and the hand, Ezra, do not look for any interval.'

* At this point the character of the dialogue changes in just the same way that the character of the first dialogue changes; see the comment on 4: 33–50. Ezra abandons his argument for the time being and begins instead to ask for information about the end. Three questions are raised: (1) how near are we to the end? (5: 50–5); (2) through whom will the end come? (5: 56 – 6: 6); (3) what interval will there be between this age and the new age? (6: 7–10).

50. *our mother:* Ezra takes up the analogy of the woman in order to ask once more how near we are to the end of this age; cp. 4: 44–5.

51–5. The reply is given by means of a further development of the analogy: children born in later life are inferior ('smaller') to those born to a woman when she is young; the fact that Ezra's generation is inferior to earlier generations is an indication that 'creation is growing old'. This means

[a] The beginning of a man . . . heel: *reading based on other Vss.; Lat. defective.*

that the present age is drawing to its close, the point already made in a different way in 4: 50.

54–5. *if you are smaller than those born before you:* the idea that earlier generations were superior to those that have followed is a familiar one. Superiority in size is implied by Gen. 6: 4 according to which there were 'Nephilim' (footnote 'giants') on the earth before the flood. In a similar way the Bible holds that the length of men's lives has progressively declined since the time of the generations before the Flood; cp. the ages of the patriarchs in Gen. 5 with Gen. 6: 3 and Ps. 90: 10.

5: 56 – 6: 6. Ezra's second question, 'show me through whom you will visit your creation' (5: 56), and God's answer, 'through me and through me alone the end shall come' (6: 6), apparently have a polemical purpose, although it is not clear whether the polemic is directed against Jewish or, as seems more likely, Christian expectations that God would use an intermediary in order to bring this age to an end (cp. the Christian belief in the second coming of Jesus to judge the world; see e.g. Matt. 24: 30–1). Whatever the case may be, it is to be observed that the author of 2 Esdras 3–14 did assign some functions to an intermediary in the events before the end; see 7: 28–9; 12: 31–4; 13: 25–52.

56. *If I have won your favour, my lord:* more or less the same formula (in the Latin the expressions are not quite the same) occurs several times in 2 Esdras 3–14, usually, as here, at the beginning of sections which are intended to provide information (cp. 6: 11; 7: [75], [102]; 12: 7; 14: 22; and contrast 8: 42). *visit:* more is conveyed than by our English word 'visit'; in the Old Testament God sometimes 'visits' his people in order to bless them, but much more frequently in order to judge them. However, the N.E.B. has usually paraphrased the passages in which this word occurs; cp. e.g. Gen. 21: 1 ('showed favour to'); Jer. 6: 15 ('on the day of my reckoning'). In a similar way the N.E.B. has used the word 'judge', instead of 'visit', in 2 Esdras 6: 18, although the

Latin word is the same as the one which occurs in 5: 56. What Ezra is asking about in 5: 56 is the final judgement and the end of the present age.

6: 1–6. What will happen at the end of this world is brought into relationship with what happened at its beginning. God states that before the world was created he planned these things ('Then did I think my thought'); just as he 'alone' brought the world into being, so he 'alone' will bring about its 'end'.

1–5. The description of the time before creation is similar to the description in Prov. 8: 24–9 (although the N.E.B. translation does not fully bring out the points of contact), and Prov. 8 may have been in the mind of the author when he wrote this passage.

4. *footstool:* cp. Lam. 2: 1 'Zion was his footstool', and for the choice of Zion cp. 5: 25.

5. *God's seal:* perhaps intended to serve as a protective mark for the righteous at the last judgement; cp. Ezek. 9: 4–6; Rev. 7: 2–4.

7. *the interval that divides the ages:* Ezra's third question is concerned with the nature oₗ the transition from this age to the new age. The answer is given in allegorical language and falls into two parts (verses 8*a* and 8*b*–10).

8*a.* *between Abraham and Abraham:* i.e. between Abraham and his family. There will in effect be no *interval* between the present age and the next age, but the one will follow immediately on the other just as Abraham was followed immediately by Isaac. The point is made explicitly in a less well-attested variant which reads 'between Abraham and Isaac'.

8*b*–10. The answer is reinforced by the application to the problem of a passage from the Old Testament which, in the light of other evidence, was apparently traditionally interpreted to refer to the transition from this age to the age to come, i.e. Gen. 25: 26, 'Immediately afterwards his brother was born with his hand grasping Esau's heel, and they called

him Jacob'. Just as 'Jacob's hand was grasping Esau's heel at
the moment of their birth' (verse 8*b*), so there will be no
interval between the ages – the same point that is made in
verse 8*a*. However, it is possible that the argument is carried
a stage further in verse 9.

9. The names *Esau* and *Jacob* are perhaps to be understood
as symbols for Rome and Israel. If this is so, *the end of the first
age* will be the period when Rome rules the world, and *the
beginning of the next age* will be the period when Israel rules
(perhaps the same as the period of the Messiah; see 7: 28).
This interpretation would provide an answer to the second
part of the question raised in verse 7, 'When will the first age
end and the next age begin?', but it is to be observed that
the idea that the next age will begin with the rule of Israel
does not occur elsewhere in 2 Esdras 3–14. Furthermore,
according to 7: 26–[44] the four-hundred-year rule of the
Messiah marks the end of the present age; this will be followed by an interval of silence for seven days, and only then
will the day of judgement take place and the new age begin
(7: 28–33). These ideas seem to be at variance with the ideas
expressed in 6: 7–10, and it would appear that the author of
2 Esdras 3–14 has not completely integrated his thoughts
about what will happen at the end. *

MORE SIGNS OF THE END

'My lord, my master,' I said, 'if I have won your 11
favour, make known to me the last of your signs, of 12
which you showed me a part that former night.'

'Rise to your feet,' he replied, 'and you will hear a 13
loud resounding voice. When it speaks, do not be 14-15
frightened if the place where you stand trembles and
shakes; it speaks of the end, and the earth's foundations
will understand that it is speaking of them. They will 16
tremble and shake; for they know that at the end they

147

17 must be transformed.' On hearing this I rose to my feet
and listened; and a voice began to speak. Its sound was
18 like the sound of rushing waters. The voice said:

'The time draws near when I shall come to judge those
19 who live on the earth, the time when I shall inquire into
the wickedness of wrong-doers, the time when Zion's
20 humiliation will be over, the time when a seal will be set
on the age about to pass away. Then I will perform these
signs: the books shall be opened in the sight of heaven,
21 and all shall see them at the same moment. Children only
one year old shall be able to talk, and pregnant women
shall give birth to premature babes of three and four
22 months, who shall live and leap about. Fields that were
sown shall suddenly prove unsown, and barns that were
23 full shall suddenly be found empty. There shall be a loud
trumpet-blast and it shall strike terror into all who hear
24 it. At that time friends shall make war on friends as
though they were enemies, and the earth and all its
inhabitants shall be terrified. Running streams shall stand
still; for three hours they shall cease to flow.

25 'Whoever is left after all that I have foretold, he shall
be preserved, and shall see the deliverance that I bring
26 and the end of this world of mine. They shall all see the
men who were taken up into heaven without ever
knowing death. Then shall men on earth feel a change of
27 heart and come to a better mind. Wickedness shall be
28 blotted out and deceit destroyed, but fidelity shall flour-
ish, corruption be overcome, and truth, so long unfruit-
ful, be brought to light.'

✻ The dialogue closes with a continuation of the description of the signs that will precede the end; cp. 4: 51 – 5: 13. This passage occupies the same position in the second dialogue as the corresponding description in the first dialogue.

11–12. *make known to me the last of your signs:* Ezra's request for more information follows quite naturally on the questions that immediately precede (cp. 5: 50; 5: 56; 6: 7), and it can hardly be maintained that this passage on the signs is introduced abruptly; contrast 4: 51–2. There is thus even less reason here than in the case of the first dialogue for saying that the description of the signs is an interpolation in its present context (see above, pp. 131–2).

13–18a. Ezra is told to prepare to listen to the answer to his question.

13. *Rise to your feet:* cp. Dan. 10: 11; in a very similar situation Daniel is told 'stand up'. *he replied:* the speaker is apparently the angel who now resumes the dialogue, although this is not made clear. But it makes sense to assume that it is the angel who tells Ezra to prepare to hear the voice of God. *a loud resounding voice:* although not stated explicitly, it is clear from the content of the signs (cp. verses 18b, 20) that the voice is that of God; cp. the 'loud voice' in Rev. 1: 10.

14–16. According to the Old Testament the shaking of the earth was one of the natural disturbances which regularly accompanied God's manifestation of himself; cp. e.g. Judg. 5: 4–5, and see above on 3: 18–19. In the same way it was also believed that when God comes to carry out his judgement, the earth would once more be shaken; cp. Isa. 13: 13:

> 'Then the heavens shall shudder,
>   and the earth shall be shaken from its place
> at the fury of the LORD of Hosts, on the day of his anger.'

Because *the earth's foundations will understand* what the divine voice is saying, *They will tremble and shake* in anticipation of what will happen *at the end* when God comes to judge the world and bring this age to a conclusion.

17. *the sound of rushing waters:* the author uses traditional language to describe the sound of God's voice; cp. Ezek. 43 : 2 (where the N.E.B. translates 'the sound of a mighty torrent'); Rev. 1 : 15.

18b–28. The divine reply. Ezra's question about the signs is only answered directly in verses 20b–24. Before this there is an introduction referring to the time when the signs will occur (verses 18b–20a), and after this there is a description of the period which will follow the judgement (verses 25–8).

18b–20a. The performance of the signs will be an indication that the judgement is about to be held and that the present age is about to pass away.

18b. *judge:* in the Latin, the same word that is translated 'visit' in 5 : 56 (see the comment on that passage).

19. *Zion's humiliation:* the reference to Jerusalem is a reminder that the starting-point of the book is the author's concern at the situation of the Jews in the period after the war of A.D. 66–73. In the view of the author the only escape from this situation would be found in the judgement and the ending of this age.

20a. *a seal will be set on the age:* i.e. as an indication that the present age is done with.

20b–24. The common characteristic of all but two of the signs is the reversal of what would naturally be expected; see 5 : 4b–9a and the comment on 5 : 1–12. For the signs see also Mark 13 : 3–27 (and parallels).

20b. *the books shall be opened:* in Jewish belief of the inter-testamental period the good and evil deeds of men were recorded in books which were to be opened at the judgement; cp. e.g. Dan. 7 : 10; Rev. 20 : 12. The opening of the books is not strictly one of the signs that the judgement is about to take place, but forms the beginning of the judgement itself. However, it is a mistake to expect that the signs should be listed in any sort of logical or temporal order. *in the sight of heaven:* i.e., apparently, in the presence of the heavenly host; cp. the situation described in Dan. 7 : 10:

'Thousands upon thousands served him
and myriads upon myriads attended his presence.
The court sat, and the books were opened.'

all: the reference is probably to the angels, but it is just possible
that all mankind is intended.

23. *trumpet-blast:* the sounding of the trumpet was a
traditional feature of Jewish and Christian expectations
concerning the end. According to Isa. 27: 13, 'a blast shall
be blown on a great trumpet' to summon the Jews scattered
in Assyria and Egypt to worship the Lord in Jerusalem.
In a similar way the Son of Man sends out the angels 'With
a trumpet blast' to gather the elect (Matt. 24: 31), but in
Christian tradition the sounding of the trumpet came to be
associated particularly with the resurrection of the dead (cp.
e.g. 1 Thess. 4: 16). In 2 Esdras 3–14 the sound of the trumpet
causes *terror* because it is an indication that the judgement
is imminent.

24a. Cp. Matt. 24: 6, 'The time is coming when you will
hear the noise of battle near at hand and the news of battles
far away.'

24b. *three hours:* perhaps intended to denote in symbolic
language the length of time that the signs would last (cp. the
symbolic use of a 'week' to denote an era of history in the
so-called Apocalypse of Weeks, in 1 Enoch 93 + 91: 11–17,
in which world history is divided into ten 'weeks'). It is in
any event difficult to think that literally three hours are
meant.

25-8. The author now transfers his attention from the
signs that will precede the end to the end itself and the period
which will follow.

25. *Whoever is left after all that I have foretold:* only those
who survive the signs described in 6: 20b–24 and 5: 1–12 will
see the *deliverance* which God brings and the end of the
present world.

26. *the men who were taken up into heaven without ever know-*

ing death: i.e. Enoch (Gen. 5: 24) and Elijah (2 Kings 2: 1–12). It is not clear why these two should be mentioned just at this point, although the author appears to regard translation to heaven before death as a particular mark of divine favour, and apparently believed, although there is no Old Testament tradition to this effect, that Ezra himself was translated directly to heaven; see 14: 9 and the comment on that passage.

26b–28. Conditions in the new age will be the exact opposite of conditions in the present evil age because men themselves will have changed.

26b. *Then shall men on earth feel a change of heart and come to a better mind:* literally 'and the heart of the earth's inhabitants shall be changed and converted to a different mind'; cp. Ezek. 36: 26–7. ✱

THE CONCLUSION OF THE SECOND DIALOGUE

29 While the voice was speaking to me, the ground under
30 me began to quake.[a] Then the angel said to me, 'These, then, are the revelations I have brought you this night.[b]
31 If once again you pray and fast for seven days, then I will
32 return to tell you even greater things.[c] For be sure your voice has been heard by the Most High. The Mighty God has seen your integrity and the chastity you have observed
33 all your life. That is why he has sent me to you with all
34 these revelations, and with this message: "Be confident, and have no fear. Do not rush too quickly into unprofitable thoughts now in the present age; then you will not act hastily when the last age comes."'

[a] the ground ... quake: *reading based on other Vss.; Lat. obscure.*
[b] *So one Vs.; Lat.* this coming night.
[c] *So other Vss.; Lat. adds* in the day-time.

✻ After the revelation from God the angel now speaks once more and gives Ezra some advice.

29. The fulfilment of what was anticipated in verses 14–16.

30–1. Essentially the same thing that is said in 5: 13 at the end of the first section.

32–3. The fact that Ezra is privileged to receive *these revelations* is attributed to his *integrity* and *chastity*; similar statements are to be found in the concluding verses of some of the other sections; cp. 10: 39, 57; 12: 36; 13: 53–6; see also the comment on 8: 62. Ezra's righteous standing before God is further stressed in other passages; cp. 7: [76–7]; 8: 47–9. Behind these statements we should perhaps see the author's convictions about his own standing before God.

34. Ezra is in effect advised not to be over-inquisitive *now in the present age* so as not to endanger his salvation *when the last age comes.* ✻

THE THIRD DIALOGUE (6: 35 – 9: 25)

✻ The third, and by far the longest, of the dialogues follows the broad pattern that has been established in the first two. It differs from these by its much greater concentration on the problem of sin and its consequences: why do the majority of men sin and thus incur eternal punishment and why are so few saved? In the course of the dialogue the author also tells us a good deal of his beliefs about the after-life and the end of the present age. This is the most important of the three dialogues and contains the heart of the discussion of the problems which concerned the author. ✻

EZRA'S THIRD PRAYER

Thereupon I wept and fasted again for seven days in the 35 same way as before, thus completing the three weeks enjoined on me. On the eighth night I was again dis- 36

37 turbed at heart, and spoke to the Most High. With spirit
38 aflame and in great agony of mind I said:

'O Lord, at the beginning of creation you spoke the
word. On the first day you said, "Let heaven and earth
39 be made!", and your word carried out its work. At that
time the hovering spirit was there, and darkness circled
round; there was silence, no sound as yet of human
40 voice.[a] Then you commanded a ray of light to be
brought out of your store-chambers, to make your works
41 visible from that time onwards. On the second day you
created the angel[b] of the firmament, and commanded
him to make a dividing barrier between the waters, one
part withdrawing upwards and the other remaining
42 below. On the third day you ordered the waters to collect
in a seventh part of the earth; the other six parts you
made into dry land, and from it kept some to be sown
43 and tilled for your service. Your word went forth, and
44 at once the work was done. A vast profusion of fruits
appeared instantly, of every kind and taste that can be
desired, with flowers of the most subtle colours and
mysterious scents. These were made on the third day.
45 On the fourth day by your command you created the
splendour of the sun, the light of the moon, and the stars
46 in their appointed places; and you ordered them to be
at the service of man, whose creation was about to take
47 place. On the fifth day you commanded the seventh
part, where the water was collected, to bring forth living
48 things, birds and fishes. And so, at your command, dumb
lifeless water brought forth living creatures, and gave the
49 nations cause to tell of your wonders. Then you set apart

[a] *So some Vss.; Lat. adds* from you.   [b] *Literally* spirit.

two creatures: one you called Behemoth and the other
Leviathan. You put them in separate places, for the 50
seventh part where the water was collected was not big
enough to hold them both. A part of the land which was 51
made dry on the third day you gave to Behemoth as his
territory, a country of a thousand hills. To Leviathan you 52
gave the seventh part, the water. You have kept them to
be food for whom you will and when you will. On the 53
sixth day you ordered the earth to produce for you
cattle, wild beasts, and creeping things. To crown your 54
work you created Adam, and gave him sovereignty over
everything you had made. It is from Adam that we, your
chosen people, are all descended.

'I have recited the whole story of the creation, O Lord, 55
because you have said that you made this first world for
our sake, and that all the rest of the nations descended 56
from Adam are nothing, that they are no better than
spittle, and, for all their numbers, no more than a drop
from a bucket. And yet, O Lord, those nations which 57
count for nothing are today ruling over us and devouring
us; and we, your people, have been put into their power – 58
your people, whom you have called your first-born, your
only son, your champion, and your best beloved. Was 59
the world really made for us? Why, then, may we not
take possession of our world? How much longer shall
it be so?'

*   35–38*a*. The preparation for the prayer. See the comment on 5: 20–2. *thus completing the three weeks:* only two
weeks of fasting have been mentioned so far (here and in
5: 20), and it is therefore possible that the introduction

(3: 1–3) to the first dialogue originally contained a reference to a week of fasting which has disappeared from the book in its present form. Whether this is so or not, the mention here of 'three weeks' suggests a conscious dependence on Dan. 10: 2–3; Daniel, in order to prepare himself for a revelation, was mourning and fasting 'for three whole weeks'.

38b–59. The prayer. The author retells the story of creation (verses 38b–54) in order to state in a new way the problem that concerned him: if the world was created for Israel's sake, why is she ruled over by other nations and unable to enter into possession of the world (verses 55–9)? The prayer is similar in character and purpose to those in the first two dialogues, and the problem remains the same. In contrast to the first dialogue, and in common with the second, there is no suggestion that Israel's fate was the result of her sin.

38b–54. The account of creation closely follows the narrative in Gen. 1: 1 – 2: 4a which was quite clearly in the mind of the author as he wrote this passage.

38b–40. The first day. The creation of heaven and earth and of light; see Gen. 1: 1–5.

40. *store-chambers:* light, like the wind, was thought to be kept in store-chambers from which it was brought out at God's command; see the comment on 5: 37.

41. The second day. The creation of the firmament to separate the waters; see Gen. 1: 6–8. *the angel of the firmament:* in the Genesis account God creates a firmament (the N.E.B. translation 'a vault' perhaps conveys better what was meant by this word) to separate the waters above heaven from the waters below, but in 2 Esdras 3–14 God creates a spirit or angel *to make a dividing barrier between the waters.* This development corresponds to ideas found in other intertestamental writings according to which natural processes were thought to be under the control of spirits; thus e.g. in 1 Enoch 60: 15–21 the thunder and lightning, the sea, the hoar-frost etc. are all controlled by spirits; cp. verse 16, 'And the spirit of the

sea is male and strong, and according to the power of its
strength (the spirit) turns it back with a rein, and likewise
it is driven forward and scattered amongst all the mountains
of the earth.'

42–4. The third day. The separation of the waters and the
dry land and the creation of plants; see Gen. 1: 9–13. *seventh
part ... six parts:* these figures are not mentioned in Genesis,
and the origin of this tradition is unknown. But seven has
commonly been regarded as a significant number and is
used frequently in the apocalyptic writings; cp. e.g. 1 Enoch
77: 4–8 'seven high mountains', 'seven rivers', 'seven great
islands'.

45–6. The fourth day. The creation of the sun, moon and
stars; see Gen. 1: 14–19.

46. *to be at the service of man:* i.e. by distinguishing day and
night; cp. Gen. 1: 18.

47–52. The fifth day. The creation of birds and fishes and of
two other creatures; see Gen. 1: 20–3.

47. *commanded ... the water ... to bring forth ... birds and
fishes:* it is a little strange to be told that birds as well as fishes
came from the water, but the author has apparently com-
pressed and confused what is said in Genesis.

49–52. *two creatures ... Behemoth ... Leviathan:* these are
not mentioned in Genesis, but the author is building on the
reference to 'the great sea-monsters' in Gen. 1: 21. In the
intertestamental period there was an apparently widespread
belief that as one of his acts of creation God made two monsters who were to be kept until the end of this world when
they would provide food for the righteous at a great banquet
which God would hold; cp. 2 Baruch 29: 4, 'And Behemoth
shall be revealed from his place and Leviathan shall ascend
from the sea, those two great monsters which I created on the
fifth day of creation, and shall have kept until that time, and
then they shall be food for all that are left' (translation from
R. H. Charles, *Apocrypha and Pseudepigrapha*, vol. 2, p. 497);
see also 1 Enoch 60:

'And on that day two monsters will be separated from one another: a female monster, whose name (is) Leviathan, to dwell in the depths of the sea above the springs of the waters; and the name of the male (is) Behemoth, who occupies with his breast an immense desert, named Dendayn, on the east of the garden where the chosen and righteous dwell, where my great-grandfather was received, who was the seventh from Adam, the first man whom the Lord of Spirits made. And I asked that other angel to show me the power of those monsters, how they were separated on one day and thrown, one into the depths of the sea, and the other on to the dry ground of the desert' (verses 7-9).

'And the angel of peace who was with me said to me: "These two monsters, prepared for the great day of the Lord, will provide food [possibly 'will be fed'] that the punishment of the Lord of Spirits may rest upon them, that the punishment of the Lord of Spirits may not come in vain"' (verse 24; the translation of this verse is based on the evidence of a manuscript that has only recently come to light).

For the idea of a banquet at the end of this age see Isa. 25: 6. The tradition about Behemoth and Leviathan makes use of a number of Old Testament motifs, particularly (1) the belief, also found outside the Old Testament, that the act of creation involved the slaying of a monster which was thought to dwell in, or to personify, the sea; cp. e.g. Pss. 74: 12-17; 89: 9-11; eventually this belief was referred to the future and it came to be held that at the day of judgement God would repeat what he had done at creation; see Isa. 27: 1; (2) the passage about Leviathan (N.E.B. 'the whale') in Job 41: 1-6 and Behemoth (N.E.B. 'the crocodile') in Job 40: 15-24 and 41: 7-34 (but see the N.E.B. footnotes and the commentary on Job in this series, pp. 220-7). *a country of a thousand hills:* based on Ps. 50: 10:

'for all the beasts of the forest are mine
and the cattle in thousands on my hills.'

In Jewish tradition 'the cattle' (Hebrew *behemoth*) was taken
as the name of the sea-monster, while the last words of the
verse can be understood as 'on a thousand hills'.

52. *You have kept them to be food for whom you will and when
you will:* cp. 2 Baruch 29: 4 and 1 Enoch 60: 24, quoted above.

53–4. The sixth day. The creation of animals and of Adam;
see Gen. 1: 24–31.

55–9. The author's purpose in retelling the story of creation
is now made clear: it is the prelude to a statement of the
belief that the world was created for Israel's sake. If this is so,
why is Israel controlled and oppressed by other nations and
unable to take possession of the world? The problem is
essentially the same as in the first and second dialogues
(cp. 3: 28–36 and 5: 28–30), but is here made more acute by
being considered within the wider context of God's original
intentions for the nations of the world which he had created.

55. *because you have said that you made this first world for our
sake:* cp. 7: 11. Although not found in the Old Testament,
this belief was current in the first century A.D.; cp. e.g. Assumption of Moses 1: 12, 'For he has created the world on behalf
of his people'; it was based on such passages as Deut. 10:
15–16; 14: 2 which stress Israel's special position among the
nations. *this first world:* the text is uncertain; the Latin, which
may not be in order, has 'the first-born world', one Arabic
version has 'the first world', but the other versions only have
'this (or 'the') world'. If 'first' is original, it serves to emphasize the contrast between this world and the world to come;
see the comment on 4: 26–32.

56. *spittle:* the author was using Isa. 40: 15, but the text
follows the Septuagint version, not the Hebrew. For the end
of the verse the Septuagint has 'and they shall be counted as
spittle', while the Hebrew, in the N.E.B. translation, reads
'coasts and islands weigh as light as specks of dust'. In Hebrew

the words for 'spittle' (*raq*) and 'specks of dust' (*daq*) are very similar. *a drop from a bucket:* cp. Isa. 40: 15a:

> 'Why, to him nations are but drops from a bucket,
>   no more than moisture on the scales'

57. *those nations which count for nothing are today ruling over us and devouring us:* the author was no doubt thinking particularly of the Romans.

58. *your first-born:* cp. Exod. 4: 22, 'Israel is my first-born son.' *your only son:* Israel is not so described in the Old Testament, but cp. Psalms of Solomon 18: 4, 'Your discipline is upon us as (upon) a first-born, an only son' (the Psalms of Solomon are a collection of poems belonging in all probability to the mid-first century B.C.; see in this series *The Making of the Old Testament*, pp. 97–8). *your champion:* the meaning of the Latin word (*aemulatorem*) is not clear; it perhaps conveys the idea of being zealous on God's behalf (cp. Num. 25: 10–13; 1 Macc. 2: 24, 26–7). *your best beloved:* the epithet as such is not applied to Israel in the Old Testament, but the thought is commonplace; cp. Hos. 11: 1–4. ✶

THE DIVINE REPLY

7 When I had finished speaking, the same angel was sent
2 to me as on the previous nights. He said to me, 'Rise to your feet, Ezra, and listen to the message I have come to
3 give you.' 'Speak, my lord', I said.

He said to me: 'Imagine a sea set in a vast open space,
4 spreading far*ᵃ* and wide, but the entrance to it narrow like
5 the gorge of a river. If anyone is determined to reach this sea, whether to set eyes on it or to gain command of it, he cannot arrive at its open waters except through the
6 narrow gorge. Or again, imagine a city built in a plain, a

[a] spreading far: *reading based on other Vss.; Lat.* deep.

city full of everything you can desire, but the entrance to 7
it narrow and steep, with fire to the right and deep water
to the left. There is only the one path, between the fire 8
and the water; and that is only wide enough for one man
at a time. If some man has been given this city as a 9
legacy, how can he take possession of his inheritance
except by passing through these dangerous approaches?'
'That is the only way, my lord', I agreed. 10

He said to me: 'Such is the lot of Israel. It was for 11
Israel that I made the world, and when Adam transgressed my decrees the creation came under judgement.
The entrances to this world were made narrow, painful, 12
and arduous, few and evil, full of perils and grinding
hardship. But the entrances to the greater world are 13
broad and safe, and lead to immortality. All men must 14
therefore enter this narrow and futile existence; otherwise they can never attain the blessings in store. Why 15
then, Ezra, are you so deeply disturbed at the thought
that you are mortal and must die? Why have you not 16
turned your mind to the future instead of the present?'

* In the reply the author again argues by means of analogy.
The world was indeed made for Israel's sake, but because of
Adam's sin 'creation came under judgement' (verse 11), and
life in this world became full of difficulty. Israel must endure
the difficulties of this world in order to enjoy the blessings of
the world to come.

1. *the same angel was sent to me as on the previous nights:* cp. 4:
1; 5: 31. Although Uriel is sent to Ezra, we again observe in
this dialogue that it is often God who is thought to be speaking to Ezra; cp. e.g. verse 11 and see the comment on 5: 40.

2. *Rise to your feet:* see the comment on 6: 13.

3*b*–10*a*. For the two analogies cp. Matt. 7: 13–14. Both express the same point, that the way to life is narrow and difficult. However, the explanation of the analogies, at least in the text followed by the N.E.B., modifies this theme to some extent; see the comment on verses 12–13.

11. *Such is the lot of Israel:* Ezra's prayer concerned Israel, and the reply refers in the first instance to Israel. But, as we shall see, the debate is very rapidly widened in scope.

12–13. *The entrances to this world . . . But the entrances to the greater world: entrances* hardly seems the right word in either case bcause the picture suggested by the two analogies (and below in verse 18) is of this world itself as the entrance to the world to come. Possibly *entrances* was copied by mistake because of the occurrence of the word in verses 4 and 7. There is some evidence for a variant reading 'ways', and it would be easier to make sense of this as referring to the life of this world and of the future world.

12. *narrow, painful, and arduous, few and evil, full of perils and grinding hardship:* cp. Gen. 3: 17–19.

14. *All men* (literally 'the living'): it is significant that the author no longer speaks of 'Israel'; contrast verse 11. From this point on in the third dialogue it is the fate, not of Israel, but of mankind in general that is at issue.

15–16. A further change of emphasis can be observed in these verses which have traditionally been seen as marking a turning-point in the structure of 2 Esdras 3–14. Ezra is reproved for occupying himself with *the present* rather than *the future*, and the remainder of 2 Esdras 3–14 is in fact largely concerned with the future – the fate of men, the end of this world, and the transition to the world to come. But it is the problems raised by his beliefs about the future that the author takes up first. ✻

THE JUSTICE OF GOD'S DEALINGS WITH MEN

'My lord, my master,' I replied, 'in your law you have 17
laid it down that the just shall come to enjoy these
blessings but the ungodly shall be lost. The just, therefore, 18
can endure this narrow life and look for the spacious life
hereafter; but those who have lived a wicked life will
have gone through the narrows without ever reaching
the open spaces.'

He said to me: 'You are not a better judge than God, 19
nor wiser than the Most High. Better that many now 20
living should be lost, than that the law God has set before
them should be despised! God has given clear instructions 21
for all men when they come into this world, telling them
how to attain life and how to escape punishment. But the 22
ungodly have refused to obey him; they have set up their
own empty ideas, and planned deceit and wickedness; 23
they have even denied the existence of the Most High
and have not acknowledged his ways. They have re- 24
jected his law and refused his promises, have neither put
faith in his decrees nor done what he commands. There- 25
fore, Ezra, emptiness for the empty, fullness for the full!

---

* 17–18. Ezra does not dispute what has just been said to
him, but uses the language of the analogies to raise a further
problem. He argues in effect that the wicked are treated
unfairly. It is all very well for *the just* to have to *endure this
narrow life*, because they ultimately attain *the spacious life
hereafter*. But the wicked suffer the difficulties of this world
without receiving any compensation. The underlying concern here, and throughout much of the third dialogue, is
whether the punishment of the wicked, for the author of

2 Esdras 3–14 the majority of mankind, can be reconciled with God's justice. *in your law:* the words that follow are not of course a quotation from the Pentateuch, but the idea contained in them reflects a basic principle of the legislation of Deuteronomy.

19–25. The answer is blunt; it is man's own fault. God had given men the law which was the means by which they could have obtained salvation, but the refusal of men to obey the law made their punishment inevitable.

20. *Better that many ... should be lost, than that the law ... should be despised:* the uncompromising tone of these words reflects the importance attached by the author to the law.

21. *God has given clear instructions:* i.e. in the law revealed to Moses at Sinai.

23. *they have even denied the existence of the Most High:* cp. 8: 58; Pss. 14: 1; 53: 1.

25. *emptiness for the empty, fullness for the full:* Ezra's sympathy for the wicked (verse 17–18) is sharply rejected; it is quite right that the wicked perish, and the righteous are rewarded. Cp. Mark 4: 25 (and parallels), 'For the man who has will be given more, and the man who has not will forfeit even what he has.' ✻

THE MESSIANIC KINGDOM AND THE JUDGEMENT

26 'Listen! The time shall come when the signs I have foretold will be seen; the city which is now invisible*a* shall appear and the country now concealed be made
27 visible. Everyone who has been delivered from the evils I have foretold shall see for himself my marvellous acts.
28 My son the Messiah*b* shall appear with his companions and bring four hundred years of happiness to all who
29 survive. At the end of that time, my son the Messiah shall

[a] *So some Vss.; Lat.* the city, the bride, which is now seen ...
[b] *So some Vss.; Lat.* My son Jesus.

die, and so shall all mankind who draw breath. Then the 30
world shall return to its original silence for seven days as
at the beginning of creation, and no one shall be left
alive. After seven days the age which is not yet awake 31
shall be roused and the age which is corruptible shall die.
The earth shall give up those who sleep in it, and the dust 32
those who rest there in silence; and the storehouses shall
give back the souls entrusted to them. Then the Most 33
High shall be seen on the judgement-seat, and there shall
be an end of all pity and patience. Judgement alone shall 34
remain; truth shall stand firm and faithfulness be strong;
requital*a* shall at once begin and open payment be made; 35
good deeds shall awake and wicked deeds shall not be
allowed to sleep.*b* Then the place of torment shall appear, [36]
and over against it the place of rest; the furnace of hell
shall be displayed, and on the opposite side the paradise
of delight.

'Then the Most High shall say to the nations that have [37]
been raised from the dead: "Look and understand who
it is you have denied and refused to serve, and whose
commandment you have despised. Look on this side, [38]
then on that: here are rest and delight, there fire and
torments." That is what he will say to them on the day
of judgement.

'That day will be a day without sun, moon, or stars; [39]
without cloud, thunder, or lightning; wind, water, or [40]
air; darkness, evening, or morning; without summer, [41]
spring, or winter; without heat, frost, or cold; without

[a] *Probable meaning; literally* work.
[b] *The passage from verse* [36] *to verse* [105], *missing from the text of
the Authorized Version, but found in ancient witnesses, has been restored.*

[42] hail, rain, or dew; without noonday, night, or dawn;
without brightness, glow, or light. There shall be only
the radiant glory of the Most High, by which all men
[43] will see everything that lies before them. It shall last as
[44] it were for a week of years. Such is the order that I have
appointed for the Judgement. I have given this revelation
to you alone.'

✴ The argument breaks off and is not resumed until verse 45.
Instead we are given more information about the end, more
precisely about the reign of the Messiah which will mark the
end of the present age, and about the judgement which will
follow. Like the passages on the signs (see the comment on
4: 51–2) this passage has sometimes been thought to have been
interpolated by the final editor of 2 Esdras 3–14. However, it
follows fairly naturally on what precedes and is best understood as going some way to explain what 'emptiness for the
empty, fullness for the full' means. Throughout the third
dialogue argument and information about the end are inter-
woven, and it seems unlikely that verses 26–[44] are not
original in their context.

26–30. The reign of the Messiah. Jews of the intertestamental period had no single belief about what would happen
when God brought this age to an end. Thus sometimes it was
thought that at the end there would be a great battle in which
God's enemies would be destroyed (cp. Ezek. 38–9), and
sometimes that there would be a trial in which the wicked
would be found guilty and condemned to punishment (cp.
Dan. 7: 9–12). Again, sometimes it was thought that God
would act on his own, and sometimes that he would make
use of an agent (here there is the added complication that
there was no single idea of what kind of person the agent
would be, what he would do, or what he would be called).
Finally, sometimes it was thought that the new age would be
more or less a continuation of the present age, only conditions

on earth would be perfect, and sometimes that there would be a radical break between this age and the new age. It is characteristic of 2 Esdras 3-14 that the author has combined several of these different ideas to produce a distinctive pattern of his own. The end of this age will be marked by the four-hundred-year rule of the Messiah. Then, following the death of the Messiah and a period of silence for seven days, there will be the great last judgement. Only after this does the new age begin. A comparable pattern of expectation, but adapted to Christian beliefs, occurs in Rev. 20.

26. *the signs:* those described in 5: 1-12 and 6: 18b-28. More signs are described in 9: 1-6. *the city which is now invisible:* the heavenly Jerusalem; cp. 8: 52; 10: 27, 38-55; 13: 36. The expectation of a new Jerusalem no doubt reflects the circumstances in which the book was written, namely at a time when the city lay in ruins as a result of its destruction by the Romans (cp. the prophecies concerning the rebuilding of Jerusalem which followed its earlier destruction by the Babylonians; see e.g. Isa. 54: 11-17; Zech. 2: 1-5). The text of the Latin version, given in the N.E.B. footnote, has possibly been influenced by Rev. 21: 2, 'I saw the holy city, new Jerusalem, coming down out of heaven from God, made ready like a bride adorned for her husband.' *the country now concealed:* the heavenly paradise; see the comment on verse [36]. It is a little surprising that the heavenly Jerusalem and paradise should be mentioned just at this point, i.e. as if they belonged to the period of the reign of the Messiah, since elsewhere in 2 Esdras 3-14 they clearly belong to the new age itself, and this latter only begins after the end of the messianic kingdom. However, inconsistencies of this kind occur elsewhere in 2 Esdras 3-14, and it is a mistake to expect that the events of the end should always be presented in a strictly logical order. For the heavenly Jerusalem and the heavenly paradise in combination cp. 8: 52.

27. *Everyone who has been delivered . . . shall see for himself my marvellous acts:* cp. 6: 25.

28. *the Messiah:* the term 'Messiah', a transliteration of the
Hebrew word meaning 'anointed', is used in the Old Testament in the first instance as a title of the king (cp. e.g. 1 Sam.
24: 6, 'the LORD's anointed'). However, when the monarchy
ceased to exist the title was transferred to the high priest (cp.
e.g. Lev. 4: 3, 'the anointed priest'), while at the same time
passages mentioning the anointed king (cp. e.g. Ps. 2) were
interpreted to refer to an ideal ruler of the future who, so it
was held, would restore the fortunes of Israel. By the time of
the intertestamental period 'Messiah' was used almost in a
technical way as a title for this ideal ruler; cp. e.g., apart from
2 Esdras 3–14, 1 Enoch 48: 10, a passage which refers to the
wicked, 'for they denied the Lord of Spirits and his Messiah';
2 Baruch 72: 2, 'After the signs have come, of which thou
wast told before, when the nations become turbulent, and the
time of My Messiah is come, he shall both summon all the
nations, and some of them he shall spare, and some of them
he shall slay' (translation from R. H. Charles, *Apocrypha and
Pseudepigrapha*, vol. 2, p. 518). As a quasi-technical term,
'Messiah' has to be ranged alongside other titles, e.g. 'Son
of David' (see Matt. 12: 23), 'Son of Man' (see Mark 8: 38),
which are applied to the agent who, it was believed, would act
on God's behalf when this age was brought to an end. The
functions assigned to the figures bearing these titles are not
precisely defined, but to some extent overlap, and it is important that each writing in which a concept such as that of the
Messiah occurs should be considered carefully on its own
merits. In the case of 2 Esdras 3–14 the role of the Messiah is
described not only here, but also in 12: 31–4 and 13: 25–52
(in this last passage called 'my son'). From these other passages it emerges that one important function of the Messiah
in 2 Esdras 3–14 was to judge and destroy the Romans and
other nations (cp. Ps. 2: 8–9 which refers to the 'anointed
king'). The judgement and destruction of the nations by the
Messiah (apparently at the beginning of his reign) is in addition
to the judgement of all men by God at the end of this age.

Here the task of the Messiah is to *bring four hundred years of happiness*; this is an allusion to the reign of the Messiah; cp. 12: 34. There is a description of the idyllic conditions that will exist on earth in the reign of the Messiah in 2 Baruch 73–4. In assigning a role to a Messiah the author of 2 Esdras 3–14 has taken over a traditional idea; the fact that he has done so is best understood as a further reaction to the political and physical circumstances in which the Jews in Palestine were living at the time at which he wrote. *My son the Messiah:* the fact that the Messiah is called 'my son' (cp. 13: 32, 37, 52; 14: 9) is possibly because of a deliberate Christian alteration to the text; this is clearly the case in the Latin version which reads 'My son Jesus' (see the N.E.B. footnote). In 1 Enoch 105: 1 'my son' is also used as a messianic title, but again Christian influence cannot be excluded. On the other hand the messianic interpretation of Ps. 2 (see above), in which God says of the anointed king 'You are my son' (verse 7; cp. Acts 13: 33), provides a possible Jewish background for the use of this title, and it may be wrong to suspect Christian influence. *his companions:* cp. 13: 52, 'his company'. Possibly angels are meant (cp. 2 Thess. 1: 7) or the men, such as Enoch and Elijah, 'who were taken up into heaven without ever knowing death' (6: 26). *four hundred years:* it was not only the author of 2 Esdras 3–14 who assigned this length to the reign of the Messiah; the same idea is also found in some rabbinic sayings, where it emerges that the figure is based on a combination of Gen. 15: 13, 'your descendants will be aliens living in a land that is not theirs; they will be slaves, and will be held in oppression there for four hundred years', and Ps. 90: 15:

'Repay us days of gladness for our days of suffering,
for the years thou hast humbled us.'

(The sense is 'as many as the days . . . as many as the years . . .')
In Christian tradition (Rev. 20: 4) Christ is to reign for a thousand years, and one of the Arabic versions of 2 Esdras 3–14, which has been influenced by this Christian view, has

'one thousand' instead of 'four hundred'. *who survive:* i.e. who survive the horrors described in 5: 1–12 and 6: 18*b*–28.

29. *my son the Messiah shall die:* the reign of the Messiah is quite explicitly of limited duration; it is merely the prelude to the last judgement and the new age which the judgement inaugurates.

30. The world will return to the condition of silence that existed at the time of creation; cp. 6: 39. The *seven days* correspond to the week of creation; the end of this world will be the same as its beginning.

31–[44]. The last judgement. This is held by God on all men, who for this purpose will have risen from the dead.

31. *the age which is not yet awake . . . the age which is corruptible:* the new age and the present age.

32. The resurrection of the dead. *the storehouses:* cp. verse [95] and the comment on 4: 35–6. *shall give back the souls entrusted to them:* cp. 4: 42.

33*a. the Most High shall be seen on the judgement-seat:* cp. Dan. 7: 9–10 and the repeated descriptions of judgement in 1 Enoch 37–71, e.g. 47: 3, 'And in those days I saw the Head of Days sit down on the throne of his glory, and the books of the living were opened before him, and all his host, which (dwells) in the heavens above, and his council were standing before him.'

33*b*–34. God's judgement will be in accordance with the strictest standards of impartiality.

35. *good deeds . . . wicked deeds:* the good and wicked deeds of men on which the judgement will be based will be revealed.

[36–105]. This passage was deliberately removed from the Latin manuscript on which nearly all the surviving Latin manuscripts are dependent because it contains a denial of the value of prayers for the dead (cp. verses [102–5]). However, the Latin version of this passage was discovered in the last century, and it has also been preserved in the other versions.

[36]. The places in which men will be finally punished or rewarded are pictured as being opposite each other. The two

halves of the verse are parallel and thus *the place of torment* is the same as *the furnace of hell*, and *the place of rest* the same as *the paradise of delight. the furnace of hell:* literally 'the furnace of Gehenna'. 'Gehenna' is the Greek and Latin form of the Hebrew *ge' hinnom* ('Valley of Hinnom'), the name of a valley to the south of Jerusalem which was also known as *ge' ben-hinnom* ('Valley of Ben-hinnom'). In the latter part of the monarchical period this valley was used for the sacrifice of children by fire, and because of this it was desecrated by Josiah (see 2 Kings 23: 10) and condemned by Jeremiah; see Jer. 7: 31–2:

'(the men of Judah) have built a shrine of Topheth in the Valley of Ben-hinnom, at which to burn their sons and daughters; that was no command of mine, nor did it ever enter my thought. Therefore a time is coming, says the LORD, when it shall no longer be called Topheth or the Valley of Ben-hinnom, but the Valley of Slaughter.'

Because of its evil associations, and the reputation it was given by Jeremiah, the valley later became in Jewish thought the traditional place of final punishment where the wicked would burn for ever; cp. e.g. Matt. 5: 22; 18: 9 (where the N.E.B. translates 'Gehenna' by 'hell'); 1 Enoch 27: 2–3:

'This accursed valley is for those who are cursed for ever; here will be gathered together all who speak with their mouths against the Lord words that are not fitting and say hard things about his glory. Here they will gather them together, and here (will be) their place of judgement. And in the last days there will be the spectacle of the righteous judgement upon them before the righteous for ever, for evermore.'

In 1 Enoch 90: 26–7, within the context of an allegorical account of the last judgement (90: 20–7), there is a vivid description of an abyss of fire to the south of Jerusalem in which wicked Israelites were punished:

'And I saw at that time how a similar abyss was opened in
the middle of the earth which was full of fire, and they
brought those blind sheep, and they were all judged and
found guilty and thrown into that abyss of fire, and they
burned; and that abyss was on the south of that house.
And I saw those sheep burning, and their bones were
burning' (the 'blind sheep' are wicked Israelites, and the
'house' is Jerusalem).

the paradise of delight: the word *paradise* is derived from
pairidaêza, a Persian word which simply means 'garden'.
In the intertestamental period this word was used to refer
both to the garden where Adam and Eve dwelt (cp. 3: 6) and
to the place of bliss where the righteous will dwell in the
future. But these conceptions overlap, and even where the
future reference is predominant, the word is not used with
any precision in the different writings where it occurs. In
2 Esdras 3–14 it refers primarily to the place where the
righteous will dwell in the world to come, i.e. to the final
place of rest of the righteous; cp. verse [123] and 8: 52; cp.
also Rev. 2: 7, 'To him who is victorious I will give the
right to eat from the tree of life that stands in the Garden
(Greek 'paradise'; see above) of God.'

[39–42a]. Cp. Gen. 8:22:

> 'While the earth lasts
> seedtime and harvest, cold and heat,
> summer and winter, day and night,
> shall never cease.'

The day of judgement will bring an end to the conditions
that obtain 'while the earth lasts'; instead conditions will be
as they were before creation.

[42b]. *the radiant glory of the Most High:* cp. Isa. 60: 19–20;
Rev. 21: 23 – but these passages are not concerned with
the day of judgement, but with the replacement of ordinary
light (sun and moon) by the light of God's presence in the
new age.

[43]. *a week of years:* i.e. seven years. The duration of the
judgement apparently corresponds to the length of time it
took for the world to be created (cp. verse 30), but with each
day as the equivalent of one year. This follows the principle
of Dan. 9: 2, 24–7 in which the seventy years of Jer. 25:
11–12; 29: 10 are reinterpreted as seventy weeks of years.

[44]. *revelation to you alone:* cp. 12: 36; 13: 53–6. ✲

THE ARGUMENT RESUMED

I replied: 'My lord, I repeat what I said before: "How [45]
blest are the living who obey the decrees you have laid
down!" But as for those for whom I have been praying, [46]
is there any man alive who has never sinned, any man who
has never transgressed your covenant? I see now that [47]
there are few to whom the world to come will bring
happiness, and many to whom it will bring torment. For [48]
the wicked heart has grown up in us, which has estranged
us from God's ways,*a* brought us into corruption and the
way of death, opened out to us the paths of ruin, and
carried us far away from life. It has done this, not merely
to a few, but to almost all who have been created.'

The angel replied: 'Listen to me and I will give you [49]
further instruction and correction. It is for this reason [50]
that the Most High has created not one world but two.
There are, you say, not many who are just, but only a [51]
few, whereas the wicked are very numerous; well then,
hear the answer. Suppose you had a very few precious [52]
stones; would you add to their number by putting common lead and clay among them*b*?' 'No,' I said, 'no one [53]

[a] *Literally* from these things.
[b] by putting...them: *probable reading, based on other Vss.; Lat.
obscure.*

[54] would do that.' 'Look at it also in this way,' he continued; 'speak to the earth and humbly ask her; she will
[55] give you the answer. Say to her: "You produce gold,
[56] silver, and copper, iron, lead, and clay. There is more
silver than gold, more copper than silver, more iron than
[57] copper, more lead than iron, more clay than lead." Then
judge for yourself which things are valuable and desirable – those that are common, or those that are rare.'
[58] 'My lord, my master,' I said, 'the common things are
[59] cheaper, and the rarer are more valuable.' He replied,
'Consider then what follows from that: the owner of
something hard to get has more cause to be pleased than
[60] the owner of what is common. In the same way, at my
promised judgement,[a] I shall have joy in the few who are
saved, because it is they who have made my glory prevail,
and through them that my name has been made known.
[61] But I shall not grieve for the many who are lost; for they
are no more than a vapour, they are like flame or smoke;
they catch fire, blaze up, and then die out.'

✳ [45–8]. The argument of verses 17–25 is now resumed,
and Ezra takes up once more the point he had made in verses
17–18. It is all very well for those who keep God's laws, but
is there anyone who has not sinned? The world to come will
bring torment to almost all mankind, and implicitly Ezra
asks whether this can be justified.

[45]. *I repeat what I said before:* the allusion is to verse 17,
although the following words are not an exact quotation.

[46–8]. Ezra hesitates between the view that all men
are doomed to perish because they have sinned, and
the view that a very few men may escape this fate to enjoy

[a] *Reading based on other Vss.; Lat.* creation.

the life of the world to come, but elsewhere in his speeches it is the former idea that is predominant (cp. 8: 35). By contrast the angel consistently takes the view that men are capable of earning their own salvation and is quite unconcerned that only a few will do so. The tension between the views of Ezra and the angel appears to represent a tension within the mind of the author himself, a tension that is never completely resolved, and on this matter the debate ends in something of an impasse; cp. 9: 14–16 with 9: 22 and see the comments on both passages.

[48]. *the wicked heart:* see the comment on 3: 16–22.

[49–61]. The angel once more uses an analogy to argue that it corresponds to a 'law of nature' that only a few are saved. A question-and-answer method is used, and the argument is split into three sections: (1) it would be wrong to increase the number of the saved by adding the wicked to them (verses [51–3]); (2) things that are precious are by nature few in number (verses [54–8]); (3) a consequence of this is that it is entirely right to rejoice over the few who will be saved rather than to worry about the many who will perish (verses [59–61]). An argument from nature of this kind has already been used in 5: 45–9. For the attitude reflected in the words of the angel cp. Matt. 22: 14, 'For though many are invited, few are chosen', and contrast the thought of the parables in Luke 15: 1–10 which emphasize God's concern that the very last sinner should be saved; cp. especially verse 7, 'there will be greater joy in heaven over one sinner who repents than over ninety-nine righteous people who do not need to repent'.

[49]. The angel again begins his reply in the manner of a wisdom teacher; see the comment on 5: 32.

[50]. *It is for this reason:* i.e. because the majority of men are wicked. The angel implicitly accepts that Ezra's analysis of the situation (verses [45–8]) is correct, as the words of verse [51] make clear. *the Most High has created not one world but two:* a fundamental statement of the belief in the two

ages; cp. 8: 1 and the comment on 4: 26–32. It was because the majority of men were sinners that God had to create not only this world (for the many sinners), but also the world to come (for the few righteous). The creation of the two ages was predetermined by God because of his knowledge of the way men would act in this world (cp. verses [70] and [74]).

[54–8]. For the analogy cp. also 8: 2–3.

[61]. *vapour . . . flame or smoke:* cp. Hos. 13: 3 (with reference to the idolaters in the northern kingdom):

'Therefore they shall be like the morning mist
   or like dew that vanishes early,
like chaff blown from the threshing-floor
   or smoke from a chimney.'   *

THE PITIABLE FATE OF MEN

[62]   Then I said: 'Mother Earth, what have you brought forth! Is the mind of man, like the rest of creation, a
[63] product of the dust? Far better then if the very dust had never been created, and so had never produced man's
[64] mind! But, as it is, we grow up with the power of thought and are tortured by it; we are doomed to die
[65] and we know it. What sorrow for mankind; what happiness for the wild beasts! What sorrow for every mother's
[66] son; what gladness for the cattle and flocks! How much better their lot than ours! They have no judgement to expect, no knowledge of torment or salvation after death.
[67] What good to us is the promise of a future life if it is
[68] going to be one of torment? For every man alive is burdened and defiled with wickedness, a sinner through
[69] and through. Would it not have been better for us if there had been no judgement awaiting us after death?'

The angel replied: 'When the Most High was creating [70] the world and Adam and his descendants, he first of all planned the judgement and what goes with it. Your own [71] words, when you said that man grows up with the power of thought, will give you the answer. It was with con- [72] scious knowledge that the people of this world sinned, and that is why torment awaits them; they received the commandments but did not keep them, they accepted the law but violated it. What defence will they be able to [73] make at the judgement, what answer at the last day? How patient the Most High has been with the men of [74] this world, and for how long! – not for their own sake, but for the sake of the destined age to be.'

* [62–9]. In the face of the seemingly heartless attitude of the angel, Ezra laments that it would have been better if man had been born without a mind, because he not only has to face the judgement, but to live his life in the conscious expectation of it. The lot of the animals, who have no expectation of a future judgement, appears in these circumstances to be superior to that of men. In any case the whole idea of a future life with the theoretical possibility of reward or punishment seems pointless if, in fact, punishment is to be the fate of all men, and Ezra questions whether it would not have been better if there had been no judgement at all.

[62–3]. *Is the mind of man, like the rest of creation, a product of the dust?:* in the Latin a conditional sentence; the N.E.B. has conveyed the sense by turning it into a rhetorical question expecting the answer Yes. The allusion is to Gen. 2: 7, 'Then the LORD God formed a man from the dust of the ground' and Gen. 2: 19, 'So God formed out of the ground all the wild animals and all the birds of heaven.' Since *the mind of man,* like man himself and the other creatures, is *a product of the dust,* it would have been better *if the very dust had never been created, and so had never produced man's mind!* Cp. 7: [116], where the creation of man himself is despaired of, and 4: 12.

[65–66a]. The idea that the *lot* of animals is superior to that of men is in sharp contrast with Gen. 1: 26–8 where man, whose creation forms the climax of all God's acts of creation, is placed in charge of the animals.

[67–8]. Here Ezra comes down quite definitely on the side of the view that all men have sinned and therefore are doomed to eternal punishment; see the comments on verses [46–8].

[70–4]. The reply of the angel consists largely of a reiteration of the view, already stated in verses 19–25, that it is man's own fault that he faces condemnation and eternal punishment; man had knowingly sinned, although he had been given the law, and would therefore have no defence to offer on the day of judgement.

[70]. *he first of all planned the judgement:* the angel begins by taking up, and bluntly dismissing, the point Ezra had made last of all. There is no question of there not being a judgement; it belongs amongst the things determined by God when he *was creating the world. and what goes with it:* probably a reference to paradise and Gehenna (cp. verse [36]) which, according to rabbinic teaching, were created before the world was made.

[71–2]. *Your own words ... will give you the answer:* as in 8: 37–40 (cp. 8: 26–30) the angel turns Ezra's own words against him. The fact that *man grows up with the power of thought*, far from being a reason for lamenting his fate, is a reason why he deserves to be punished, for he can legitimately be accused of sinning *with conscious knowledge. the commandments ... the law:* cp. 3: 19–22. The law given at Sinai offered the means of salvation, but men had quite consciously not observed it.

[73]. *the last day:* i.e. the day of judgement.

[74]. God had, in fact, so far dealt very patiently with men, but this was *not for their own sake, but for the sake of the destined age to be.* As is emphasized elsewhere in 2 Esdras 3–14,

178

God's dealings with this world are in accordance with his predetermined plan (cp. the comment on 4: 37). ✲

THE FATE OF MEN AFTER DEATH

Then I said: 'If I have won your favour, my lord, make [75] this plain to me: at death, when every one of us gives back his soul, shall we be kept at rest until the time when you begin to create your new world, or does our torment begin at once?' 'I will tell you that also', he replied. 'But [76] do not include yourself among those who have despised my law; do not count yourself with those who are to be tormented. For you have a treasure of good works [77] stored up with the Most High, though you will not be shown it until the last days. But now to speak of death: [78] when the Most High has given final sentence for a man to die, the spirit leaves the body to return to the One who gave it, and first of all to adore the glory of the Most High. But as for those who have rejected the ways of the [79] Most High and despised his law, and who hate all that fear God, their spirits enter no settled abode, but roam [80] thenceforward in torment, grief, and sorrow. And this for seven reasons. First, they have despised the law of the [81] Most High. Secondly, they have lost their last chance of [82] making a good repentance and so gaining life. Thirdly, [83] they can see the reward in store for those who have trusted the covenants of the Most High. Fourthly, they [84] begin to think of the torment that awaits them at the end. Fifthly, they see that angels are guarding the abode of the [85] other souls in deep silence. Sixthly, they see that they are [86] soon*a* to enter into torment. The seventh cause for grief, [87]

[a] *So some Vss.; Lat. obscure.*

179

the strongest cause of all, is this: at the sight of the Most High in his glory, they break down in shame, waste away in remorse, and shrivel with fear remembering how they sinned against him in their lifetime, and how they are soon to be brought before him for judgement on the last day.

[88]   'As for those who have kept to the way laid down by the Most High, this is what is appointed for them when
[89] their time comes to leave their mortal bodies. During their stay on earth they served the Most High in spite of constant hardship and danger, and kept to the last letter
[90] the law given them by the lawgiver. Their reward is this:
[91] first they shall exult to see the glory of God who will receive them as his own, and then they shall enter into
[92] rest in seven appointed stages of joy. Their first joy is their victory in the long fight against their inborn impulses to evil, which have failed to lead them astray from
[93] life into death. Their second joy is to see the souls of the wicked wandering ceaselessly, and the punishment in
[94] store for them. Their third joy is the good report given of them by their Maker, that throughout their life they
[95] kept the law with which they were entrusted. Their fourth joy is to understand the rest which they are now to share in the storehouses, guarded by angels in deep silence, and the glory waiting for them in the next age.
[96] Their fifth joy is the contrast between the corruptible world they have escaped and the future life that is to be their possession, between the cramped laborious[a] life from which they have been set free and the spacious life which
[97] will soon be theirs to enjoy for ever and ever. Their sixth

[a] *So some Vss.; Lat. obscure.*

180

joy will be the revelation that they are to shine like stars, never to fade or die, with faces radiant as the sun. Their [98] seventh joy, the greatest joy of all, will be the confident and exultant assurance which will be theirs, free from all fear and shame, as they press forward to see face to face the One whom they served in their lifetime, and from whom they are now to receive their reward in glory.

'The joys I have been declaring are the appointed [99] destiny for the souls of the just; the torments I described before are the sufferings appointed for the rebellious.'

Then I asked: 'When souls are separated from their [100] bodies, will they be given the opportunity to see what you have described to me?' 'They will be allowed seven [101] days,' he replied; 'for seven days they will be permitted to see the things I have told you, and after that they will join the other souls in their abodes.'

---

* The argument is once more interrupted, to be resumed this time only in verse [116]. But again, as in the case of verses 26–[44], the digression is not irrelevant to its context. In the previous section (verses [62–74]) the discussion centred on the fact that mankind, considered by Ezra in its totality to be sinful, was destined to suffer torment. Now Ezra asks for more information about this torment, in particular whether it takes effect at the moment of death or only at the beginning of the new age (verse [75]). In a long reply (verses [76–99]) the angel first rejects the implication in the question that Ezra belongs amongst the sinners and then contrasts the differing fates of the wicked and the righteous in the interval between death and the last judgement. The information is supplemented in a further question and answer (verses [100–1]).

[75]. *If I have won your favour, my lord:* see the comment

on 5: 56. *the time when you begin to create your new world*
(literally 'to renew the creation'): for the idea cp. Rev. 21: 1,
'Then I saw a new heaven and a new earth, for the first
heaven and the first earth had vanished.' The time when the
new age begins is, of course, also the time when the last
judgement will occur; cp. verses 31–3.

[76]. A comparable injunction not to class himself with the
sinners occurs in 8: 47–9. For Ezra's righteous standing
before God see also the comment on 6: 32–3.

[77]. *a treasure of good works:* the author of 2 Esdras 3–14, in
common with other Jews of his day, believed that by the
strict observance of the law it was possible for an individual
to acquire, as it were, a credit balance of good works and to
earn thereby the reward in the world to come of life; cp. 8:
33, 'For the reward which will be given to the just, who have
many good works stored up with thee, will be no more than
their own deeds have earned.' One important way in which
such a treasure could be acquired was by the giving of alms,
as is indicated in the words of Jesus in Luke 12: 33, 'Sell your
possessions and give in charity. Provide for yourselves purses
that do not wear out, and never-failing treasure in heaven.'
But in this matter the author of 2 Esdras 3–14 regarded 'faith'
or 'fidelity' (in the Latin the same word is used) as being
equally important; cp. 9: 7, 'Whoever comes safely through
and escapes destruction, thanks to his good deeds or the faith
he has shown', and see also 6: 5; 13: 23 (what is apparently
intended in these passages is faithfulness to the law, although
this is not made explicit). However, Ezra was one of the very
few who would earn salvation in this way. The author
struggled to believe that there would be others who would
take part in the life of the world to come as a result of God's
mercy (cp. 7: [132–40], especially verses [137–40]), but in the
end seems to have been unable to accept this; see further the
comment on 7: [132] – 8: 3. *until the last days:* i.e. at the
judgement; cp. verse 35.

[78]. At death the spirits of all men initially return to God

in order to appear before him for a brief moment to worship him. Thereafter the fates of the wicked and the righteous are very different. *the spirit leaves the body to return to the One who gave it:* cp. Eccles. 12: 7, 'before the dust returns to the earth as it began and the spirit returns to God who gave it', and Gen. 2: 7, 'Then the LORD God formed a man from the dust of the ground and breathed into his nostrils the breath of life.'

[79–98]. The two passages which set out the fates of the wicked and the righteous (verses [79–87] and [88–98]) have a similar form in that the suffering or joy which the individual experiences after death is in each case described in seven stages. These seven stages have been taken as a refinement of an older belief in seven hells and seven heavens (there is a description of the seven heavens in the Testament of Levi 2: 7 – 3: 10); but seven was in any case regarded as a significant number, and there may be no more to the use of seven in these descriptions in 2 Esdras 3–14 than this. (The Testament of Levi forms part of the Testaments of the Twelve Patriarchs, in its present form a Christian work of the second century A.D., but containing much older Jewish material.)

[79–87]. The wicked. In the interval between death and the last judgement the spirits of the wicked, unlike those of the righteous, have 'no settled abode', but wander about 'in torment, grief, and sorrow' (verse [80]). To this extent the answer to Ezra's question (verse [75]) is that torment begins at death. However, it is made clear that a far worse torment awaits the wicked after the last judgement; see verses [84] and [86] and the comment on verse [36]. The reasons for the anguish which the wicked suffer in the interim are described in verses [81–7].

[85]. *in deep silence:* see the comment on verse [95].

[87]. *at the sight of the Most High:* cp. verse [78].

[88–98]. The righteous. As we have already learnt (see 4: 35), the righteous spend the interval between death and the last judgement in 'storehouses' where they are guarded by angels (see verse [95]); they are in a state of joy and look forward to the life of glory which awaits them in the world to come. The seven stages of their joy are described in verses [92–8].

[88]. *to leave their mortal bodies:* implicit here is the view that the body is merely the prison of the soul, and nothing further is said about the body after death. By contrast, in 1 Cor. 15: 53 Paul argues that at the resurrection men's bodies will undergo transformation: 'This perishable being must be clothed with the imperishable, and what is mortal must be clothed with immortality.'

[91]. *first they shall exult to see the glory of God:* cp. verse [78].

[92]. *their inborn impulses to evil:* another term for the evil inclination which leads men to commit sin; see the comment on the 'wicked heart' (3: 20) in the discussion on 3: 16–22. *from life into death:* life and death in the world to come are meant. Those who succeed in the struggle against the inclination to evil are able to rejoice because they have not lost their place in the new age.

[93]. *Their second joy is to see ... the punishment:* cp. Ps. 118: 7:

> 'The LORD is on my side, he is my helper,
> and I shall gloat over my enemies.'

[95]. *the rest which they are now to share in the storehouses, guarded by angels in deep silence:* after death the souls of the righteous wait for the resurrection and the day of judgement in storehouses; cp. 4: 35, 'the righteous in the storehouse of souls' ask how long they are to stay there, and 7: 32, on the day of judgement 'the storehouses shall give back the souls (i.e. of the righteous) entrusted to them'; cp. also 7: [85], [101], where this same place is referred to as an 'abode'. Comparable ideas about the fate of the righteous after death are to be found in other Jewish writings of the period. Thus e.g. in 1 Enoch 22, both righteous and wicked wait for the day

of judgement in a special place in the west of the earth; this
place is divided into four sections (two for the righteous, and
two for the wicked), and, as in Dan. 12: 2, not all rise from
the dead. According to 2 Baruch the righteous wait in
'treasuries' in much the same way as in 2 Esdras 3–14; cp.
e.g. 30: 2,

> 'Then (i.e. when the Messiah returns in glory) all who have
> fallen asleep in hope of Him shall rise again. And it shall
> come to pass at that time that the treasuries will be opened
> in which is preserved the number of the souls of the righteous,
> and they shall come forth'

(translation from R. H. Charles, *Apocrypha and Pseudepigrapha*,
vol. 2, p. 498).

in deep silence: 'quietness' rather than 'silence' would better
convey the sense, as the Syriac version makes explicit. After
death the righteous enjoy their rest undisturbed by the cares
and troubles of this life.

[96]. *between the cramped laborious life ... and the spacious
life:* cp. 7: 3*b*–16 and 17–18.

[97]. *to shine like stars:* cp. Dan. 12: 2–3:

> 'many of those who sleep in the dust ... will wake ...
> The wise leaders shall shine like the bright vault of heaven,
>   and those who have guided the people in the true path
>   shall be like the stars for ever and ever.'

[98]. *to see face to face the One whom they served:* cp. 1 John
3: 2, 'we know that when he appears (see the N.E.B. footnote) we shall be like him, because we shall see him as he is'.
their reward: see 8: 33 and the comment on 7: [77].

[100–1]. Although not made explicit, it is clear that this
question and answer refer only to the souls of the righteous
because, as we now know, the souls of the wicked have no abode,
but wander about continually until the day of judgement
(see verse [80]). *They will be allowed seven days:* an old tradition
probably underlies this idea. Cp. the Greek version of the

Life of Adam (a Jewish work which apparently dates from before A.D. 70) 43:3, 'You shall not mourn beyond six days, but on the seventh day rest and be joyful, for on that day God and we angels rejoice with the righteous soul that has departed from the earth.' What is implied here is that the righteous soul only enters God's presence on the seventh day. This is not an exact parallel, but it does indicate that the seven days after death was a traditional length of time. ✻

THE RIGHTEOUS CANNOT INTERCEDE
FOR THE WICKED

[102]   Then I asked: 'If I have won your favour, my lord, tell me more. On the day of judgement will the just be able to win pardon for the wicked, or pray for them to [103] the Most High? Can fathers do so for their sons, or sons for their parents? Can brothers pray for brothers, relatives and friends*a* for their nearest and dearest?'

[104]   'You have won my favour,' he replied, 'and I will tell you. The day of judgement is decisive,*b* and sets its seal on the truth for all to see. In the present age a father cannot send his son in his place, nor a son his father, a master his slave, nor a man his best friend, to be ill*c* for [105] him, or sleep, or eat, or be cured for him. In the same way no one shall ever ask pardon for another; when that day comes, every individual will be held responsible for his own wickedness or goodness.'

[106] 36   To this I replied: 'But how is it, then, that we read of intercessions in scripture? First, there is Abraham, who prayed for the people of Sodom; then Moses, who prayed [107] 37 for our ancestors when they sinned in the desert. Next,

[a] friends: *so some Vss.; Lat.* the faithful.   [b] *So one Vs.; Lat.* stern.
[c] *So some Vss.; Lat.* to understand.

186

there is Joshua, who prayed for the Israelites in the time
of Achan, then Samuel in the time of Saul,[a] David during   38 [108]
the plague,[b] and Solomon at the dedication of the temple.
Elijah prayed for rain for the people, and for a dead man   39 [109]
that he might be brought back to life. Hezekiah prayed   40 [110]
for the nation in the time of Sennacherib; and there are
many more besides. If, then, in the time when corruption   41 [111]
grew and wickedness increased, the just asked pardon for
the wicked, why cannot it be the same on the day of
judgement?'

The angel gave me this answer: 'The present world is   42 [112]
not the end, and the glory of God does not stay in it
continually.[c] That is why the strong have prayed for the
weak. But the day of judgement will be the end of the   43 [113]
present world and the beginning of the eternal world to
come, a world in which corruption will be over, all   44 [114]
excess abolished, and unbelief uprooted, in which justice
will be full-grown, and truth will have risen like the sun.
On the day of judgement, therefore, there can be no   45 [115]
mercy for the man who has lost his case, no reversal for
the man who has won it.'

* Ezra's concern at the fate that awaits sinners (for Ezra, as
we have seen, this means virtually all mankind) leads him to
ask a further question: on the day of judgement will it be
possible for a righteous man to intercede on behalf of the
wicked? To this the reply is a decisive No; 'when that day
comes, every individual will be held responsible for his own
wickedness or goodness' (verse [105]). Ezra objects that

[a] in the time of Saul: *so some Vss.; Lat.* omits.
[b] during the plague: *so some Vss.; Lat.* for the destruction.
[c] does...continually: *so some Vss.; Lat.* regularly stays in it.

during the course of Israel's history it had not infrequently been the case that 'the just asked pardon for the wicked' (verse [111]) and asks why the same principle cannot apply. But the angel dismisses the parallel. The day of judgement marks the beginning of the new age in which conditions will be transformed. Although in the present age men had been permitted to pray on behalf of others, in the new age the judgement will be strictly according to justice (verses [112–14]). The attitude of the author reflected in these verses is in sharp contrast with the view held by other Jews at that time who did believe that the prayers of the righteous could benefit the wicked at the judgement. Thus, e.g., in the Testament of Abraham (a Jewish work of the first century A.D.) 12–14 a soul whose sins and righteous deeds are found to be equal is saved through the prayers of Abraham.

[102]. *If I have won your favour:* see the comment on 5: 56.

[105]. *every individual will be held responsible for his own wickedness or goodness:* similar statements are to be found already in the Old Testament, but in a rather different theological context. In the Old Testament stress is laid on the individual's responsibility, over against the idea of inherited guilt (cp. Deut. 24: 16), or, particularly in the period of the exile, on both responsibility and the reality of release from the past guilt of the community (cp. Jer. 31: 29–30; Ezek. 18: 20). Here these ideas are reapplied to the final moment of judgement.

[106]. *Abraham, who prayed for the people of Sodom:* see Gen. 18: 16–33. *Moses, who prayed for our ancestors when they sinned in the desert:* see Exod. 32: 11–14.

[107]. *Joshua, who prayed for the Israelites in the time of Achan:* see Josh. 7: 6–9.

[108]. *Samuel in the time of Saul:* the precise allusion is uncertain; see 1 Sam. 7: 9 (but this antedates the appearance of Saul); 12: 19–25; cp. also Ps. 99: 6, 'Samuel among those who call on his name'. *David during the plague:* see 2 Sam. 24: 17. *Solomon at the dedication of the temple:* see 1 Kings 8: 22–3, 30.

[109]. *Elijah prayed for rain for the people:* see 1 Kings 18: 36–7, 42*b*. *and for a dead man that he might be brought back to life:* see 1 Kings 17: 20–1.

[110]. *Hezekiah prayed for the nation:* see 2 Kings 19: 15–19.

[112]. *The present world is not the end:* the angel explains the fact that righteous men had in the past prayed on behalf of the wicked by stressing the transitory and imperfect character of life in this world. *and the glory of God does not stay in it continually:* the author refers to God's presence in the world in terms familiar from certain parts of the Old Testament according to which God was thought to manifest himself to his people by means of his glory (see e.g. Exod. 24: 15–18; Ezek. 1: 26–8). According to the Old Testament it was believed that sin led to the withdrawal of God's presence (see e.g. Hos. 5: 6, 15; Ezek. 11: 22–3, the climax of the description of the sin of Jerusalem in Ezek. 8–11); for the author of 2 Esdras 3–14 this was an indication of the imperfect character of this world, and the reason *why the strong have prayed for the weak.* In the Latin text of this verse in 2 Esdras (see the N.E.B. footnote) the negative has been omitted by mistake.

[113–14]. *the day of judgement will be the end of the present world and the beginning of the eternal world to come:* cp. verses 31–3. *a world in which corruption will be over . . . truth will have risen like the sun:* conditions in the world to come will be so transformed that all the imperfections of the present world will disappear, and the judgement itself will be according to the strictest standards of justice and impartiality (cp. verses 33*b*–34). The implication is clear; there will be no place then for one man to pray on behalf of another. ✲

THE ARGUMENT RESUMED ONCE MORE

I replied, 'But this is my point, my first point and my **46 [116]** last: how much better it would have been if the earth had never produced Adam at all, or, since it has done so, if he

[117] 47 had been restrained from sinning! For what good does it
do us all to live in misery now and have nothing but
[118] 48 punishment to expect after death? O Adam, what have
you done? Your sin was not your fall alone; it was ours
[119] 49 also, the fall of all your descendants. What good is the
promise of immortality to us, when we have committed
[120] 50 mortal sins; or the hope of eternity, in the wretched and
[121] 51 futile state to which we have come; or the prospect of
dwelling in health and safety, when we have lived such
[122] 52 evil lives? The glory of the Most High will guard those
who have led a life of purity; but what help is that to us
[123] 53 whose conduct has been so wicked? What good is the
revelation of paradise and its imperishable fruit, the
[124] 54 source of perfect satisfaction and healing? For we shall
never enter it, since we have made depravity our home.
[125] 55 Those who have practised self-discipline shall shine with
faces brighter than the stars; but what good is that to us
[126] 56 whose faces are darker than the night? For during a lifetime of wickedness we have never given a thought to the
sufferings awaiting us after death.'

[127] 57   The angel replied, 'This is the thought for every man
[128] 58 to keep in mind during his earthly contest: if he loses, he
must accept the sufferings you have mentioned, but if he
[129] 59 wins, the rewards I have been describing will be his. For
that was the way which Moses in his time urged the
people to take, when he said, "Choose life and live!"
[130] 60 But they did not believe him, nor the prophets after him,
[131] 61 nor me when I spoke to them. Over their damnation
there will be no sorrow; there will only be joy for the
salvation of those who have believed.'[a]

[a] *So some Vss.; Lat.* for those who are convinced of salvation.

✻ [116–26]. The argument of verses 17–25, [45–74] is now again taken up in a more direct way. Ezra has just learnt (verses [75–115]) of the fate that awaits sinners after death, and this leads him to complain bitterly that it would have been better if Adam had never been born, or at any rate had been prevented from sinning and thereby implicating all his descendants in sin. Ezra concedes that 'Those who have practised self-discipline' (verse [125]) will be rewarded, but for the sinful majority of mankind promises of eternal bliss are empty and meaningless. In essence what Ezra is arguing is that the conditions of life imposed on man by God are unfair.

[116]. *how much better it would have been if the earth had never produced Adam:* cp. verse [63] and 4: 12.

[118]. *Your sin was not your fall alone; it was ours also, the fall of all your descendants:* the author refers once more to the idea that men sin as a result of the fact that Adam sinned; cp. 3: 21; Rom. 5: 12–14. As we saw in the comment on 3: 16–22, this is only one of his explanations for the existence of sin, the other being the idea of the wicked heart.

[122]. *The glory of the Most High:* see the comment on verse [112].

[123]. *paradise:* see the comment on verse [36]. *and its imperishable fruit:* the belief that the fruit of paradise is imperishable has a parallel in Ezekiel's vision of the spring of life-giving water flowing from the temple; see Ezek. 47: 1–12, especially verse 12, 'Beside the torrent on either bank all trees good for food shall spring up. Their leaves shall not wither, their fruit shall not cease.' Cp. also Rev. 22: 1–5, particularly verse 2.

[125]. *shall shine with faces brighter than the stars:* cp. Dan. 12: 2–3 (see the comment on verse [97]); Matt. 13: 43, 'And then (i.e. after the wicked have been destroyed) the righteous will shine as brightly as the sun in the kingdom of their Father.'

[127–31]. The angel does not respond directly to Ezra's complaint, but merely continues the line of argument that he has already developed in verses 19–25, [70–4]: man is responsible for his own destiny, and it lies entirely within his own hands whether his fate in the world to come is damnation or salvation. Thus in direct contrast to Ezra the angel insists that it is perfectly possible for a man to secure his own salvation. Cp. Ecclus. 15: 14–17:

> 'When he made man in the beginning,
> he left him free to take his own decisions;
> if you choose, you can keep the commandments;
> whether or not you keep faith is yours to decide.
> He has set before you fire and water;
> reach out and take which you choose;
> before man lie life and death,
> and whichever he prefers is his.'

[127]. *his earthly contest:* i.e. with the forces of evil, and more particularly with the wicked heart; cp. verse [92] and 3: 20.

[128]. *the sufferings you have mentioned . . . the rewards I have been describing:* no particular passages are in mind, but throughout the preceding dialogue Ezra has consistently taken the side of the sinners (with whom he identifies himself), whereas the angel has taken the side of the righteous.

[129]. *For that was the way which Moses . . . urged the people to take . . . "Choose life, and live!":* cp. Deut. 30: 19, 'I summon heaven and earth to witness against you this day: I offer you the choice of life or death, blessing or curse. Choose life and then you and your descendants will live.' However, by 'life' the author of 2 Esdras 3–14 was thinking of life in the world to come, an idea which is not present in the passage in Deuteronomy.

[130]. *But they did not believe him, nor the prophets after him:* cp. 1: 32. The rejection of the word of God delivered by the prophets forms a frequent theme in the Old Testament; cp. e.g. 2 Chron. 36: 15–16; 'The LORD God of their fathers had warned them betimes through his messengers, for he took pity on his people and on his dwelling-place; but they

never ceased to deride his messengers, scorn his words and
scoff at his prophets'; cp. also Matt. 23: 37, 'O Jerusalem,
Jerusalem, the city that murders the prophets and stones the
messengers sent to her!' *nor me*: the angel speaks as if he were
God; see the comment on 5: 40.

[131]. Cp. verses 25, [60–1]. *for the salvation of those who
have believed*: so the Syriac and Ethiopic versions. The meaning
of the Latin text is not entirely clear; the N.E.B. footnote
gives a possible interpretation, but it may be that the Latin is
corrupt, and that it is based on a misunderstanding of a
Greek text similar to that presupposed by the Syriac and
Ethiopic. ✶

EZRA APPEALS TO GOD'S MERCY

'My lord,' I replied, 'I know that the Most High is 62 [132]
called "compassionate", because he has compassion on
those yet unborn; and called "merciful", because he 63 [133]
shows mercy to those who repent and live by his law;
and "patient", because he shows patience to those who 64 [134]
have sinned, his own creatures as they are; and "bene- 65 [135]
factor", because he prefers giving to taking; and "rich 66 [136]
in forgiveness", because again and again he forgives sinners, past, present, and to come. For without his con- 67 [137]
tinued forgiveness there could be no hope of life for the
world and its inhabitants. And he is called "generous", 68 [138]
because without his generosity in releasing sinners from
their sins, not one ten-thousandth part of mankind could
hope to be given life; and he is also called "judge", for 69 [139]
unless he grants pardon to those who have been created
by his word, and blots out their countless offences, I 70 [140]
suppose that of the entire human race only very few
would be spared.'

8 The angel said to me in reply: 'The Most High has made this world for many, but the next world for only
2 a few. Let me give you an illustration, Ezra. Ask the earth, and it will tell you that it can produce plenty of clay for making earthenware, but very little gold-dust.
3 The same holds good for the present world: many have been created, but only a few will be saved.'

✻ In the face of the hard and inflexible attitude of the angel, Ezra does not attempt to pursue the argument directly, but instead describes and acknowledges the compassionate mercy of God apart from which 'only very few would be spared' (verse [140]). Implicit in his words is the conviction that the destruction of the great majority of mankind is incompatible with God's mercy; rather he believes that through the compassion of God sinners will be pardoned and 'given life' (verse [138]) in the world to come. But the response of the angel remains negative; his short reply consists merely of a restatement of the view that it is in the nature of things that 'only a few will be saved' (8: 3, cp. 7: [49–61]). The conflict between the attitude of Ezra and the attitude of the angel doubtless reflects an unresolved tension in the mind of the author; he attempts here to find an answer to his problems in an appeal to God's mercy, but in the end cannot accept this solution.

[132–40]. This passage is probably based directly on Exod. 34: 6–7, 'Then the LORD passed in front of him and called aloud, "JEHOVAH, the LORD, a god compassionate and gracious, long-suffering, ever constant and true, maintaining constancy to thousands, forgiving iniquity, rebellion, and sin, and not sweeping the guilty clean away"' (some of the similarities between Exod. 34: 6–7 and the passage in 2 Esdras are more obvious in the underlying texts and versions than in the N.E.B. translation itself). Exod. 34: 6–7 had apparently already been utilized in several passages in the Old Testament which refer to God's mercy (cp. e.g. Neh. 9: 17; Pss. 103: 8; 145: 8–9), and by the time of 2 Esdras the list of attributes had become to a great extent traditional.

[133]. *"merciful"*: in Exod. 34: 6 the word rendered 'gracious'.

[134]. *"patient"*: in Exod. 34: 6 the word rendered 'long-suffering'. *his own creatures as they are:* cp. Ps. 145: 8–9:

> 'The LORD is gracious and compassionate,
>   forbearing, and constant in his love,
> The LORD is good to all men,
>   and his tender care rests upon all his
>   creatures.'

[135]. *"benefactor"*: the origin of this title is unclear (it is not present in Exod. 34: 6–7). *he prefers giving to taking:* cp. Acts 20: 35, 'Happiness lies more in giving than in receiving', but the context suggests that what is particularly in mind in 2 Esdras 3–14 is the idea of granting pardon instead of exacting punishment.

[136]. *"rich in forgiveness"*: in Exod. 34: 6 the words rendered 'ever constant'.

[137–40]. In contrast to the angel Ezra here argues for the view that through God's mercy *sinners* will *be given life*; cp. 8: 36.

[137]. *life:* both here and in the next verse life in the world to come is meant; those who have not been condemned at the last judgement will enjoy the delights of paradise; cp. verses [36], [123–4]; 8: 52.

138. *"generous"*: the origin of this title is also uncertain, but the whole verse seems to go back ultimately to the words in Exod. 34: 7 which the N.E.B. translates 'maintaining constancy to thousands', but which might also be translated 'maintaining steadfast love to thousands'.

[139–40]. *"judge"*: although attested by all the versions, this is not quite the word we expect, and it is possible that the

text is in some way corrupt. However, these two verses
appear to be based on Exod. 34: 7, 'forgiving iniquity,
rebellion, and sin, and not sweeping the guilty clean away'.
created by his word: cp. Gen. 1: 26–7.

8: 1. *The Most High has made this world for many, but the
next world for only a few:* cp. 7: [50–1].

2. *plenty of clay ... very little gold-dust:* cp. 7: [51–61],
particularly verses [54–7].

3. *many have been created, but only a few will be saved:* cp.
Matt. 22: 14, 'For though many are invited, few are chosen.' ✳

EZRA AGAIN APPEALS TO GOD'S MERCY

4 I said: 'My soul, drink deep of understanding and eat
5 your fill of wisdom! Without your consent*a* you came
here, and unwillingly you go away; only a brief span of
6 life is given you. O Lord above, if I may be allowed to
approach you in prayer, plant a seed in our hearts and
minds, and make it grow until it bears fruit, so that fallen
7 man may obtain life. For you alone are God, and we are
all shaped by you in one mould, as your word declares.
8 The body moulded in the womb receives from you both
life and limbs; that which you create is kept safe amid
fire and water; for nine months the body moulded by
9 you bears what you have created in it. Both the womb
which holds safely and that which is safely held will be
safe only because you keep them so. And after the womb
10 has delivered up what has been created in it, then from
the human body itself, that is from the breasts, milk, the
11 fruit of the breasts, is supplied by your command. For a
certain time what has been made is nourished in that
way; and afterwards it is still cared for by your mercy.

[a] Without your consent: *so one Vs.; Lat.* To obey.

You bring it up to know your justice, train it in your 12
law, and correct it by your wisdom. It is your creature 13
and you made it; you can put it to death or give it life,
as you please. But if you should lightly destroy one who 14
was fashioned by your command with so much labour,
what was the purpose of creating him?

'And now let me say this: about mankind at large, 15
you know best; but it is for your own people that I 16
grieve, for your inheritance that I mourn; my sorrow is
for Israel and my distress for the race of Jacob. For them 17
and for myself, therefore, I will address my prayer to
you, since I perceive how low we have fallen, we dwellers
on earth; and I know well how quickly your judgement 18
will follow. Hear my words then, and consider the prayer 19
which I make to you.'

Here begins the prayer which Ezra made, before he
was taken up to heaven.

'O Lord, who dost inhabit eternity, to whom the sky 20
and the highest heavens belong; whose throne is beyond 21
imagining, and whose glory is past conceiving; who art
attended by the host of angels trembling as they turn 22
themselves into wind and fire at thy bidding; whose word
is true and constant; whose commands are mighty and
terrible; whose glance dries up the deeps, whose anger 23
melts the mountains, and whose truth stands for ever:[a]
hear thy servant's prayer, O Lord, listen to my petition, 24
for thou hast fashioned me, and consider my words.
While I live I will speak; while understanding lasts, I will 25
answer.

'Do not look upon thy people's offences, look on those 26

[a] *So some Vss.; Lat.* bears witness.

27 who have served thee faithfully; pay no heed to the
godless and their pursuits, but to those who have observed
28 thy covenant and suffered for it. Do not think of those
who all their life have been untrue to thee, but remember
those who have acknowledged and feared thee from the
29 heart. Do not destroy those who have lived like animals,
but take account of those who have borne shining witness
30 to thy law. Do not be angry with those judged to be
worse than beasts; but show love to those who have put
31 unfailing trust in thy glory. For we and our fathers have
lived in mortal sin,*a* yet it is on our account that thou art
32 called merciful; for if it is thy desire to have mercy on us
sinners, who have no just deeds to our credit, then indeed
33 thou shalt be called merciful. For the reward which will
be given to the just, who have many good works stored
up with thee, will be no more than their own deeds have
earned.

34 'What is man, that thou shouldst be angry with him?
or the race of mortals, that thou shouldst treat them so
35 harshly? The truth is, no man was ever born who did
36 not sin; no man alive is innocent of offence. It is through
thy mercy towards those with no store of good deeds
to their name that thy justice and kindness, O Lord, will
be made known'.

37 The angel said to me in reply: 'Much of what you have
38 said is just, and it will be as you say. Be sure that I shall
not give any thought to sinners, to their creation, death,
39 judgement, or damnation; but I shall take delight in the
just, in their creation, their departure from this world,
40 their salvation, and their final reward. So I have said, and

[a] in mortal sin: *so some Vss.; Lat. obscure.*

so it is. The farmer sows many seeds in the ground and 41
plants many plants, but not all the seeds sown come up
safely in season, nor do all the plants strike root. So too
in the world of men: not all who are sown will be
preserved.'

✻ The debate of the previous section (7: [132]-8: 3) is
here renewed with an explicit appeal by Ezra for God to show
mercy to his people (verses 4–36) and a further negative response from the angel (verses 37–41). Ezra's appeal falls into
three parts, verses 4–14, 15–19a, 19b–36.

4–14. After a short introduction (verses 4–5) Ezra asks God
to make it possible for 'fallen man' to 'obtain life' (verse 6).
God has created man with infinite care (verses 7–13), and the
destruction of man seems in these circumstances incomprehensible (verse 14).

4–5. Ezra begins by addressing his soul and urging it to
absorb all the 'understanding' and 'wisdom' that it is capable
of absorbing in view of the uncertainty and brevity of life.
Ezra despairs because he feels he lacks the ability to make
sense of the problems which face him, but he seems at the
same time to be complaining that life is not long enough for
him ever to acquire the insight necessary to solve these
problems. The thought that man's ability to understand God's
ways is restricted by the uncertainty and brevity of life is also
found in 2 Baruch 14: 8–11:

'But who, O Lord, my Lord, will comprehend thy
    judgement,
Or who will search out the profoundness of thy way?
Or who will think out the weight (?) of thy path?
Or who will be able to think out thy incomprehensible
    counsel?
Or who of those that are born has ever found
The beginning or end of thy wisdom?
For we have all been made like a breath. For as the breath
ascends involuntarily, and again dies, so it is with the

nature of men, who depart not according to their own will, and know not what will befall them in the end' (translation from R. H. Charles, *Apocrypha and Pseudepigrapha*, vol. 2, p. 490).

4. *drink deep of understanding and eat your fill of wisdom!*: for the imagery cp. the invitation of Wisdom in Prov. 9: 5-6:

> 'Come, dine with me (literally 'eat of my bread')
> and taste the wine that I have spiced.
> Cease to be silly, and you will live,
> you will grow in understanding.'

5. *Without your consent*: so the Syriac version; the Latin 'To obey' (see the footnote) derives from a misreading of the underlying Greek text. *you came here*: the words used imply a belief in the pre-existence of the soul: cp. Wisd. of Sol. 8: 19-20, 'As a child I was born to excellence, and a noble soul fell to my lot; or rather, I myself was noble, and I entered into an unblemished body.' Cp. also the comment on 7: [88].

6. Ezra appeals to God to bring about such a change in *fallen man* that he *may obtain life* in the world to come. *plant a seed in our hearts and minds, and make it grow until it bears fruit*: the transformation of man is described by means of the same imagery as that used in 4: 30 to describe Adam's fall, 'A grain of the evil seed was sown in the heart of Adam from the first; how much godlessness has it produced already!' For the thought of 8: 6 cp. Ezek. 36: 26-7, 'I will give you a new heart and put a new spirit within you; I will take the heart of stone from your body and give you a heart of flesh. I will put my spirit into you and make you conform to my statutes, keep my laws and live by them.' *until it bears fruit*: man is to be transformed so that he will produce the good works (cp. 7: [77]; 8: 33) which will ensure his salvation. *life*: as elsewhere, life in the new age is meant.

7-14. Ezra bases his appeal (verse 6) on the fact that man's creation and continued existence depend entirely on God. It is inconceivable that God should have taken the care that he did to create man only to destroy him; cp. Job 10: 8–12.

7. *For you alone are God, and we are all shaped by you in one mould* (literally 'and we are one work of your hands'), *as your word declares:* not an exact quotation, but cp. e.g. Isa. 44: 6:

> 'I am the first and I am the last,
> and there is no god but me'

and Isa. 45: 11:

> 'Thus says the LORD ...
> Would you dare question me concerning my children,
> or instruct me in my handiwork?'

8. *amid fire and water:* an allusion to two of the elements of which the body was thought to be composed; according to Philo, a Jewish writer who lived in Alexandria in the first century A.D., the human body was formed from earth, water, air and fire (cp. *On the Creation of the World* 146; see the Loeb Classical Library translation of Philo, vol. I, pp. 115, 117). In 2 Esdras 3–14 the thought is that the embryo, consisting of the elements fire and water, is *kept safe* by God.

12. *train it in your law:* God's concern for man is shown not only by the fact that he creates and sustains him, but also by the fact that he instructs him in the law. The implication of this verse is that the law was intended for all men; cp. 7: 21, [72]; in other passages (3: 19; 5: 27) the law is seen as the special gift of Israel.

13. *you can put it to death or give it life, as you please:* in the context the reference is to God's power to destroy or maintain physical life; contrast the many passages, e.g. verse 6, where 'life' means life in the age to come. Cp. 1 Sam. 2: 6:

> 'The LORD kills and he gives life,
> he sends down to Sheol, he can bring the dead up again'

and see the comments on this verse in the commentary on 1 Samuel in this series.

15–29a. Ezra does not pause for a reply to what he has just

said, but states that he will leave in God's hands the fate of 'mankind at large' (verse 15), and that his concern is 'for Israel' (verse 16). He announces that he will pray on Israel's behalf as well as his own.

16. *your own people ... your inheritance:* the thought that Israel is God's people is commonplace in the Old Testament, but cp. e.g. Deut. 32: 8–9:

> 'When the Most High parcelled out the nations,
> when he dispersed all mankind,
> he laid down the boundaries of every people
> according to the number of the sons of God;
> but the LORD's share was his own people,
> Jacob was his allotted portion'

(The last line could be translated 'Jacob was his allotted inheritance'.)

17. *and for myself:* as in the prayer which follows (cp. verses 31–2) Ezra classes himself with the sinners. Cp. 7: [75] and contrast the rebukes of the angel in 8: 47–9 and 7: [76].

19*b*–36. Ezra's prayer begins with an invocation to God who is asked to hear the words of his servant (verses 20–5). There follows a petition that God will show mercy to his people by ignoring their sins and by paying attention only to those who have served him and kept his law (verses 26–30). The petition is supported by a confession of sin, with which Ezra associates himself, and an appeal to God to treat sinners with mercy even though they have no good deeds to their credit (verses 31–6). The prayer was used independently of 2 Esdras 3–14 for liturgical purposes; as such it was often copied separately, with the title 'the Confession of Esdras', amongst the collections of canticles and hymns which are to be found in manuscripts of the Vulgate (for the Vulgate see above, the Footnotes to the N.E.B. text, p. xi).

19*b*. *Here begins the prayer which Ezra made, before he was taken up to heaven:* these words are not part of the prayer itself, but a title. The occurrence of this title is an indication of the independent use of the prayer for liturgical purposes (see above). According to this title it was believed that Ezra, like Enoch (Gen. 5: 24) and Elijah (2 Kings 2: 1–12), had been translated to heaven; such a belief is indicated in 2 Esdras 14: 9, and stated explicitly in some words at the end of ch. 14 which occur in the oriental versions of 2 Esdras (e.g. the Syriac), but not in the Latin version, and hence not in the N.E.B. which is based on the Latin version. Cp. the comment on 14: 9 and 14: 48.

20–3. Several of the attributes by which God is invoked are reminiscent of descriptions of God in the Old Testament and one (in verse 22) is actually based on a particular Old Testament passage, namely Ps. 104: 4.

20. *to whom the sky and the highest heavens belong:* cp. Deut. 10: 14, 'To the LORD your God belong heaven itself, the highest heaven, the earth and everything in it.'

21. *whose throne is beyond imagining, and whose glory is past conceiving:* cp. the description of God seated upon his throne in Ezek. 1 (particularly verses 22–28a) which concludes with the words 'it was like the appearance of the glory of the LORD'. In Ezekiel 'glory' is a technical term used to describe the way in which God manifested himself to his people (cp. the comment above on 7: [112]); it was conceived of as a brilliant light or fire encircling God. In Rev. 21: 23 the glory of God provides the light for the new Jerusalem: 'And the city had no need of sun or moon to shine upon it; for the glory of God gave it light, and its lamp was the Lamb.' *who art attended by the host of angels:* cp. 1 Kings 22: 19; Dan. 7: 10.

22. *as they turn themselves into wind and fire at thy bidding:* based on Ps. 104: 4, but understood in a different way from the N.E.B. translation:

> 'who makest the winds thy messengers
> and flames of fire thy servants'

Ps. 104: 4 is also used in Heb. 1: 7; Hebrews, like the Septuagint version of Ps. 104, understood the passage in the same way as 2 Esdras.

23. *whose glance dries up the deeps:* cp. Isa. 51: 10:

> 'Was it not you
> who dried up the sea, the waters of the great abyss?'

whose anger melts the mountains: cp. Mic. 1: 4, part of a description of the coming of God to judge his people:

> 'Beneath him mountains dissolve
> like wax before the fire'

stands for ever: the Latin 'bears witness' (see the footnote) goes back to a misreading of the original Hebrew text.

26–30. Essentially the same point is made in the five petitions which all have an antithetic structure, one clause contrasting with the other in each case. For the thought cp. Gen. 18: 22–33; cp. also 2 Baruch 14: 7, 'And if others did evil, it was due to Zion that on account of the works of those who wrought good works she should be forgiven, and should not be overwhelmed on account of the works of those who wrought unrighteousness' (translation from R. H. Charles, *Apocrypha and Pseudepigrapha*, vol. 2, p. 490).

27. *who have observed thy covenant and suffered for it:* cp. the stories of martyrdom in the Maccabaean period (2 Macc. 6: 10 – 7: 42).

29. *those who have lived like animals:* cp. the Psalmist's description of himself in Ps. 73: 22:

> 'I would not understand, so brutish was I,
> I was a mere beast in thy sight, O God.'

In 2 Esdras 3–14 the contrast with bearing witness to the law suggests that what is in mind is lack of understanding leading to disregard for the law.

30. *those judged to be worse than beasts:* Jews worse even than those mentioned in the previous verse. *who have put unfailing trust in thy glory:* that is, in the power and might of God. For this use of 'glory' cp. Wisd. of Sol. 9: 11 where Solomon prays that wisdom may guard him 'in her glory'.

31–6. Ezra supports his petition by a twice-repeated confession of sin (verses 31, 35) and a twice-repeated appeal to God to treat sinners with mercy even though they have 'no store of good deeds to their name' (verses 32–3, 36); man is too insignificant for God to be angry with him (verse 34). The appeal made in these verses is essentially a repetition of the appeal made in 7: [132–40], but, as we shall see, it is again rejected.

31. *For we and our fathers have lived in mortal sin:* cp. Ps. 106: 6. Ezra again includes himself amongst the sinners, as he does also in the next verse; see the comment on verse 17. *yet it is on our account that thou art called merciful:* a reminder to God of his past mercies to his people.

32–3. *no just deeds to our credit . . . many good works stored up with thee:* as we have seen (cp. the comment on 7: [77]) the author of 2 Esdras 3–14 believed that a few very righteous men would earn their place in the life of the world to come by means of their good works. Ezra's appeal is for the vast majority of mankind who would not be in this position.

34. Based on Job 7: 17–18:

> 'What is man that thou makest much of him
> and turnest thy thoughts towards him,
> only to punish him morning by morning
> or to test him every hour of the day?'

This in its turn is related to Ps. 8: 4:

> 'what is man that thou shouldst remember him,
> mortal man that thou shouldst care for him?'

35. *no man was ever born who did not sin:* the absolute terms of this confession (cp. 7: [46], [68]) are strictly speaking inconsistent with what is said in the immediate context. In verses 26–30 Ezra has just appealed to God to take account of those who have kept his law, while verses 32–3 and 36 assume the existence of a group of righteous men whose good works will be sufficient to earn their salvation. Ezra is in effect appealing to God to count men as just, although they are in fact sinners; cp. Rom. 4: 6-8.

36. Cp. the comment on verses 32–3.

37–41. In his reply the angel ignores the main point of Ezra's prayer, i.e. the appeal for God to show mercy to his people. Instead he turns Ezra's own words against him to reiterate the point that God is not concerned with the damnation of sinners, but only with the salvation of the just (verses 37–40, cp. 7: 25, [60–1], [131]), and he uses an analogy to reiterate the point that only a few will be saved (verse 41; cp. 7: [51–61]; 8: 1–3).

37–40. *Much of what you have said is just, and it will be as you say:* the words of Ezra's petition in verses 26–30 are used against him in a contrary sense to that intended; the same stylistic device occurs in 7: [71–2]; cp. 7: [64].

38. The author again forgets that the speaker is supposed to be the angel, not God; cp. the comment on 5: 40.

39. *their departure from this world:* literally 'their pilgrimage', but the parallelism with 'death' in verse 38 indicates how 'pilgrimage' is to be understood.

40. *So I have said:* so the Latin and all the other versions except the Ethiopic, the allusion being to such passages as 7: [131]. The Ethiopic 'So you have said' repeats the thought of verse 37, 'and it will be as you say'. The reading of the Ethiopic has sometimes been preferred as being more appropriate in the context, but it is not clear that this is right.

41. *The farmer sows many seeds in the ground:* for the analogy cp. the parable of the sower, Matt. 13: 4–9, 18–23. The author of 2 Esdras 3–14 has already used the analogy of sowing seed, but in a rather different way, in 4: 28–39; see the comment on 4: 28. ✶

EZRA'S FINAL APPEAL FOR MERCY

42 To that I replied: 'If I have won your favour, let me
43 speak. The farmer's seed may never come up because it
is given no rain at the right time, or it may rot because
44 of too much rain. But man, who was formed by your

hands and made in your image, and for whose sake you
made everything – will you compare him with seed sown
by a farmer? Surely not, O Lord above! Spare your own 45
people and pity them, for you will be pitying your own
creation.'

He answered: 'The present is for those now alive, the 46
future for those yet to come. You cannot love my 47
creation with a love greater than mine – far from it! But
never again rank yourself among the unjust, as you have
so often done. Yet the Most High approves of the 48, 49
modesty you have rightly shown; you have not sought
great glory by including yourself among the godly. In 50
the last days, then, the inhabitants of the world will be
punished for their arrogant lives by bitter sufferings. But 51
you, Ezra, should direct your thoughts to yourself and
the glory awaiting those like you. For all of you, paradise 52
lies open, the tree of life is planted, the age to come is
made ready, and rich abundance is in store; the city is
already built, rest from toil is assured, goodness and wisdom are brought to perfection. The root of evil has been 53
sealed off from you; for you there is no more illness,
death[a] is abolished, hell has fled, and decay is quite forgotten. All sorrows are at an end, and the treasure of 54
immortality has been finally revealed. Ask no more 55
questions, therefore, about the many who are lost. For 56
they were given freedom and used it to despise the Most
High, to treat his law with contempt and abandon his
ways. Yes, and they trampled on his just servants; they 57, 58
said to themselves, "There is no God", though well
aware that they must die. Yours, then, will be the joys 59

[a] death: *so some Vss.; Lat. omits.*

207

I have predicted; theirs the thirst and torments which are prepared. It is not that the Most High has wanted any 60 man to be lost, but that those he created have themselves brought dishonour on their Creator's name, and shown ingratitude to the One who had put life within their 61, 62 reach. My day of judgement is now close at hand, but I have not made this known to all; only to you and a few like you.'

✽ 42–5. Ezra protests at the implications of the analogy of verse 41. Many things may happen to prevent a seed coming up, or a plant reaching maturity, but he cannot believe that God treats men with such indifference (verses 42–45*a*). He makes a final impassioned appeal for God to show mercy to his people (verse 45*b*).

42. *If I have won your favour:* see the comment on 5: 56.

43. *The farmer's seed may never come up:* cp. Matt. 13: 4–7.

45. Cp. Joel 2: 17, an appeal to God's care for what he has created:

> 'Spare thy people, O Lord, thy own people,
> expose them not to reproach'

46–62. Ezra's appeal for mercy for God's 'own people' is once more rejected, and he is urged to think about the glorious future which awaits him rather than to concern himself with the fully justified fate of the wicked. The reply falls into three parts (verses 46–47*a*, 47*b*–54, 55–62) and seems at times to be spoken by God and at times by the angel; for the alternation see the comment on 5: 40.

46–47*a*. Ezra's objection to the analogy of the seeds is dismissed.

46. *The present is for those now alive, the future for those yet to come* (or 'Things present are for those now alive, things future for those yet to come'): the meaning is that the analogy only has relevance in the present age; full understanding of

what will apply in the future age will be possible only for those who will participate in the life of that age. Cp. the arguments in 4: 1–32; 5: 31–40.

47a. *You cannot love my creation with a love greater than mine:* Ezra's understanding of the situation is also erroneous, because, whatever he might think, God's love for mankind is still far greater than his own (cp. 5: 33b–34).

47b–54. Ezra is rebuked for associating himself with the sinners, but at the same time commended for his modesty in so doing (verses 47b–49). Those who are arrogant will suffer punishment, but Ezra ought to direct his thoughts to the glorious future which awaits him and those like him (verses 50–4).

47b. *But never again rank yourself among the unjust, as you have so often done:* cp. verses 17 and 31–2, and see also 7: [75–6].

48–9. *the modesty you have rightly shown; you have not sought great glory:* the same attitude that is frequently commended in the gospels; cp. e.g. Matt. 23: 12, 'For whoever exalts himself will be humbled; and whoever humbles himself will be exalted.'

50. In contrast to Ezra those who do lead *arrogant lives* will have to endure *bitter sufferings* at the time of judgement.

51. *to yourself and the glory awaiting those like you:* for Ezra and the righteous like him glory lies in store in the new age; the content of this glory is described in detail in verses 52–4, first positively (verse 52), then negatively (verse 53); verse 54 provides a concluding summary.

52. The blessings of the new age are thought of as being already in existence; cp. 1 Pet. 1: 4–5:

'The inheritance to which we are born is one that nothing can destroy or spoil or wither. It is kept for you in heaven, and you, because you put your faith in God, are under the protection of his power until salvation comes – the salvation which is even now in readiness and will be revealed at the end of time.'

paradise: as elsewhere in 2 Esdras 3–14, the place of rest of the righteous in the world to come; cp. 7: [36], [123] and the comment on 7: [36]. *the tree of life:* cp. 7: [123]; Rev. 2: 7 (quoted in the comment on 7: [36]; Rev. 22: 2. *the city:* the new Jerusalem; the expectation of a new Jerusalem forms part of the beliefs associated with the new age (cp. 7: 26; 10: 27, 38–59; 13: 36; Rev. 21: 1–4 and see also the comment on 7: 26).

53. *The root of evil has been sealed off from you:* 'of evil' has been supplied in the translation, but accurately conveys the sense; cp. 3: 22 'a rooted wickedness' (literally 'the wickedness of the root' or 'the wicked root'). *root* is used here almost as a technical term to describe what it is that causes men to sin; in the new age this root will no longer be able to affect men. *for you there is no more illness, death is abolished, hell has fled, and decay is quite forgotten:* not only the cause, but also the consequences of sin will be removed in the new age. In the Latin version *death* has been omitted by mistake (see the N.E.B. footnote); for the thought cp. Isa. 25: 8, 'he will swallow up death for ever'; Rev. 21: 4. Cp. also Rev. 20: 14, at the judgement 'Death and Hades' are destroyed by being thrown 'into the lake of fire' ('Hades' was the name given in the Graeco-Roman world to hell or the underworld and is similar to 'Sheol' in Old Testament thought).

55–62. Contemplation of the future which lies in store for him ought to lead Ezra to put out of his mind the fate of 'the many who are lost'. Their fate is in any case their own fault; they used the freedom they had been given to disobey God and thereby brought their punishment on themselves. Ezra's appeal for mercy (verse 45) is thus dismissed. As we have seen (cp. 7: 19–25, [70–4], [127–31]), the idea that man is entirely responsible for his destiny in the world to come forms a constant theme in the replies of the angel in the third dialogue, and 8: 55–62 does not really advance the argument any further.

56. *For they were given freedom:* for the thought cp. 7: [127–9]. *to treat his law with contempt:* cp. 7: 24, [72].

58. *they said to themselves, "There is no God"*: cp. 7: 23; Pss. 14: 1; 53: 1. *though well aware that they must die*: death in the age to come as a punishment for denying the existence of God seems to be what is meant.

59. *the joys I have predicted*: cp. verses 51–4. *the thirst and torments which are prepared*: cp. 7: [36], [84], [86]. *It is not that the Most High has wanted any man to be lost*: cp. Ezek. 18: 23, 'Have I any desire, says the Lord GOD, for the death of a wicked man? Would I not rather that he should mend his ways and live?'; cp. also Matt. 18: 14.

60. *the One who had put life within their reach*: God had provided the opportunity of life in the age to come for all men, but the majority by their own actions had lost this.

61. *My day of judgement is now close at hand*: the idea that the end of this age and the judgement would come quickly is commonplace in Jewish and Christian writings of this period; cp. e.g. Matt. 24: 34, 'I tell you this: the present generation will live to see it all.'

62. *not made this known to all: only to you and a few like you*: these words reflect the author's own understanding of his work; like the authors of the other apocalypses (see pp. 105–8), he regarded himself as the recipient of a secret revelation intended for a very limited circle of readers. Cp. 12: 36–8; 13: 53–6; 14: 26, 46–7. ✳

MORE ABOUT THE SIGNS OF THE END

'My lord,' I replied, 'you have now revealed to me 63 the many signs which you are going to perform in the last days; but you have not told me when that will be.'

The angel answered: 'Keep a careful count yourself; **9** when you see that some of the signs predicted have already happened, then you will understand that the time 2 has come when the Most High will judge the world he has created. When the world becomes the scene of earth- 3

quakes, insurrections, plots among the nations, unstable
4 government, and panic among rulers, then you will recognize these as the events which the Most High has foretold
5 since first the world began. Just as everything that is
done on earth has its beginning and end clearly marked,[a]
6 so it is with the times which the Most High has determined: their beginning is marked by portents and
miracles, their end by manifestations of power.

7 'Whoever comes safely through and escapes destruction, thanks to his good deeds or the faith he has shown,
8 will survive all the dangers I have foretold and witness
the salvation that I shall bring to my land, the country
9 I have marked out from all eternity as my own. Then
those who have misused my law will be taken by surprise; their contempt for it will bring them continual
10 torment. All who in their lifetime failed to acknowledge
11 me in spite of all the good things I had given them, all
who disdained my law while freedom still was theirs, who
scornfully dismissed the thought of penitence while the
12 way was still open – all these will have to learn the truth
13 through torments after death. Do not be curious any
more, Ezra, to know how the godless will be tormented,
but only how and when the just will be saved; the world
is theirs and it exists for their sake.'

* The statement that the 'day of judgement' is 'close at
hand' (8: 61) leads Ezra to ask when the 'signs' preceding the
end of this age will occur (8: 63). He is told to work this out
for himself from the fulfilment of the signs which have been
foretold and about which he is now given further information
(9: 1–6). In the following verses (9: 7–12) the contrasting fates

[a] has . . . marked: *so one Vs.; Lat. defective.*

of the righteous and the wicked in the period after the last days are described. Finally Ezra is again told not to bother about 'how the godless will be tormented, but only how and when the just will be saved' (9: 13).

This passage about the signs occupies a place in the last part of the third dialogue comparable to that occupied by the earlier passages about the signs in the first and second dialogues (cp. 4: 51 – 5: 13; 6: 11–28). As we saw earlier (see on 4: 51–2), it has sometimes been argued that all the passages about the signs were interpolated by the final editor of 2 Esdras 3–14. This view seems, however, unlikely. So far as 8: 63 – 9: 13 is concerned, the passage fits quite naturally into its context – 8: 63 follows naturally on 8: 61, while 9: 13 brings the discussion firmly back to the main theme of the third dialogue – and is hardly to be regarded as an interpolation.

63. *you have now revealed to me the many signs which you are going to perform in the last days:* cp. 5: 1–12; 6: 18b–28. *but you have not told me when that will be:* Ezra had in fact already asked more than once when the end would be, but had been given only rather vague replies; cp. e.g. 4: 44–52. Here also Ezra is not given a direct reply to his question, but on this occasion he is told to work out the answer for himself from his observation of the fulfilment of the signs (9: 1–2); cp. Mark 13: 3–8, but contrast Acts 1: 7, 'It is not for you to know about dates or times, which the Father has set within his own control.'

9: 1. *the signs:* for the significance of the signs see the comment on 4: 51–2.

3. The signs have a conventional character and occur frequently in lists of this kind, e.g. Mark 13: 7–8:

'When you hear the noise of battle near at hand and the news of battles far away, do not be alarmed. Such things are bound to happen; but the end is still to come. For nation will make war upon nation, kingdom upon kingdom; there will be earthquakes in many places; there will be famines. With these things the birth-pangs of the new age begin.'

When the world becomes the scene of earthquakes: cp. 5: 8; 6: 14–16 and see the comments on both passages. *insurrections, plots among the nations:* cp. 5: 5. *unstable government, and panic among rulers:* cp. 5: 1.

4. *the events which the Most High has foretold since first the world began:* the author appears to allude to the revelations that are associated with figures of the primaeval period such as Adam or Enoch; see the comments on the apocalyptic writings above, pp. 105–8.

5–6. The N.E.B. translation follows the Syriac version, although the text is somewhat uncertain. According to the Syriac Ezra is told that the 'last days' (8: 63) have a clearly defined beginning and end just like everything else that takes place on earth; the beginning of the last days will be indicated *by portents and miracles,* and the end *by manifestations of power;* the occurrence of these events, so it is implied, will enable Ezra to recognize the last days for what they are. Verses 5–6 thus appear to continue the thought of verses 1–4 and provide a further answer to the question posed in 8: 63. *the times which the Most High has determined:* i.e. the last days. *portents and miracles:* an alternative way of referring to the 'signs'. *by manifestations of power* (literally 'in act and in signs'): the great act of judgement (cp. 9: 2) by which this age will be brought to an end and the new age inaugurated.

7–8. The righteous who *survive all the dangers* of the last days will *witness* the inauguration of the new age. Here the new age is described in traditional terms as the establishment of a messianic kingdom based on the land of Israel, cp. Ezek. 36: 24–8. *Whoever comes safely through:* cp. 6: 25. *his good deeds or the faith he has shown:* see the comment on 7: [77]. *my land:* for the idea of Israel as God's land cp. e.g. Jer. 2: 7:

> 'I brought you into a fruitful land
>> to enjoy its fruit and the goodness of it;
>> but when you entered upon it you defiled it
>> and made the home I gave you loathsome.'

The last two lines read literally, 'but you entered and defiled my land and made my inheritance loathsome'. Elsewhere in 2 Esdras 3–14 it is indicated that salvation will be restricted to those who are in the land of Israel; cp. 12: 34; 13: 48–9.

9–12. The advent of the last days will make the wicked realize too late the error of their ways, and they will be compelled to suffer 'continual torment'.

9. *my law:* literally 'my ways'.

10. *All who in their lifetime failed to acknowledge me:* cp. Matt. 10: 32–3.

11. *all who disdained my law while freedom still was theirs:* the angel reiterates the view that men had the opportunity of salvation through the observance of the law, and that their failure to make use of this opportunity was entirely their own fault; cp. e.g. 7: [72]; 8: 56–60. *while the way was still open:* i.e. before death.

12. *all these will have to learn the truth through torments after death:* the author does not here make the clear distinction that he does in 7: [75–87] between the torments which face the wicked between death and the last judgement and the torments which face them after the last judgement.

13. The angel brings the discussion back to the main theme of the third dialogue (Ezra's concern at the fate of the sinful majority of mankind) and tells him once more not to worry about the torments of the wicked, but only about the salvation of the righteous; cp. 8: 51, 55.　✻

THE ARGUMENT RECAPITULATED

I answered, 'I repeat what I have said again and again: 14, 15 the lost outnumber the saved as a wave exceeds a drop of 16 water.'

The angel replied: 'The seed to be sown depends on 17 the soil, the colour on the flower, the product on the workman, and the harvest on the farmer. There was once 18

a time before the world had been created for men to dwell in; at that time I was planning it for the sake of
19 those who now exist. No one then disputed my plan, for no one existed. I supplied this world with unfailing food and a mysterious law; but those whom I created turned
20 to a life of corruption. I looked at my world, and there it lay spoilt, at my earth in danger from men's wicked
21 thoughts; and at the sight I could scarcely bring myself to spare them. One grape I saved out of a cluster, one
22 tree out of a forest.[a] So then let it be: destruction for the many who were born in vain, and salvation for my grape and my tree, which have cost me such labour to bring to perfection.

✳ *14–16. the lost outnumber the saved as a wave exceeds a drop of water:* despite the injunction of the angel in verse 13, Ezra refuses to be silenced, but restates in forceful terms the essence of the problem that occupies the central place in the third dialogue: why is it that virtually all mankind is doomed to perish? Ezra still finds it impossible to reconcile the fate of mankind with his notions of God's justice, and his words constitute a defiant refusal to accept the arguments that have been put to him and a demand for a more convincing explanation. *the lost outnumber the saved* (literally, 'those who are lost are more than those who will be saved'): Ezra's accusation picks up directly the words of the angel in verse 13, 'how and when the just will be saved'.

17–22. The angel does not respond to Ezra's demand, but repeats the view that man is responsible for his own destiny. It is because of sin and the effects of sin that mankind faces destruction, and it is only through God's grace that a very small number will be saved.

17. The reply of the angel begins with a wisdom saying

[a] *So some Vss.; Lat.* tribe.

which illustrates in a striking way the principle of cause and effect. The application of the principle is given in verses 18–21. The use of sayings cast in a striking and pithy form is a characteristic feature of 2 Esdras 3–14; cp. 7: 25; 8: 46. *The seed to be sown depends on the soil* (literally, 'As is the field, so is the seed', and similarly in the following examples): the N.E.B. translation does not really convey the sense; the thought is rather that what a seed produces depends on the soil – as the other three examples indicate.

18–21. The application of the principle stated in verse 17: because the majority of men have sinned, so they will suffer punishment in the world to come. Despite the fact that God provided men 'with unfailing food and a mysterious law' (the means of physical life and the means of salvation), men 'turned to a life of corruption'. They brought ruin to the earth and thereby provoked God's anger, so much so that it was only with difficulty that a small remnant was spared. Man's total responsibility for this state of affairs is underlined by reference to the conditions that existed before the earth was created; 'at that time' God was planning the earth for the sake of men, and there was no opposition to God because man himself did not yet exist.

19b–20a. *but those whom I created turned to a life of corruption. I looked at my world, and there it lay spoilt:* cp. Gen. 6: 11–12, 'Now God saw that the whole world was corrupt and full of violence. In his sight the world had become corrupted, for all men had lived corrupt lives on earth.'

21. *I could scarcely bring myself to spare them. One grape I saved out of a cluster, one tree out of a forest:* these words, as also those of verse 22, imply that the salvation even of the few is only the result of God's grace; elsewhere it is stated that the salvation of the few will be the fully deserved reward of their deeds and their faith; cp. 8: 33; 9: 7. *forest:* the Latin 'tribe' (see the footnote) derives from a corruption in the Greek text which underlies the Latin version.

22. *So then let it be: destruction for the many who were born in*

vain, and salvation for my grape and my tree: the angel reaffirms his view in words as adamant as those of Ezra in verses 14–16; cp. 7: 25, 'Therefore, Ezra, emptiness for the empty, fullness for the full!'; also 7: [60–1]; 7: [131]. *which have cost me such labour to bring to perfection:* see on verse 21. ✻

THE CONCLUSION OF THE THIRD DIALOGUE

23, 24 'You, Ezra, must wait one more week. Do not fast this time, but go to a flowery field where no house stands, and 25 eat only what grows there – no meat or wine – and pray unceasingly to the Most High. Then I will come and talk to you again.'

✻ The conclusion of the third dialogue differs significantly from the corresponding passages in the previous dialogues (cp. 5: 14–19; 6: 29–34). As before Ezra is told to wait seven days for a further revelation and to pray, but this time he is told not to fast. Instead he is to 'go to a flowery field' and to 'eat only what grows there – no meat or wine'. This formal change marks a correspondingly significant change in the character of 2 Esdras. From now on Ezra abandons his complaints and accepts the viewpoint of God; the dialogue form is given up, and Ezra becomes the recipient of revelations in vision form, as is often the case in the so-called apocalyptic writings; see pp. 105–8.

24. The command not to eat meat or drink wine, but to eat only what grows in the field (literally 'of the flowers of the field'), has probably been included by the author under the influence of the story of Daniel and his three companions; cp. Dan 1: 5, 8–16. However, Ezra's diet also corresponds to the diet of man in the period before the flood; see Gen. 1: 29; 9: 3. ✻

Visions of the last days

☆ As we have seen, the debate between Ezra and the angel has reached something of an impasse, with neither side prepared to accept the viewpoint of the other; cp. 9: 14–16 with 9: 22. Now, however, the character of the debate changes, and Ezra, who throughout the three dialogues has accused God of injustice, comes to accept that the ways of God are just (see 10: 15–16). No reason is given for Ezra's change of attitude. Instead, just as in the end Job comes to realize not through argument but through his experience of God that he had been in the wrong, so Ezra comes through experience to acknowledge that God's treatment of man is fair. The transition is marked in the fourth section of 2 Esdras 3–14 (9: 26 – 10: 59). Ezra begins, as before, with complaint (9: 28–37), but confronted by the vision of the woman in distress (9: 38 – 10: 4) his attitude changes, and he urges the woman to 'accept God's decree as just' (10: 16). From this point on Ezra ceases complaining; his questions are no longer intended to accuse, but to elicit information. The change in the content of 2 Esdras 3–14 corresponds to a change in its form. The fourth, fifth, and sixth sections of 2 Esdras 3–14 (9: 26 – 10: 59; 11–12; 13) consist of a series of allegorical visions; in the interpretations of these visions (particularly of the last two) Ezra is given detailed information about the events of the end. The way for this has, however, already been prepared in the dialogues, namely in the sections which provide information, particularly about the signs of the end (cp. 4: 33 – 5: 13; 5: 50 – 6: 28; 7: 26–[44]; 7: [75–115]; 8: 63 – 9: 13). It is to be observed also that from the fourth section onwards the fate of mankind in general recedes into the background, and the concern is primarily with Israel.

The contrast in character between the different parts of

2 Esdras 3-14 (particularly between 3: 1 – 10: 59 and 11-12; 13; 14) led some older scholars to argue that 2 Esdras 3-14 was not a unity, but a compilation of several different writings. This view, however, fails to take account of the links that exist between the different parts of the book. It also fails to take account of its essential dramatic unity. The conflicts within the mind of the author that are revealed in the three dialogues (3: 1 – 9: 25) find their resolution in the crucial fourth section (9: 26 – 10: 59); thereafter the author is able to devote his attention exclusively to the events of the end which alone will provide the final answer to the problems that concern him. To say this is not to deny that the author has made use of older traditions, nor to deny that his ideas are not always consistent. But there are no strong reasons for not regarding 2 Esdras 3-14 as essentially the work of one author.   *

THE VISION OF THE WOMAN IN
DISTRESS (9: 26 – 10: 59)

EZRA'S PERPLEXITIES

So I went out, as the angel told me, to a field called Ardat. There I sat among the flowers; my food was what grew in the field, and I ate to my heart's content.
27 The week ended, and I was lying on the grass, troubled
28 again in mind with all the same perplexities. I broke my
29 silence and addressed the Most High. 'O Lord,' I said, 'you showed yourself to our fathers in the desert at the time of the exodus from Egypt, when they were travelling
30 through the barren and untrodden waste. You said, "Hear
31 me, Israel; listen to my words, race of Jacob. This is my law, which I sow among you to bear fruit and bring you
32 glory for ever." But our fathers who received your law did not keep it; they did not observe your commandments. Not that the fruit of the law perished; that was

impossible, for it was yours. Those who received it 33
perished, because they failed to keep safe the good seed
that had been sown in them. Now the usual way of 34
things is that when seed is put into the earth, or a ship on
the sea, or food or drink into a jar, then if the seed, or the
ship, or the contents of the jar should be destroyed, what 35
held or contained them does not perish with them. But
with us sinners it is different. Destruction will come upon 36
us, the recipients of the law, and upon our hearts, the
vessel that held the law. The law itself is not destroyed, 37
but survives in all its glory.'

*   The fourth section begins in the same way as the first three
with a prayer in which Ezra, as he lies 'on the grass, troubled
again in mind with all the same perplexities' (verse 27),
attempts once more to set out the problem which concerns
him. Israel had been given the law, but had failed to observe
it; as a result Israel, but not the law, had been destroyed. Ezra
is perplexed by this state of affairs; he argues by analogy from
the natural world that it is contrary to 'the usual way of
things' (verse 34) that those who had received the law should
perish, but the law itself should survive.

26. Ezra fulfils the instructions given him in verses 23–5.
Ardat: the versions provide a number of variants for this
name, and its exact form remains uncertain. However, it is
difficult to identify Ardat with any known locality, and it
seems likely that the name has a symbolic meaning – although
what this is cannot now be ascertained. *my food was what grew
in the field:* see the comments on verses 23–5.

27. *and I was lying on the grass, troubled again in mind with
all the same perplexities:* cp. 3: 1; 5: 21; 6: 36–7.

29. *you showed yourself to our fathers in the desert at the time
of the exodus from Egypt:* cp. Exod. 19: 9; Deut. 4: 12–13.

30–1. Not an actual quotation, although for the opening

words *Hear me, Israel* cp. Deut. 4: 1; 5: 1; 6: 4; cp. also Ps. 50: 7. Verse 31 does, however, sum up in terms of the theology of 2 Esdras 3–14 the basis of the covenant relationship between God and Israel as it is expressed in Deuteronomy (cp. e.g. 7: 12–16) and elsewhere in the Old Testament. In the wilderness God gave Israel the law; obedience to the law would bring Israel *glory for ever*. By *glory* the author probably had in mind participation in the life of the world to come; cp. 7: [95]. For the gift of the law cp. also 3: 17–22; 5: 27; in the present passage the gift of the law is expressed in terms of the imagery of sowing; cp. 3: 20; 8: 6 and contrast 4: 28–32 where the same imagery is used of the 'wicked heart'.

32. *the fruit of the law:* obedience to the law leading to participation in the life of the new age; the existence of the new age was not affected by Israel's failure to keep the law.

36–7. Cp. 2 Baruch 14: 19, 'And now I see that as for the world which was made on account of us, lo! it abides, but we, on account of whom it was made, depart' (from R. H. Charles, *Apocrypha and Pseudepigrapha*, vol. 2, p. 491). ✶

THE VISION

38 While these thoughts were in my mind, I looked round, and on my right I saw a woman in great distress, mourning and loudly lamenting; her dress was torn, and
39 she had ashes on her head. Abandoning my meditations,
40 I turned to her, and said: 'Why are you weeping? What
41 is troubling you?' 'Sir,' she replied, 'please leave me to my tears and my grief; great is my bitterness of heart,
42 great my distress.' 'Tell me,' I asked, 'what has hap-
43 pened to you?' 'Sir,' she replied, 'I was barren and
44 childless through thirty years of marriage. Every hour of every day during those thirty years, day and night alike,
45 I prayed to the Most High. Then after thirty years, my

God answered my prayer and had mercy on my distress;
he took note of my sorrow and granted me a son. What
happiness he brought to my husband and myself and to
all our neighbours! What praise we gave to the Mighty
God! I took great pains over his upbringing. When he 46, 47
came of age, I chose a wife for him, and fixed the date
of the wedding.

'But when my son entered his wedding-chamber, he **10**
fell down dead. So we all put out our lamps, and all my 2
neighbours came to comfort me; I controlled my grief
till the evening of the following day. When they had all 3
ceased urging me to take comfort and control my grief,
I rose and stole away in the night, and came here, as you
can see, to this field. I have made up my mind never to 4
go back to the town, but to stay here eating nothing and
drinking nothing, and to continue my mourning and
fasting unbroken till I die.'

At that I interrupted the train of my thoughts, and I 5
spoke sternly to the woman: 'You are the most foolish 6
woman in the world,' I said; 'are you blind to the grief
and sufferings of our nation? It is for the sorrow and 7
humiliation of Zion, the mother of us all, that you should
mourn so deeply; you should share in our common 8
mourning and sorrow. But you are deep in sorrow for 9
your one son. Ask the earth and she will tell you; she
must mourn for the thousands and thousands who come
to birth upon her. From her we all originally sprang, and 10
there are more to come. Almost all her children go to
perdition, and their vast numbers are wiped out. Who 11
then has the better right to be in mourning – the earth,
who has lost such vast numbers, or you, whose sorrow

12 is for one alone? You may say to me, "But my grief is
very different from the earth's grief; I have lost the fruit
of my own womb, which I brought to birth with pain
13 and travail, but it is only in the course of nature that the
vast numbers now alive on earth should depart in the
14 same way as they have come." My answer to that is: at
the cost of pain you have been a mother, but in the same
way the earth has always been the mother of mankind,
bearing fruit to earth's creator.

15 'Keep your sorrow to yourself, therefore, and bear
16 your misfortunes bravely. If you will accept God's decree
as just, then in due time you will receive your son back
17 again, and win an honoured name among women. So go
back to the town and to your husband.'

18 'No, I will not,' she replied; 'I will not go back to the
town; I will stay here to die.'

19, 20 But I continued to argue with her. 'Do not do what
you say', I urged; 'be persuaded because of Zion's misfortunes, and take comfort to yourself from the sorrow
21 of Jerusalem. You see how our sanctuary has been laid
waste, our altar demolished, and our temple destroyed.
22 Our harps are unstrung, our hymns silenced, our shouts
of joy cut short; the light of the sacred lamp is out, and
the ark of our covenant has been taken as spoil; the holy
vessels are defiled, and the name which God has conferred on us is disgraced; our leading men[a] have been
treated shamefully, our priests burnt alive, and the Levites
taken off into captivity; our virgins have been raped and
our wives ravished, our godfearing men carried off, and
our children abandoned; our youths have been enslaved,

[a] *So some Vss.; Lat.* our children.

224

and our strong warriors reduced to weakness. Worst of 23
all, Zion, once sealed with God's own seal, has forfeited
its glory and is in the hands of our enemies. Then throw 24
off your own heavy grief, and lay all your sorrows aside;
may the Mighty God restore you to his favour, may the
Most High give you rest and peace after your troubles!'

Suddenly, while I was still speaking to the woman, I 25
saw her face begin to shine; her countenance flashed like
lightning, and I shrank from her in terror. While I 26
wondered what this meant, she suddenly uttered a loud
and terrible cry, which shook the earth. I looked up and 27
saw no longer a woman but a complete city, built*a* on
massive foundations. I cried aloud in terror, 'Where is 28
the angel Uriel, who visited me before? It is his doing
that I have fallen into this bewilderment, that all my
hopes are shattered,*b* and all my prayers in vain.'

✻ Ezra's prayer is interrupted by his observation on his right
of 'a woman in great distress' (verse 38); we subsequently
learn that this is part of a visionary experience. The woman
tells him that she is mourning her son, born after a period of
thirty years' barrenness and brought up with great care, who
had died on his wedding-night; so great is her distress that
she has resolved to die (9: 38 – 10: 4). Ezra at first reproaches
her; she ought rather to be mourning the fate of Jerusalem
(10: 5–8). But he subsequently attempts to console her by
arguing that her loss is small in comparison with the loss
perpetually suffered by the earth whose children (i.e. mankind) are constantly dying (10: 9–18), and by urging her to
take comfort in her sorrow from the misfortunes which
Jerusalem has suffered (10: 19–24). At this point, while Ezra

[a] *Probable meaning, based on other Vss.; Lat.* but a city was being
built...   [b] *Or* that my destiny turns out to be corruption.

is still talking to her, the woman is suddenly and dramatically transformed into a city. Ezra, overwhelmed by his experiences, appeals once again to Uriel for help (10: 25-8).

The vision of the Woman in Distress, like the two following visions (chs. 11–12; 13), belongs to a distinct group of what may be termed allegorical visions. Visions of this type are to be found in several apocalyptic writings (cp. e.g. Dan. 7 and 8), and it is characteristic of them that the content of the vision is to a great extent interpreted in terms of allegory. One unusual feature of the present passage is that Ezra himself plays a role in the vision he sees.

The interpretation that is given in 10: 40-54 provides an explanation of the main elements of the vision, but it is significant that a number of features are not explained: that the woman prayed ceaselessly for the birth of the child (9: 44); that the neighbours are mentioned as sharing in both the joy at the birth and the grief at the death (9: 45; 10: 2); that it is on his wedding-night that the son dies (10: 1); that the lamps are put out (10: 2); that the woman mourns until the second night and then flees, determined to die (10: 3-4). The presence of these features, which add to the vividness of the story, but are totally ignored in the interpretation, has led to the suggestion that the author took over and adapted to his purposes an old folk-tale similar in some ways to the kind of story we have in the book of Tobit (see chs. 6–8). We lack the conclusion to the story, but it is possible in the light of 10: 16 that it told how in the end the son was miraculously restored to life (cp. 2 Kings 4: 18–37).

The words of Ezra's reply to the woman in 10: 5-8 and 10: 19-24 reveal once again how deeply affected the author of 2 Esdras 3–14 was by the fall of Jerusalem in A.D. 70, and, as we have already seen, it was largely in response to this event that 2 Esdras 3–14 was written. It is important to observe, however, that despite his continued grief, Ezra no longer blames God for these events (contrast 3: 28–36). Instead Ezra advises the woman: 'Keep your sorrow to yourself, therefore, and bear your misfortunes bravely. If you will

226

accept God's decree as just, then in due time you will receive your son back again, and win an honoured name among women' (10: 15–16). Ezra (and behind him we are no doubt to see the author) is now prepared to accept the reality of what has happened and the justice of God's dealings in this matter. The reason for this change is not indicated; rather we are left to understand that through experience the author has overcome his doubts and no longer seeks to accuse God.

38. *her dress was torn, and she had ashes on her head:* the characteristic signs of mourning; cp. 2 Sam. 13: 19; Esther 4: 1.

43. *I was barren and childless through thirty years of marriage:* this is a common motif in a number of stories; cp. Sarah (Gen. 21: 1–7); Rachel (Gen: 30: 22–4); Hannah (1 Sam. 1); Elizabeth (Luke 1).

44. *I prayed to the Most High:* cp. 1 Sam. 1: 9–11.

45. *my distress . . . my sorrow:* so barrenness was regarded in Israel; cp. 1 Sam. 1: 6–8, 11; Luke 1:25. *What happiness . . . to all our neighbours:* cp. Luke 1: 58.

47. *I chose a wife for him:* the father would be the one normally expected to choose the wife; the fact that the mother does it in this case has probably been dictated by the needs of the story. *the wedding:* the Latin word (*epulum*) is perhaps better translated 'wedding-feast'; for feasts at weddings cp. Judg. 14: 10; Tobit 8: 19–20; Matt. 22: 1–10.

10: 1. *he fell down dead:* cp. the theme of Tobit 6–8.

2. *lamps:* for lamps at a wedding-feast cp. Matt. 25: 1–13.

5–14. The thought of Zion as 'the mother of us all' (verses 7–8; cp. Gal. 4: 26, 'the heavenly Jerusalem . . . is our mother') leads naturally into the thought of the earth as 'the mother of mankind' (verses 8–14, especially verse 14) – although the actual expression 'mother of mankind' is not present in the Latin text.

10. *Almost all her children go to perdition:* the exceptions in the mind of the author were presumably men such as Enoch (Gen. 5: 24) and Elijah (2 Kings 2: 11).

14. Although not stated, the implication of the argument

is that the earth bears her fruit (i.e. gives birth to mankind) *at the cost of pain* in the same way as a mother.

16. *then in due time you will receive your son back again:* either through the restoration to life of the original son, or through the birth of another son; the following words imply the latter (the woman will gain honour through giving birth), but the expression used *you will receive your son back again* is somewhat ambiguous. It is possible, as we have seen, that the folk-tale which appears to have been taken over by the author ended with an account of the restoration to life of the son. *and win an honoured name among women:* cp. the words spoken by 'the women' when a son is born to Ruth (Ruth 4: 14–15).

18. The woman is not persuaded, but merely repeats what she has already stated in verse 4.

21–3. The anguish experienced by the author at the fall of Jerusalem in A.D. 70 and the consequential loss of the temple is revealed clearly in these verses.

22. *Our harps are unstrung, our hymns silenced, our shouts of joy cut short:* the loss of the temple meant the end of the worship of God in the temple. *the light of the sacred lamp is out:* the lamps on the lamp-stand (Exod. 25: 31–7) were supposed to be tended regularly (Exod. 27: 20–1; Lev. 24: 2–4), and their extinction was an indication that the temple services had ceased. In 1 Macc. 4: 50 the relighting of the lamps on the lamp-stand was one of the measures undertaken as part of the restoration of the temple after its desecration in the time of Antiochus Epiphanes (167–164 B.C.). When the temple was destroyed in A.D. 70, the lamp-stand and the other sacred utensils came into the hands of Titus and were subsequently taken to Rome and displayed in his triumphal procession. The scene is depicted on the Arch of Titus in Rome; for a photograph see the volume in this series entitled *New Testament Illustrations*, p. 17. *and the ark of our covenant has been taken as spoil:* the mention of the Ark is an historical allusion appropriate to the supposed setting of 2 Esdras 3–14 in the

sixth century B.C., not to its actual setting at the end of the
first century A.D. The Ark was apparently destroyed at the
time of the destruction of Jerusalem in 587 B.C., if not earlier,
and in any event nothing is known of it after that date.
the holy vessels are defiled: this again is a feature appropriate to
the setting of 2 Esdras 3–14 in the sixth century; see 2 Kings
25: 14–15 which refers to the taking of the temple vessels to
Babylon, and Ezra 1: 7–11 which refers to their return.
The temple vessels also play an important part in the story
of Belshazzar's feast, Dan. 5 (cp. Dan. 1: 2). In the case
of the vessels, however, the author was probably thinking
much more of their seizure by Titus in his own day (see
above). For a list of the sacred vessels see 1 Macc. 4: 49–51.
and the name which God has conferred on us is disgraced (literally,
'and the name which is called over us is disgraced'): i.e. the
name of God. Israel is called by God's name (cp. Deut. 28: 10;
2 Macc. 8: 15), an indication that the nation belongs to him.
our leading men have been treated shamefully: cp. on the one
hand 2 Kings 25: 18–21, on the other Josephus, *Jewish War*
6: 271:

> 'While the temple blazed, the victors plundered everything
> that fell in their way and slaughtered wholesale all who
> were caught. No pity was shown for age, no reverence for
> rank; children and greybeards, laity and priests, alike were
> massacred; every class was pursued and encompassed in the
> grasp of war, whether suppliants for mercy or offering
> resistance' (Loeb Classical Library translation of Josephus,
> vol. 3, p. 455).

In 2 Esdras 3–14 the reading of the Latin 'our children' (see
the footnote; the Latin text could also be translated 'our free
men') probably goes back to the same Hebrew text as that of
the other versions. *our priests burnt alive:* perhaps an exaggeration, but Josephus (*Jewish War* 6: 280) does report that two
leading priests plunged themselves into the fire that was con-
suming the temple rather than give up or face capture.

23. *Worst of all, Zion, once sealed with God's own seal, has forfeited its glory:* the translation and meaning of this passage are a little uncertain; the N.E.B. has paraphrased, and a more literal rendering of the Latin would be 'Worst of all, the seal of Zion, for she has now been unsealed of her glory.' Possibly the 'seal of Zion' is to be understood as a mark of God's protection of Jerusalem which had been withdrawn.

24. *Then throw off your own heavy grief, and lay all your sorrows aside:* repetition of the advice of verse 15.

25–7. The woman is dramatically transformed into a city. For the vision cp. Rev. 21: 9–11:

'Then one of the seven angels ... came and spoke to me and said, "Come, and I will show you the bride, the wife of the Lamb." So in the Spirit he carried me away to a great high mountain, and showed me the holy city of Jerusalem coming down out of heaven from God. It shone with the glory of God; it had the radiance of some priceless jewel, like a jasper, clear as crystal.'

Cp. also the description of the 'man' (probably the angel Gabriel) seen by Daniel in Dan. 10: 5–6.

28. *I cried aloud in terror, 'Where is the angel Uriel ... ?':* cp. verse 25, 'and I shrank from her in terror'. Fear and consternation at the sight of the vision and an appeal for an explanation are characteristic elements in allegorical visions of this kind; cp. e.g. Dan. 7: 15–16; 8: 15–17; in 2 Esdras 3–14 cp. 12: 3*b*–9; 13: 13*b*–20. *Uriel:* cp. 4: 1. *that all my hopes are shattered:* the translation given in the footnote is a less convincing interpretation of the same Latin text. Ezra cannot understand the vision and feels that his prayer (9: 29–37) has been ignored; he does not realize that the vision is in fact an answer to his prayer.   *

THE INTERPRETATION OF THE VISION

I was still speaking when the angel appeared who had 29
visited me before. When he saw me lying in a dead faint, 30
unconscious on the ground, he grasped me by my right
hand, put strength into me, and raised me to my feet.
'What is the matter?' he asked. 'Why are you over- 31
come? What was it that disturbed your mind and made
you faint?' 'It was because you deserted me', I replied. 32
'I did what you told me: I came out to the field; and
what I have seen here and can still see is beyond my
power to relate.'

'Stand up like a man,' he said, 'and I will explain it 33
to you.'

'Speak, my lord,' I replied; 'only do not abandon me 34
and leave me to die unsatisfied. For I have seen and I hear 35
things beyond my understanding – unless this is all an 36
illusion and a dream. I beg you to tell me, my lord, the 37
meaning of my vision.'

'Listen to me,' replied the angel, 'while I explain to 38
you the meaning of the things that terrify you; for the
Most High has revealed many secrets to you. He has seen 39
your blameless life, your unceasing grief for your people,
and your deep mourning over Zion. Here then is the 40
meaning of the vision. A little while ago you saw a 41
woman in mourning, and tried to give her comfort;
now you no longer see that woman, but a whole city. 42
She told you she had lost her son, and this is the explana- 43
tion. The woman you saw is Zion, which you now see as 44
a city with all its buildings. She told you she was childless 45
for thirty years; that was because there were three thou-

sand years in which sacrifices were not yet offered in
46 Zion. But then, after the three thousand years, Solomon
built the city and offered the sacrifices; that was the time
47 when the barren woman bore her son. She took great
pains, she said, over his upbringing; that was the period
48 when Jerusalem was inhabited. Then she told you of the
great loss she suffered, how her son died on the day he
entered his wedding-chamber; that was the destruction
49 which overtook Jerusalem. Such then was the vision that
you saw – the woman mourning for her son – and you
tried to comfort her in her sufferings; this was the revela-
50 tion you had to receive. Seeing your sincere grief and
heartfelt sympathy for the woman, the Most High is now
51 showing you her radiant glory and her beauty. That was
why I told you to stay in a field where no house stood,
52 for I knew that the Most High intended to send you this
53 revelation. I told you to come to this field, where no
54 foundation had been laid for any building; for in the
place where the city of the Most High was to be revealed,
no building made by man could stand.

✣   29–37. In response to his appeal Uriel comes to Ezra and
revives him. Ezra asks to be told the meaning of his vision.

30. Collapse on the ground and revival by an angel are
traditional elements in apocalyptic visions; see on verse 28 and
cp. Dan. 8: 17–18; 10: 8–11; Rev. 1: 17.

32. *and can still see:* the vision of the city remains before
Ezra; cp. verse 55.

33. *Stand up like a man:* see the comment on 6: 13; cp.
also 7: 2.

38–54. The interpretation of the vision given by Uriel is
not completely straightforward, but the main points seem

fairly clear. Since the woman is identified as Zion (verse 44), but the birth and death of the son correspond to the building and destruction of Jerusalem (verses 46, 48), it is now generally argued that the mother is the heavenly Jerusalem and the son the earthly Jerusalem, and it is this view which is followed here. We have seen earlier that the heavenly Jerusalem belongs to the age to come, but is at the same time thought of as being already in existence (see 8: 52 and cp. also 7: 26; 13: 36). Ezra's complaint about the fate of Israel (9: 29–37) is thus answered by a revelation of the new Jerusalem: the earthly Jerusalem had indeed been destroyed, but this was not the end; the heavenly Jerusalem was waiting ready to take its place in the age to come.

38. *the things that terrify you . . . many secrets:* in both cases the things Ezra has seen in the vision.

39. *He has seen your blameless life:* see the comments on 6: 32–3. *your unceasing grief for your people, and your deep mourning over Zion:* as revealed in the dialogues (3: 1 – 9: 25) and in the introductory prayer of the present section (9: 29–37).

44. *The woman you saw is Zion:* i.e. the heavenly Jerusalem.

45. *there were three thousand years in which sacrifices were not yet offered in Zion:* i.e. the period from the creation of the world to the building of the temple. Most Latin manuscripts have 'three years' instead of 'three thousand years' (the reading of the Syriac, Ethiopic and Arabic versions), and the three years have been interpreted literally to refer to the three years between Solomon's accession and the building of the temple (1 Kings 6: 1), and at the same time to refer mystically to three world years of one thousand years each, i.e. three thousand years. This double interpretation of the three years is not convincing, but the reading 'three years' is perhaps not just a mistake, but points to the existence of an alternative understanding of what Uriel's explanation of the vision means. *in Zion:* literally, 'in her', but it is pressing the logic of the symbolism too far to argue that the author is talking

about sacrifice in the heavenly Jerusalem; what he means is that there were three thousand years before regular sacrifices were offered in the place where the earthly Jerusalem and the temple were eventually built (the author ignores the occasional sacrifices that were offered before the building of the temple, e.g. 2 Sam. 24: 25).

46. *after the three thousand years:* so the Syriac, Ethiopic and Arabic versions; the Latin manuscripts again have 'three years' (see on verse 45). *Solomon built the city and offered the sacrifices:* contrast 3: 23-4, 'you raised up ... David. You told him to build the city that bears your name and there offer to you in sacrifice what was already your own.' Neither David nor Solomon actually built Jerusalem, but both made additions to it; see 2 Sam. 5: 9, 11; 1 Kings 6-7; in 2 Esdras 10 the author probably referred to Solomon because he had in mind particularly the building of the temple. *her son:* i.e. the earthly Jerusalem.

48. *the destruction which overtook Jerusalem:* according to the supposed setting of the book the destruction of 587 B.C., but the author really has in mind the events of A.D. 70.

49. *this was the revelation you had to receive:* so the Latin (other versions omit); if the text is correct, the point being made is that the vision is the answer to Ezra's prayer.

50. The revelation of the new Jerusalem was granted to Ezra because of his *sympathy for the woman*; cp. verse 39.

51. *That was why I told you to stay in a field where no house stood:* cp. 9: 24. *

THE CONCLUSION OF THE VISION

55 'Have no fear then, Ezra, and set your trembling heart at rest; go into the city, and see the magnificence of the buildings, so far as your eyes have power to see it all.
56 Then, after that, you shall hear as much as your ears have
57 power to hear. You are more blessed than most other

men, and few have such a name with the Most High as
you have. Stay here till tomorrow night, when the Most 58, 59
High will show you in dreams and visions what he
intends to do to the inhabitants of earth in the last days.'
I did as I was told and slept there that night and the next.

* 55–6. *see the magnificence of the buildings, so far as your eyes
have power to see it all. Then, after that, you shall hear as much
as your ears have power to hear:* these words imply that what
was seen and heard in the vision could not adequately be
comprehended by a mere human being; because of their
apparent spontaneity they have been taken as an indication
that the narrative is based on an actual visionary experience.
Cp. 1 Cor. 2: 9, 'But, in the words of Scripture, "Things
beyond our seeing, things beyond our hearing, things beyond
our imagining, all prepared by God for those who love him",
these it is that God has revealed to us through the Spirit.'
The command to enter and see the city implies that the city
is thought of as still being present before Ezra; cp. verse 32.

57. See the comment on 6: 32–3.

58–9. As on previous occasions Ezra is commanded to wait
for a further revelation, but this time, for no obvious reason,
the regular pattern is broken; he is to wait only two nights,
not a week, and there is no reference either to fasting or to
eating only what grows in the field. *the Most High will show
you in dreams and visions what he intends to do to the inhabitants
of earth in the last days:* the author indicates precisely the function of the two visions which follow; they describe when and
how the end will come and thus supplement the information
already given in different places in the dialogues (cp. 4: 33 –
5: 13; 5: 50 – 6: 28; 7: 26–[44], [75–115]; 8: 63 – 9: 13).   *

THE VISION OF THE EAGLE AND THE LION
(CHS. II–I2)

✻ In a dream vision Ezra sees a monstrous creature rising from the sea, an eagle with twelve wings, eight rival wings and three heads. The wings and heads rule over the earth in turn and then disappear until, when only one head and two rival wings are left, the eagle is challenged by a lion which accuses it of tyrannizing the earth. The lion states that in accordance with God's predetermined plan the time for the disappearance of the eagle itself has now come, and the vision ends with the body of the eagle bursting into flames. As we subsequently learn, the eagle symbolizes the fourth kingdom of the vision of Dan. 7, but interpreted to refer to the Roman Empire not, as in Daniel, to the Greek Empire founded by Alexander the Great (see the comment on 12: 11–13); the lion is the Messiah. The wings and heads are Roman emperors, and the rival wings are military commanders or provincial governors who attempted to seize power. However, although there are good reasons for thinking that the first two wings represent Julius Caesar and Augustus, and that the three heads are Vespasian, Titus and Domitian, it is difficult beyond this to identify the remaining wings and rival wings with any certainty.

The concern with Roman history and the succession of emperors reveals something of the purpose of this vision. The author's intention was to provide comfort and assurance for his readers by indicating to them where they stood in time. He wrote during the reign of Domitian, and, as we shall see, he believed that the end of the Roman Empire and of the present age would follow shortly after Domitian's death. This vision offers, therefore, a rather more precise answer than we have so far been given to the question 'How long?' (cp. 4: 33).

We saw earlier that the vision of the Woman in Distress (9: 26 – 10: 59) apparently uses an old folk-tale, but the

vision of the eagle very obviously draws its inspiration from
the Old Testament. Several elements in the vision are taken
from the Son of Man vision in Dan. 7, and since an explicit
link is made with this chapter in 12: 11–12, it seems clear that
Dan. 7 was in the mind of the author as he wrote. The vision
of the Eagle thus provides us with further evidence of the
way in which the Old Testament was used in the apocalyptic
writings (see the comment on 3: 4–36). ✶

THE EAGLE

On the second night I had a vision in a dream; I saw, **11**
rising from the sea, an eagle with twelve wings and
three heads. I saw it spread its wings over the whole 2
earth; and all the winds blew on it, and the clouds*a*
gathered. Out of its wings I saw rival wings sprout, 3
which proved to be only small and stunted. Its heads lay 4
still; even the middle head, which was bigger than the
others, lay still between them. As I watched, the eagle 5
rose on its wings to set itself up as ruler over the earth and
its inhabitants. I saw it bring into subjection everything 6
under heaven; it met with no opposition at all from any
creature on earth. I saw the eagle stand erect on its talons, 7
and it spoke aloud to its wings:'Do not all wake at once,' 8
it said; 'sleep in your places, and each wake up in turn;
the heads are to be kept till the last.' I saw that the sound 9, 10
was not coming from its heads, but from the middle of
its body. I counted its rival wings, and saw that there were 11
eight of them.

   As I watched, one of the wings on its right side rose 12
and became ruler over the whole earth. After a time, its 13
reign came to an end, and it disappeared from sight com-

[a] the clouds: *so some Vss.; Lat. omits.*

pletely. Then the next one arose and established its rule,
14 which it held for a long time. When its reign was coming
to an end and it was about to disappear like the first one,
15, 16 a voice could be heard saying to it: 'You have ruled the
world for so long; now listen to my message before your
17 time comes to disappear. None of your successors will
achieve a reign as long as yours, nor even half as long.'
18 Then the third wing arose, ruled the world for a time
19 like its predecessors, and like them disappeared. In the
same way all the wings came to power in succession, and
in turn disappeared from sight.

20 As time went on, I saw the wings on the left*a* side also
raise themselves up to seize power. Some of them did
21 so, and passed immediately from sight, while others arose
22 but never came to power. At this point I noticed that
two of the little wings were, like the twelve, no longer
23 to be seen. Nothing was now left of the eagle's body
except the three motionless heads and six little wings.
24 As I watched, two of the six little wings separated from
the rest and took up a place under the head on the right.
25 The other four remained where they were; and I saw
26 them planning to rise up and seize power. One rose, but
27 disappeared immediately; so too did the second, vanishing
28 even more quickly than the first. I saw the last two
29 planning to seize the kingship for themselves. But while
they were still plotting, suddenly one of the heads woke
from sleep, the one in the middle, the biggest of the
30, 31 three. I saw how it joined with the other two heads, and
along with them turned and devoured the two little
32 wings which were planning to seize power. This head

[a] *So one Vs.; Lat.* right.

got the whole earth into its grasp, establishing an oppressive rule over all its inhabitants and a worldwide
kingdom mightier than any of the wings had ruled. But 33
after that I saw the middle head vanish just as suddenly
as the wings had done. There were two heads left, and 34
they also seized power over the earth and its inhabitants,
but as I watched, the head on the right devoured the 35
head on the left.

✽ 1. *I saw, rising from the sea:* cp. Dan. 7: 2-3, 'I saw a great
sea churned up by the four winds of heaven, and four huge
beasts coming up out of the sea'; see also Rev. 13: 1. *an eagle
with twelve wings and three heads:* cp. the descriptions of the
beasts in Dan. 7: 4-8, which likewise have monstrous characteristics: 'The first was like a lion but had an eagle's wings . . .
another, a beast like a leopard with four bird's wings on its
back; this creature had four heads, and it was invested with
sovereign power' (Dan. 7: 4, 6). The eagle was appropriate
as a symbol of Rome inasmuch as it was the Roman military
emblem. The beast which rises out of the sea in Rev. 13: 1
is likewise a symbol of Rome.

2. *I saw it spread its wings over the whole earth:* an indication
of its universal power; cp. verses 5-6. *and all the winds blew
on it:* a motif taken from Dan. 7: 2. *and the clouds gathered:*
the Syriac version reads literally 'and the clouds gathered
about it' (similarly the Ethiopic and Arabic), but the Latin
omits 'the clouds' and 'about it'. However, the significance
of the statement is not clear. In the Old Testament clouds
regularly accompany the self-revelation of God (e.g. Exod.
19: 9, 16), but also symbolize the gloom of God's day of
judgement (e.g. Joel 2: 1-2); neither idea suits the present
passage. It is just possible that the motif has been inappropri-
ately taken from Dan. 7: 13, 'and I saw one like a man coming
with the clouds of heaven'.

3. *rival wings* (so the Latin; the other versions support the

reading 'little wings'): military commanders or provincial governors who attempted to seize power; the fact that they *proved to be only small and stunted* indicates their lack of success.

4. *Its heads lay still:* because the time for their rule had not yet come; cp. verses 8–9.

5–6. An allusion to the world-wide power exercised by the Romans in the first century A.D.

8. The emperors obviously could not all rule at the same time, but this fact has to be accommodated to the symbolism of the vision.

9. *the heads are to be kept till the last:* because we know that 2 Esdras 3–14 was written against the background of the Jewish war of A.D. 66–73 and its aftermath (see pp. 102–4), it is possible to identify the three heads as Vespasian and his two sons, Titus and Domitian, with a fair degree of certainty. The author, writing in the time of Domitian, believed that the reigns of these three emperors marked the climax of Roman rule, and expected that the end of this age would follow the death of Domitian; see 12: 28.

10. *the sound was not coming from its heads, but from the middle of its body:* because the Roman Empire itself is speaking, not one of the emperors.

11. *rival wings:* so the Latin, but other versions have 'little wings', and this (or a similar expression) is the term used from now on in the Latin. *eight:* who these were is extremely uncertain.

12–13a. The first wing can be identified as Julius Caesar because the next wing is clearly Augustus.

13b–17. The long reign indicates that the second wing represents Augustus who came to power after the death of Caesar in 44 B.C. and was in effect sole ruler from 31 B.C. to A.D. 14, although the formal recognition of his status dates only from 27 B.C.

19. *all the wings came to power in succession, and in turn disappeared:* it is not clear whether *all the wings* means all twelve

wings or only, as the N.E.B. implies, the six on the right side
(see the comment on verse 20). In either case there are considerable problems in identifying the twelve wings and eight
little wings. Since the first two wings are Caesar and Augustus,
and since the three heads are Vespasian, Titus and Domitian,
it is possible that the twelve wings are Caesar, Augustus,
Tiberius, Gaius, Claudius, Nero, Vindex, Nymphidius, Galba,
Piso (i.e. M. Piso Licinianus), Otho and Vitellius. The identification of the first six (Caesar and the emperors Augustus,
Tiberius, Gaius, Claudius and Nero) is virtually certain, that
of the second six much less so; these are men who in the
troubled years of 68 and 69 either became emperor for a short
period or were involved in attempts to seize power. However, the main difficulty with this view is the identity of the
eight little wings, and if this view is correct, it would probably
have to be said that we are not in a position to determine
whom they symbolize. Alternatively it might be argued that
Vindex, Nymphidius, Galba, Piso, Otho and Vitellius are

The Roman emperors from Augustus to Domitian	
(Murder of Julius Caesar	44 B.C.)
Augustus	27 B.C.–A.D. 14
Tiberius	A.D. 14–37
Gaius	37–41
Claudius	41–54
Nero	54–68
(Revolt of Vindex and conspiracy of	
Nymphidius	68)
Galba	68–9
Otho	69
Vitellius	69
Vespasian	69–79
Titus	79–81
Domitian	81–96

more naturally identified with six of the eight little wings. But on this view the twelve wings become a problem, for there are now apparently only six rulers left prior to Vespasian (i.e. Caesar, Augustus, Tiberius, Gaius, Claudius, Nero) whom they could represent. This difficulty could be explained by assuming that the numbers were revised after the death of Domitian in an attempt to bring the vision up to date when it had become clear that the end of this age had not yet arrived; against this, apart from the question of the numbers, there are no hints in the text to suggest that it has been revised. There are clearly difficulties involved in both explanations, as well as in others that might be suggested, and no certain conclusion can be reached. On any view it is possible that the figure 'twelve' was used primarily because it was regarded as a significant number (cp. 2 Baruch 53 where the whole of history from Adam to the period after the exile is divided up into twelve periods).

20. *I saw the wings on the left side also raise themselves up to seize power:* the N.E.B. translation implies that the first six (those on the right side) of the twelve wings are referred to in verses 12–19, and the second six (those on the left side) in verse 20. Such a view is certainly possible. However, the reading 'on the left side' is supported only by some Ethiopic manuscripts; the Latin, Syriac and Armenian versions (the Arabic does not mention the side), as well as the remaining Ethiopic manuscripts, all have 'on the right side', and this much stronger attestation suggests that there is no parallelism between the right and left sides in verses 12–19 and 20. Besides this, there are indications that the rival or little wings are meant in verse 20; for *the wings* the Latin actually has 'the wings which followed', the Syriac 'the little wings'; the Latin is ambiguous, but the Syriac quite explicit. Verse 20 could certainly be interpreted without difficulty as referring to the little wings, and if this is so, (1) 'all the wings' in verse 19 means all twelve wings, (2) the detail 'on its right side' (verses 12, 20) has no particular significance.

22. *two of the little wings:* possibly Vindex and Nymphidius who were both involved in plots in the last months of Nero's reign. For a vivid description of the events of this period see the accounts by Suetonius (*The Lives of the Caesars*) and Tacitus (*The Histories*); see the Note on Further Reading, p. 306.

23. This verse refers to the period immediately after the death of Nero in June 68.

24. *two of the six little wings . . . took up a place under the head on the right:* the head on the right is Domitian (emperor from 81 to 96), but there has been no entirely convincing identification of the two little wings which joined him, nor is it clear why they should be mentioned here rather than later.

26. *One rose, but disappeared immediately:* possibly Galba who became emperor after the death of Nero, but was murdered in January 69.

27. *the second, vanishing even more quickly than the first:* possibly M. Piso Licinianus who was nominated co-ruler by Galba, but was likewise murdered.

28. *the last two:* possibly Otho and Vitellius who were emperors for brief periods during 69; the former took his own life, the latter was murdered.

29. *one of the heads . . . the one in the middle, the biggest of the three:* Vespasian, the general in command of the operations against the Jews, who was declared emperor by his legions and was the one ultimately successful in the struggle for power in the year 69. He reigned until 79.

30. *the other two heads:* his sons, Titus and Domitian.

32. *an oppressive rule:* the author's attitude towards Vespasian was no doubt strongly influenced by the measures taken against the Jews in the aftermath of the Jewish war.

35. *the head on the right devoured the head on the left:* according to rumour the death of Titus (*the head on the left*) was supposed to have been brought about by Domitian (*the head on the right*). The former was emperor from 79 to 81, the latter from

81 to 96. Verse 35 forms the conclusion of the description of
the past; the author has now reached the time at which he
is writing and what follows is his prophecy of the events that
would take place in the last days; cp. the comparable transition that occurs in Dan. 11 between verse 39 and verse 40.   ✧

THE LION

36   Then I heard a voice which said to me: 'Look carefully
37 at what you see before you.' I looked, and saw what
seemed to be a lion roused from the forest; it roared as
it came, and I heard it address the eagle in a human voice.
38 'Listen to what I tell you', it said. 'The Most High says
39 to you: Are you not the only survivor of the four beasts
to which I gave the rule over my world, intending
40-41 through them to bring my ages to their end? You are the
fourth beast, and you have conquered all who went
before, ruling over the whole world and holding it in
the grip of fear and harsh oppression. You have lived*a*
long in the world, governing it with deceit and with no
42 regard for truth. You have oppressed the gentle and
injured the peaceful, hating the truthful and loving liars;
you have destroyed the homes of the prosperous, and
razed to the ground the walls of those who had done
43 you no harm. Your insolence is known to the Most
44 High, and your pride to the Mighty One. The Most High
has surveyed the periods he has fixed: they are now at an
45 end, and his ages have reached their completion. So you,
eagle, must now disappear and be seen no more, you and
your terrible great wings, your evil small wings, your

[a] You are the fourth ... lived: *so some Vss.; Lat.* The fourth beast
came and conquered ... It has lived ...

cruel heads, your grim talons, and your whole worthless body. Then all the earth will feel relief at its deliverance 46 from your violence, and look forward hopefully to the judgement and mercy of its Creator.'

While the lion was still addressing the eagle, I looked **12** 1 and saw the one remaining head disappear. Then the 2 two*a* wings which had gone over to him arose and set themselves up as rulers. Their reign was short and troubled, and when I looked at them they were already 3 vanishing. Then the eagle's entire body burst into flames, and the earth was struck with terror.

* 37. *a lion:* identified in 12: 31–2 with the Messiah. The symbolism perhaps goes back to the prophecy concerning Judah in Gen. 49: 9; cp. Rev. 5: 5 where the Messiah is described as 'the Lion from the tribe of Judah, the Scion of David'.

39–40*a*. *Are you not the only survivor of the four beasts ... ? You are the fourth beast:* the eagle is identified as the fourth beast, i.e. the fourth kingdom, of Dan. 7: 7; cp. 12: 10–12.

40*b*–43. The author, writing under the impact of the events of the Jewish war, accuses the Romans of ruling with cruelty and injustice. In the Latin version of part of verses 40 and 41 the third person was used by mistake instead of the second person; see the footnote.

44–5. The end of the Roman Empire is in accordance with God's plan. The thought underlying these verses is one common to many apocalyptic writings: God has determined in advance the duration of this world and the course of human history (cp. verse 39, 'Are you not the only survivor of the four beasts to which I gave the rule over my world, intending through them to bring my ages to their end?'). However,

[*a*] *So other Vss.; Lat. corrupt.*

245

despite holding this deterministic view, the author also believed that men were responsible for their own destiny, as we have seen. So here the downfall of Rome is presented both as part of God's plan and at the same time as a consequence of its despotic and arrogant behaviour.

46. *all the earth will . . . look forward hopefully to the judgement and mercy of its Creator:* not the last judgement, but the judgement of the Roman Empire; this would be followed by the reign of the Messiah; cp. 12: 31–4.

12: 1–3*a. I looked and saw the one remaining head disappear:* the death of Domitian still lay in the future; it would be one of the events of 'the last days'; see verse 28. *the two wings:* see the comment on 11: 24; the death of these two would also be one of the events of the last days; cp. verses 29–30. *Then the eagle's entire body burst into flames:* cp. the fate of the fourth beast in Dan. 7: 11, 'I went on watching until the beast was killed and its carcass destroyed: it was given to the flames.'   ✲

THE INTERPRETATION OF THE VISION

So great was my alarm and fear that I awoke, and said
4 to myself: 'See the result of your attempt to discover the
5 ways of the Most High! My mind is weary; I am utterly exhausted. The terrors of this night have completely
6 drained my strength. So I will now pray to the Most
7 High for strength to hold out to the end.' Then I said: 'My Master and Lord, if I have won your favour and stand higher in your approval than most men, if it is
8 true that my prayers have reached your presence, then give me strength; reveal to me, my Lord, the exact interpretation of this terrifying vision, and so bring full
9 consolation to my soul. For you have already judged me worthy to be shown the end of the present age.'

He said to me: 'Here is the interpretation of your 10
vision. The eagle you saw rising from the sea represents 11
the fourth kingdom in the vision seen by your brother
Daniel. But he was not given the interpretation which I 12
am now giving you or have already given you. The 13
days are coming when the earth will be under an empire
more terrible than any before. It will be ruled by twelve 14
kings, one after another. The second to come to the 15
throne will have the longest reign of all the twelve. That 16
is the meaning of the twelve wings you saw.

'As for the voice which you heard speaking from the 17
middle of the eagle's body, and not from its heads, this
is what it means: After this second king's reign, great 18
conflicts will arise, which will bring the empire into
danger of falling; and yet it will not fall then, but will be
restored to its original strength.

'As for the eight lesser wings which you saw growing 19
from the eagle's wings, this is what they mean: The 20
empire will come under eight kings whose reigns will be
trivial and short-lived; two of them will come and go 21
just before the middle of the period, four will be kept
back until shortly before its end, and two will be left
until the end itself.

'As for the three heads which you saw sleeping, this is 22
what they mean: In the last years of the empire, the Most 23
High will bring to the throne three kings, who will
restore much of its strength, and rule*a* over the earth and 24
its inhabitants more oppressively than anyone before.
They are called the eagle's heads, because they will com- 25

[*a*] who ... rule: *so some Vss.; Lat.* and he will restore ... and they
will rule ...

plete and bring to a head its long series of wicked deeds.

26 As for the greatest head, which you saw disappear, it signifies one of the kings, who will die in his bed, but in

27 great agony. The two that survived will be destroyed by

28 the sword; one of them will fall by the sword of the other, who will himself fall by the sword in the last days.

29 'As for the two little wings that went over to the head

30 on the right side, this is what they mean: They are the ones whom the Most High has reserved until the last days, and their reign, as you saw, was short and troubled.

31 'As for the lion which you saw coming from the forest, roused from sleep and roaring, which you heard addressing the eagle, taxing it with its wicked deeds and

32 words, this is the Messiah whom the Most High has kept back until the end. He will address*a* those rulers, taxing them openly with their sins, their crimes, and their

33 defiance. He will bring them alive to judgement; he will

34 convict them and then destroy them. But he will be merciful to those of my people that remain, all who have been kept safe in my land; he will set them free and give them gladness, until the final day of judgement comes, about which I told you at the beginning.

35 'That, then, is the vision which you saw, and its mean-

36 ing. It is the secret of the Most High, which no one except

37 yourself has proved worthy to be told. What you have seen you must therefore write in a book and deposit it

38 in a hiding-place. You must also disclose these secrets to those of your people whom you know to be wise

39 enough to understand them and to keep them safe. But stay here yourself for seven more days, to receive what-

[a] He will address: *probable reading; Lat. defective.*

ever revelation the Most High thinks fit to send you.'
Then the angel left me.

* 3*b*–9. Ezra wakes in terror and prays to God to be shown
the meaning of the vision; as we have seen, these are common
motifs in visions of this kind; cp. the comment on 10: 28.

7. *if I have won your favour:* see the comment on 5: 56.
and stand higher in your approval than most men: as he had been
repeatedly assured; cp. 7: [76]; 8: 47–9; 10: 57. *if it is true
that my prayers have reached your presence:* cp. 6: 32.

9. *For you have already judged me worthy to be shown the end
of the present age:* Ezra is apparently alluding to the information given him during the course of the three dialogues.

10–34. The interpretation is given in language that is indirect in character and in some respects no clearer than the
vision itself, although no doubt the author's contemporaries
understood exactly what was meant. The use of language of
this kind is typical of such visions (cp. e.g. the interpretation
in Dan. 7: 23–7) and forms part of the whole apocalyptic
approach, namely that the revelations which are given are
mysteries intended, not for the general public, but only for a
restricted group of wise men who are capable of understanding them (cp. e.g. verses 36–8 and see the comment on
8: 62).

10. *He said to me:* we are not told who the speaker is, and
from this point on it is left quite unclear whether it is the
angel or God who answers Ezra.

11–13. *The eagle . . . represents the fourth kingdom in the
vision seen by your brother Daniel. But he was not given the
interpretation which I am now giving you:* the author indicates
clearly his use and reinterpretation of the vision of Dan. 7.
The eagle is the fourth kingdom (Dan. 7: 7–8, 11, 19–27), but
whereas in Daniel this is the Greek Empire founded by
Alexander the Great, in 2 Esdras 3–14 it is the Roman Empire.
In a somewhat similar way the author of Rev. 13: 1–10 has
drawn on Dan. 7 in his description of the beast which sym-

bolizes the Roman Empire, although in Revelation the term 'fourth kingdom' is not used. For the eagle as a symbol of Rome see on 11: 1. *The days are coming:* the vision is supposed to have been received during the exile in Babylon, i.e. at a time long before the Roman Empire came into existence.

14–16. *twelve kings . . . twelve wings:* see the comment on 11: 19. *The second . . . will have the longest reign of all the twelve:* i.e. Augustus; see on 11: 13*b*–17.

17. *As for the voice which you heard speaking from the middle of the eagle's body, and not from its heads:* these words suggest a reference to 11: 10, but cp. also 11: 15. However, the following verse is not an interpretation of the speech in 11: 7–9 (which in any case would be out of place at this point), nor of the speech in 11: 16–17; see below.

18. *After this second king's reign:* so the Latin, but the Syriac and Armenian versions read 'In the middle of the time of that kingdom', and these versions probably preserve the original text. The author has used a detail taken from 11: 10 (the middle of the eagle's body) as the basis of a piece of interpretation which has no real counterpart in the vision itself. From an historical point of view verse 18 seems to refer to the troubled period which followed the death of Nero, and to the restoration under Vespasian, events which are dealt with in more detail in verses 19–21 and 22–8.

19–21. *eight lesser wings . . . eight kings:* see the comment on 11: 19. *two of them will come and go just before the middle of the period:* possibly Vindex and Nymphidius; see the comment on 11: 22. *four will be kept back until shortly before its end:* possibly Galba, Piso, Otho and Vitellius; see the comment on 11: 26–8. *and two will be left until the end itself:* cp. 11: 24; 12: 2; as we have seen, there has been no convincing identification of these two little wings.

22–5. *three heads . . . the Most High will bring to the throne three kings:* the Flavian emperors, Vespasian, Titus and Domitian (cp. 11: 29–35 and see the comment on 11: 9). The deterministic view of history held by the author is reflected clearly here; it was God who controlled what happened to the Romans, and thus he who brought the kings to the throne. *In the last years of the empire:* the author of 2 Esdras 3–14 believed that the end of the Roman Empire (and of the present age) would follow immediately after the rule of these three emperors; cp. verse 25. *who will restore much of its strength:* the Flavian emperors brought a period of peace and stability after the disorders of 68 and 69. In the Latin version the text of verse 23 is slightly out of order; see the footnote. *and rule . . . more oppressively than anyone before:* the accusation again reflects the impact of the events of the war of A.D. 66–73; cp. 11: 32.

26. *the greatest head:* Vespasian; cp. 11: 32–3. *who will die in his bed, but in great agony:* Vespasian died of fever.

27. *The two that survived:* Titus and Domitian; cp. 11: 34.

28. *one of them will fall by the sword of the other:* the death of Titus; see the comment on 11: 35. *who will himself fall by the sword in the last days:* the death of Domitian (cp. 12: 1–2*a*) which for the author still lay in the future; it would be one of the events of *the last days*, i.e. of the end of the present age.

29–30. *the two little wings:* cp. 11: 24; 12: 2*b*–3*a*. As we have seen, there has been no convincing identification of these two; for the author their death also lay in the future. *until the last days:* here literally 'for its end', i.e. for the end of the eagle.

31–4. The Messiah; cp. 7: 26–44 and see the comment on 7: 28 where the name and functions of this figure are discussed. In the present passage his tasks are to judge, convict and destroy the Roman Empire (verses 31–3), and to bring deliverance and happiness to the remnant of God's people who survive (verse 34).

31–3. *As for the lion . . . this is the Messiah:* cp. 11: 36–46 and for the symbolism see the comment on 11: 37. *whom the Most High has kept back until the end:* these words imply that the Messiah is already in existence; he is kept by God in readiness until the time comes for him to act. In 1 Enoch the

pre-existence of the Son of Man, who is likewise kept back by
God until the end of this age, is stated rather more explicitly;
see 48: 6, 'he was chosen and hidden before him (i.e. God)
before the world was created', and 62: 7, 'For from the
beginning the Son of Man was hidden, and the Most High
kept him in the presence of his power.' *until the end:* so the
Latin, but the Syriac and other versions add 'of days', thus
making clear that the end of this age is meant; the end of this
age coincides with the end of the Roman Empire which will be
destroyed by the Messiah. The Syriac and other versions continue 'who will spring from the seed of David. He will come
and address . . . ' (the Latin is defective here, see the footnote); the belief that the Messiah would be a descendant of
David, which was based on such passages as Isa. 11: 1 and
Jer. 23: 5, was widespread (cp. e.g. Psalms of Solomon 17: 23,
'Behold, O Lord, and raise up for them their king, the son
of David, at the time when you see, O God, that he should
reign over Israel, your servant'; in the New Testament cp.
Rev. 5: 5; 22: 16, and contrast Matt. 22: 41-6 where this
belief is challenged as being inadequate). *He will address those
rulers, taxing them openly with their sins . . . He will bring them
alive to judgement:* it is interesting to observe that the Messiah
brings about the end of the Roman Empire, not in a great
battle, but through an act of judgement; cp. 13: 37. In this
respect he functions in a similar way to the Son of Man in
1 Enoch whose role is primarily that of the judge of the
wicked; cp. e.g. 69: 27, 'and the whole judgement was given
to the Son of Man, and he will cause the sinners to pass away
and be destroyed from the face of the earth'.

34. This verse describes the reign of the Messiah (see the
comment on 7: 28); the destruction of the Romans would be
followed by the liberation of those who survived the end of
this age and by the establishment of the messianic kingdom.
those of my people that remain: i.e. those who survive the woes
which will occur at the end of this age; cp. 6: 25; 7: 27-8;
9: 7-8. *all who have been kept safe in my land:* as in 9: 8 and

13: 48 the messianic kingdom will be based on the land of Israel. *my land* (literally 'my borders'): at this point the speaker is assumed to be God; for Israel as God's land see the comment on 9: 8. *give them gladness:* cp. 7: 28, the Messiah will 'bring four hundred years of happiness to all who survive'. *until the final day of judgement comes:* the reign of the Messiah is only of limited duration (cp. 7: 28); it will be followed by the day of judgement which will mark the beginning of the new age. *about which I told you at the beginning:* perhaps a specific allusion to 7: 26–[44] where the day of judgement as the sequel to the reign of the Messiah is described in some detail. But the day of judgement forms a constant theme throughout the dialogues (3: 1 – 9: 25).

35. *That, then, is the vision which you saw:* cp. 11: 1.

36. *the secret . . . which no one except yourself has proved worthy to be told:* these words no doubt reflect the author's convictions about his own status and about the revelation which he had received; see the comment on 6: 32–3.

37. The command to write an account of the vision and to hide it in a secret place is part of the apocalyptic technique; it is intended to explain how Ezra's revelation, which supposedly dated from the period of the exile, only became known at a much later date, i.e. at the end of the first century A.D., the time when it was actually composed. Similar commands, with a similar purpose, are to be found in other apocalyptic writings; cp. e.g. Dan. 12: 4, 'But you, Daniel, keep the words secret and seal the book till the time of the end.'

38. *You must also disclose these secrets to those of your people whom you know to be wise enough to understand them:* see the comment on 8: 62. The apocalyptic revelations are intended only for the wise, who alone are capable of understanding them.

39. *stay here . . . for seven more days:* cp. 5: 13; 6: 31; 9: 23, and contrast 10: 58. *the angel:* only mentioned in the Armenian version; see the comment on verse 10.   ✳

253

EZRA COMFORTS THE PEOPLE

40 　When all the people heard that seven days had passed without my returning to the town, they assembled and 41 came to me. 'What wrong or injury have we done you,' they asked me, 'that you have deserted us and settled 42 here? Out of all the prophets you are the only one left to us. You are like the last cluster in a vineyard, like a lamp in the darkness, or a safe harbour for a ship in a 43, 44 storm. Have we not suffered enough? If you desert us, we had far better have been destroyed in the fire that 45 burnt up Zion. We are no better than those who perished there.' Then they raised a loud lamentation.

46 　I replied: 'Take courage, Israel; house of Jacob, lay 47 aside your grief. The Most High bears you in mind, and 48 the Mighty One has not for ever[a] forgotten you. I have not left you, nor abandoned you; I came here to pray for Zion in her distress, and to beg for mercy for your 49 sanctuary that has fallen so low. Go to your homes now, every one of you; and in a few days' time I will come back to you.'

50 　So the people returned to the town as I told them, 51 while I remained in the field. I stayed there for seven days in obedience to the angel, eating nothing but what grew in the field, and living on that for the whole of the time.

✷ 40-5. The people come to Ezra and complain that he has abandoned them.

40. *When all the people heard that seven days had passed:* apparently an allusion to 9: 23. Ezra had waited a week before he had the vision of the Woman in Distress (cp. 9: 26-7),

[a] *So one Vs.; Lat.* in strife.

and a further two nights before the vision of the eagle (cp. 10: 58 – 11: 1). *without my returning to the town:* i.e. to Babylon (cp. 3: 1). Ezra had gone out from Babylon to the 'field called Ardat' (9: 26) and had not returned from there.

42. *Out of all the prophets you are the only one left to us:* Ezra is here regarded as a prophet; cp. 1: 1; 15: 1, and see p. 77.

43–5. The complaint of the people leads naturally into a reference to the fate of Jerusalem, the problem with which 2 Esdras 3–14 begins (cp. ch. 3). Ezra takes up this point in the course of his reply in verse 47.

46–9. Ezra assures the people that they have neither been forgotten by God, nor abandoned by himself; they should return home to await him.

47. *The Most High bears you in mind, and the Mighty One has not for ever forgotten you:* Ezra's words here allude to what had been said in verses 43–5. His positive statement contrasts strikingly with his earlier complaints about God's dealings with Israel and is a further indication of the change of attitude that occurs after 9: 25. *for ever:* so the Syriac version; the Latin 'in strife' (see the N.E.B. footnote) probably goes back to a misunderstanding of the same Greek text as that underlying the Syriac.

51. *I stayed there for seven days in obedience to the angel:* cp. verse 39. Once again it is only the Armenian version that actually refers to the angel; cp. verse 10; the Latin, Syriac and Ethiopic versions have literally 'as he had commanded me'. *eating nothing but what grew in the field:* Ezra maintains the diet prescribed in 9: 24. ✳

THE VISION OF THE MAN FROM THE SEA (CH. 13)

✳ We saw earlier that the vision of the Eagle (chs. 11–12) was intended to provide comfort for the author's contemporaries by indicating when the end of the Roman Empire – and of this age – would occur, but in the course of the vision

the role of the Messiah in the events of the end was also
described (cp. 11: 36 – 12: 3*a*; 12: 31–4). The vision of the
Man from the Sea offers a further description of the role of
the Messiah which, like the vision of the Eagle, is based on the
Son of Man vision in Dan. 7. There are, however, a number
of differences. The vision itself (13: 1–13*a*), although drawing
its primary inspiration from Dan. 7, also makes use of motifs
taken from Dan. 2 and from a wide range of other Old
Testament passages. More importantly, in the interpretation
(13: 25–53) the term 'Messiah' is not used; instead the man
from the sea is identified as 'my son' (cp. e.g. 13: 32). In
addition the functions assigned to this figure differ to some
extent from those assigned to the Messiah in the vision of the
eagle. These differences may suggest that in the composition
of this section (i.e. ch. 13) of 2 Esdras 3–14 the author drew on
other already existing traditions. More important than this is
to ask what was the author's purpose in adding the vision of
the man from the sea. In effect the vision provides a further
comment on the tasks of the Messiah which supplements the
picture already given in the preceding vision: the Messiah
will not merely judge and destroy the Romans, he will
destroy all the nations opposed to him (cp. 13: 25–38) and
will then gather in the land of Israel the twelve tribes to
participate in the messianic kingdom (cp. 13: 39–50). ✶

THE VISION

13 The seven days passed; and the next night I had a dream.
2 In my dream, a wind came up out of the sea and set the
3 waves in turmoil. And this wind brought a human figure
rising from the depths,*a* and as I watched, this man came
flying*b* with the clouds of heaven. Wherever he turned
his eyes, everything that they fell on was seized with

[*a*] And ... depths: *so other Vss.; Lat. defective.*
[*b*] *So other Vss.; Lat.* grew strong.

terror; and wherever the sound of his voice reached, all 4
who heard it melted like wax at the touch of fire.

Next I saw an innumerable host of men gathering from 5
the four winds of heaven to wage war on the man who
had risen from the sea. I saw that the man hewed out a 6
vast mountain for himself, and flew up on to it. I tried to 7
see from what quarter or place the mountain had been
taken, but I could not. Then I saw that all who had 8
gathered to wage war against the man were filled with
fear, and yet they dared to fight against him. When he 9
saw the hordes advancing to attack, he did not so much
as lift a finger against them. He had no spear in his hand,
no weapon at all; only, as I watched, he poured what 10
seemed like a stream of fire out of his mouth, a breath
of flame from his lips, and a storm of sparks from his
tongue. All of them combined into one mass – the stream 11
of fire, the breath of flame, and the great storm. It fell
on the host advancing to join battle, and burnt up every
man of them; suddenly all that enormous multitude had
disappeared, leaving nothing but dust and ashes and a
reek of smoke. I was dumbfounded at the sight.

After that, I saw the man coming down from the 12
mountain and calling to himself a different company, a
peaceful one. He was joined by great numbers of men, 13
some with joy on their faces, others with sorrow. Some
came from captivity; some brought others to him as an
offering.

* The vision falls into three parts: (1) the appearance of the
Man from the Sea (verses 1–4); (2) the defeat of the forces
opposed to him (verses 5–11); (3) the summoning of a peaceful
company (verses 12–13*a*).

2. *In my dream, a wind came up out of the sea and set the waves in turmoil:* cp. 11: 1–2 and Dan. 7: 2, 'In my visions of the night I . . . saw a great sea churned up by the four winds of heaven.'

3*a*. *And this wind brought a human figure rising from the depths:* the author of 2 Esdras 3–14 has rather dramatically altered the sense of Dan. 7, the passage on which he is at this point dependent; in Dan. 7 it is the beasts, symbolizing the forces hostile to God, who rise from the sea, not the 'one like a man' (Dan. 7: 13). *and as I watched, this man came flying with the clouds of heaven:* cp. Dan. 7: 13, 'I was still watching in visions of the night and I saw one like a man coming with the clouds of heaven'; Isa. 19: 1, 'See how the LORD comes riding swiftly upon a cloud.' In the Old Testament clouds regularly accompany a self-revelation of God (cp. e.g. Exod. 19: 9, 16); correspondingly in 2 Esdras 3–14 the fact that the man flies *with the clouds of heaven* is an indication that he, like the 'one like a man' of Dan. 7, has some kind of divine status. In the New Testament cp. Rev. 1: 7 (Jesus 'is coming with the clouds') and Matt. 24: 30. *came flying:* the Latin 'grew strong' (see the N.E.B. footnote) is merely a mistake.

3*b*–4. The things said here about the man from the sea are similar to things said in the Old Testament about God; this is not chance, but is a further indication of the divine status of the Man from the Sea. *Wherever he turned his eyes, everything that they fell on was seized with terror:* cp. Ps. 104: 32, 'When he looks at the earth, it quakes.' *and wherever the sound of his voice reached, all who heard it melted like wax at the touch of fire:* the simile of wax melting before fire is used several times in the Old Testament in passages referring to the self-revelation of God; cp. e.g. Ps. 97: 5:

'The mountains melt like wax as the LORD approaches,
    the Lord of all the earth.'

Cp. also Ps. 68: 2; Micah 1: 3–4.

5. The nations of the world gather to fight in a last great battle against *the man who had risen from the sea*. For the motif cp. Ezek. 38–9, the assault of Gog and his forces on the land of Israel, and see the comment on this passage in the commentary on Ezekiel in this series (p. 254). Cp. also Dan. 7: 21, 25. *from the four winds of heaven:* i.e. from the four quarters of heaven, a way of saying 'from the whole world'.

6. *the man hewed out a vast mountain for himself:* the author is drawing on Dan. 2. In his dream Nebuchadnezzar saw a stone, 'hewn from a mountain, not by human hands', which shattered the statue of gold, silver, bronze, iron and clay, and then became 'a great mountain filling the whole earth' (Dan. 2: 34–5). Subsequently the stone is identified as a kingdom, established by God, which destroys the kingdoms symbolized by the statue (Dan. 2: 44–5). In 2 Esdras 3–14 the mountain is identified in the interpretation as the pre-existent heavenly Jerusalem (verse 36, cp. 7: 26; 10: 27, 38–59). Verse 36 makes clear the link with Dan. 2 by adding a significant detail ('hewn out, not by the hand of man') to its description of the mountain. *and flew up on to it:* in Dan. 2 the stone shatters the statue which symbolizes the kingdoms; in 2 Esdras 3–14 the Messiah stands on the mountain in order to destroy his enemies (cp. verse 35).

7. Ezra cannot *see from what quarter or place the mountain had been taken* because, as a symbol of the new Jerusalem, it belongs to the heavenly world.

10. *he poured what seemed like a stream of fire out of his mouth, a breath of flame from his lips, and a storm of sparks from his tongue:* probably based on Isa. 11: 4, the passage referring to the ideal Davidic king:

> 'his mouth shall be a rod to strike down the ruthless,
> and with a word he shall slay the wicked.'

Cp. also Ps. 18: 8, which describes God coming to the aid of the Psalmist:

'Smoke rose from his nostrils,
devouring fire came out of his mouth,
glowing coals and searing heat.'

For a similar motif in the New Testament cp. 2 Thess. 2: 8.

11. *It fell on the host . . . and burnt up every man of them:* in Dan. 7 the fourth beast is destroyed by being burned in fire (Dan. 7: 11). Fire is mentioned elsewhere in the Old Testament as the means by which God destroys those who have incurred his anger; cp. Ezek. 39: 6 (significantly in the context of the Gog prophecy; cp. the comment on verse 5) and frequently in Amos 1–2.

12. *I saw the man . . . calling to himself a different company, a peaceful one:* after defeating his enemies the Messiah will gather those who will be his subjects in his kingdom.

13*a*. *some with joy on their faces, others with sorrow:* the former are presumably Jews, and the latter gentiles, although the gentiles are not in fact mentioned in the interpretation (but see the comment on verses 49–50). The theme of the conversion of the gentiles occurs in several Old Testament writings; in Isa. 55: 3–5 their conversion is, in an indirect way, the work of the Davidic Messiah. *Some came from captivity:* i.e. Jews in captivity; cp. Isa. 42: 6–7, referring to God's appointment of his servant:

'I have formed you, and appointed you . . .
to bring captives out of prison,
out of the dungeons where they lie in darkness.'

some brought others to him as an offering: the words are apparently based on Isa. 66: 20:

'From every nation they shall bring your countrymen . . .
as an offering to the LORD'

Thus the implication of the passage in 2 Esdras is that Gentiles will bring Jews. *

EZRA REFLECTS ON THE SIGNIFICANCE OF THE VISION

I woke up in terror, and prayed to the Most
High. I said, 'You have revealed these marvels to me, your   14
servant, all the way through; you have judged me worthy
to have my prayers answered. Now show me the mean-   15
ing of this dream also. How terrible, to my thinking, it   16
will be for all who survive to those days! But how much
worse for those who do not survive! Those who do not   17
survive will have the sorrow of knowing what is in store   18
in the last days and yet missing it. Those who do survive   19
are to be pitied for the terrible dangers and trials which,
as these visions show, they will have to face. But perhaps   20
after all it is better to endure the dangers and reach the
goal than to vanish out of the world like a cloud and
never see the events of the last days.'

'Yes,' he replied, 'I will explain the meaning of this   21
vision, and tell you all that you ask. As for your question   22
about those who survive, this is the answer: the very   23
person from whom the danger will then come will protect in danger those who have works and fidelity laid up
to their credit with the Most High. You may be assured   24
that those who survive are more highly blessed than those
who die.

✶   13*b*–20. As on previous occasions Ezra is overcome by
fear and asks to be shown the meaning of his dream; for these
typical motifs see the comment on 10: 28. But the content
of the dream also leads Ezra to reflect on the alternatives that
face men: survival until the last days, or death before the end.
Distress is inevitable in either case, but he concludes that the
former is preferable to the latter.

14. *You have revealed these marvels to me, your servant, all the way through:* cp. 8: 63. The marvels are the revelations about the end which Ezra has received throughout the preceding dialogues and visions. *you have judged me worthy to have my prayers answered:* cp. the rather more tentative words that are used in 12: 7–9.

16. *How terrible ... for all who survive to those days!:* i.e. to the time when the Messiah will destroy his enemies (verses 5–11), and more generally to the time of distress which will occur at the end of this age (cp. 5: 1–12; 6: 18b–28; 9: 1–13). Strictly speaking, Ezra, who has just asked to be told the meaning of his dream, does not at this point know that the vision of the Man from the Sea refers to the Messiah. But it would be wrong to conclude from this inconsistency – as some older scholars did – that verses 16–24 do not belong to the original text. *But how much worse for those who do not survive!:* i.e. for those who die before the time of distress at the end of this age.

17–18. *what is in store in the last days:* the blessings of the messianic kingdom (cp. 7: 28). Those who die before the end will miss not only the distress, but also the reign of the Messiah which will follow.

19. *the terrible dangers and trials:* cp. the comment on verse 16 and the passages mentioned there.

20. It is preferable to survive to the period of distress, and to live through it, in order to enjoy the blessings of the messianic kingdom, than to die before the end.

21–4. Ezra is assured that the righteous who survive to the last days will be protected.

21. *he replied:* it is again left unclear whether it is the angel or God who answers Ezra; cp. the comment on 12: 10.

23. *the very person from whom the danger will then come:* i.e. the Messiah, who will not only destroy his enemies, but will at the same time protect the righteous who are to be the subjects of his kingdom. *those who have works and fidelity laid*

up to their credit with the Most High: cp. the comment on
7: [77].

24. The conclusion which Ezra had reached in verse 20
is confirmed.   ✳

THE INTERPRETATION OF THE VISION

'This is what the vision means: The man you saw   25
rising from the depths of the sea is he whom the Most   26
High has held in readiness through many ages; he will
himself deliver the world he has made, and determine
the lot of those who survive. As for the breath, fire, and   27
storm which you saw pouring from the mouth of the
man, so that without a spear or any weapon in his hand   28
he destroyed the hordes advancing to wage war against
him, this is the meaning: The day is near when the Most   29
High will begin to bring deliverance to those on earth.
Then men will all be filled with great alarm; they will   30, 31
plot to make war on one another, city on city, region on
region, nation on nation, kingdom on kingdom. When   32
this happens, and all the signs that I have shown you
come to pass, then my son will be revealed, whom you
saw as a man rising from the sea. On hearing his voice,   33
all the nations will leave their own territories and their
separate wars, and unite in a countless host, as you saw   34
in your vision, with a common intent to go and wage
war against him. He will take his stand on the summit   35
of Mount Zion, and Zion will come into sight before all   36
men, complete and fully built. This corresponds to the
mountain which you saw hewn out, not by the hand of
man. Then my son will convict of their godless deeds   37

the nations that confront him. This will correspond to
38 the storm you saw. He will taunt them with their evil
plottings and the tortures they are soon to endure. This
corresponds to the flame. And he will destroy them
without effort by means of[a] the law – and that is like
the fire.

39 'Then you saw him collecting a different company, a
40 peaceful one. They are the ten tribes which were taken
off into exile in the time of King Hoshea, whom Shalmaneser king of Assyria took prisoner. He deported them
beyond the River, and they were taken away into a
41 strange country. But then they resolved to leave the
country populated by the Gentiles and go to a distant
42 land never yet inhabited by man, and there at last to be
obedient to their laws, which in their own country they
43 had failed to keep. As they passed through the narrow
44 passages of the Euphrates, the Most High performed
miracles for them, stopping up the channels of the river
45 until they had crossed over. Their journey through that
region, which is called Arzareth, was long, and took a
46 year and a half. They have lived there ever since, until
47 this final age. Now they are on their way back, and once
more the Most High will stop the channels of the river
to let them cross.

48 'That is the meaning of the peaceful assembly that you
saw. With them too are the survivors of your own
people, all who are found inside my sacred boundary.
49 So then, when the time comes for him to destroy the
nations assembled against him, he will protect his people
50 who are left, and show them many prodigies.'

[a] by means of: *so one Vs.; Lat.* and.

'My lord, my master,' I asked, 'explain to me why the 51
man that I saw rose up out of the depths of the sea.' He 52
replied: 'It is beyond the power of any man to explore
the deep sea and discover what is in it; in the same way
no one on earth can see my son and his company until
the appointed day. Such then is the meaning of your 53
vision.

✻ In the interpretation the man from the sea is identified as
the Messiah (verses 25–6); he will destroy his enemies (verses
27–38) and gather together the tribes of Israel to participate
in his kingdom (verse 39–50). In a further question and
answer the fact that the man comes from the sea is explained
as indicating that the Messiah will remain hidden until the
time comes for him to act (verses 51–2).

25–6. *The man ... is he whom the Most High has held in
readiness through many ages:* i.e. the man is the pre-existent
Messiah; see the comment on 12: 31–3 and cp. verse 52.
he will himself deliver the world he has made: so the Latin, the
meaning being that God himself will deliver his world (cp.
verse 29). But other versions support a translation 'through
whom he will deliver the world he has made', and this corresponds better to the general sense of the chapter (the Latin
text is based on a misunderstanding of the original). The
thought here is that the Messiah will be God's agent in the
deliverance of the world. *and determine the lot of those who
survive:* the N.E.B. translation assumes that the subject of this
clause is the same as that of the previous clause, i.e. 'the Most
High'. But the text is perhaps better translated 'and he will
determine ... ', with the Messiah as the implied subject. The
Messiah will order the conditions of life for those who are
left to participate in his kingdom.

27–8. Cp. verses 9–11.

29–31. These verses have no counterpart in the vision, and
this is perhaps an indication that they are an addition to the

original text. They describe the signs of the end and, as such, are similar in character to 5: 1–12; 6: 18b–28; 9: 1–13, passages which are in fact alluded to in verse 32.

29. *The day is near:* cp. 5: 1; 6: 18b – the same words are used in the Latin in all three cases. *when the Most High will begin to bring deliverance to those on earth:* cp. verse 26 and the comment on that verse. The fact that God, rather than the Messiah, is seen here as the deliverer (cp. 1 Thess. 4: 14) is perhaps a further indication that verses 29–31 are an addition.

30. *Then men will all be filled with great alarm:* cp. 5: 1.

31. *they will plot to make war on one another, city on city, region on region, nation on nation, kingdom on kingdom:* probably based on Isa. 19: 2:

> 'I will set Egyptian against Egyptian,
>   and they shall fight one against another,
>   neighbour against neighbour,
> city against city and kingdom against kingdom'.

Cp. Mark 13: 8 (and parallels), part of the Marcan account of the signs of the end, 'For nation will make war upon nation, kingdom upon kingdom.'

32. *and all the signs that I have shown you come to pass:* see the comment on verses 29–31. *then my son will be revealed:* cp. 7: 28 and see the comment on that verse. As we have seen (p. 169), the use of 'my son' as a title for the Messiah may reflect Christian influence, but the messianic interpretation of Ps. 2 leaves open the possibility that this is a Jewish title.

33–4. Cp. verses 4–5 and the comment on verse 5. Cp. also Zech. 14: 2 and Rev. 16: 14–16, 'These spirits . . . were sent out to muster all the kings of the world for the great day of battle of God the sovereign Lord . . . So they assembled the kings at the place called in Hebrew Armageddon.'

35. *He will take his stand on the summit of Mount Zion:* cp. verse 6. The passage possibly draws its inspiration from Zech. 14: 4.

36. *and Zion will come into sight before all men, complete and fully built:* the pre-existent heavenly Jerusalem; cp. 7: 26;

10: 27, 38–59; Rev. 21: 2, 9–10. *the mountain which you saw hewn out, not by the hand of man:* cp. Dan. 2: 34, 45, and see the comment on verse 6.

37–8. Cp. verses 10–11. It is noticeable that the interpretation at this point diverges from the sense of the vision. In the vision the *storm, flame* and *fire* combine into one and burn up the enemies of the Messiah so that nothing is left 'but dust and ashes and a reek of smoke'. Here each of the three elements is given a separate allegorical interpretation. *my son will convict of their godless deeds the nations that confront him:* as in 12: 32–3 the Messiah is presented as a judge, rather than as a military leader (see the comment on the earlier passage). *And he will destroy them without effort by means of the law:* apparently the thought is of the law as the standard by which the Messiah will exercise judgement. *by means of:* so the Syriac version; the Latin 'and' is corrupt (see the N.E.B. footnote).

39–50. Cp. verses 12–13*a*. After destroying his enemies the Messiah will bring the ten northern tribes back to the land of Israel; this is a more specific expression of the common belief in the return to Israel in the last days of all dispersed Jews; cp. e.g. Isa. 27: 13; 2 Macc. 2: 18; Matt. 24: 31. At the time at which 2 Esdras 3–14 was written there seems to have been a certain amount of speculation as to the fate of the ten tribes. The deportation of the inhabitants of the northern kingdom to Assyria is described in 2 Kings 17: 1–23, and in verse 23 they are said to be still there. But the exiles from the north are not further mentioned in the Old Testament, and in practice it is likely that they were absorbed into the local population and lost their identity. However, the ideal of the twelve tribes was still maintained (cp. e.g. Matt. 19: 28), and at the end of the first century A.D. the belief is found that the exiled northern tribes were still in existence. Thus Josephus (*Antiquities* 11: 133), having mentioned the Jews (including some from the northern tribes) who returned to Jerusalem with Ezra, states: 'But the Israelite nation as a whole remained in the country. In this way has it come about that there are two tribes in Asia and Europe subject to the Romans, while until now there have been ten tribes beyond the Euphrates – countless myriads whose number cannot be ascertained' (Loeb Classical Library translation of Josephus, vol. 6, pp. 377, 379). So also in 2 Baruch the northern tribes to whom Baruch sends a letter are thought of as dwelling beyond the river Euphrates (77: 22; 78: 1). But the legend found in 2 Esdras 13: 39–50 goes beyond these references; it is an attempt to explain both the assumed existence of the ten tribes and their actual disappearance. The expectation of the return of the ten tribes which occurs here has a parallel in a debate between two rabbis, Aqiba and Eliezer, who were more or less contemporary with the author of 2 Esdras 3–14: the former held that the ten tribes would not return, the latter that they would (Mishnah, Sanhedrin 10: 3; see H. Danby, *The Mishnah*, p. 398). The legend of the ten tribes was subsequently further elaborated, but none of the speculation about their fate has any historical foundation.

40. *the ten tribes which were taken off into exile in the time of King Hoshea, whom Shalmaneser king of Assyria took prisoner:* cp. 2 Kings 17: 1–6. *beyond the River:* i.e. beyond the Euphrates – from a Palestinian standpoint on its eastern side; this was the area in which the places mentioned in 2 Kings 17: 6 lay. Cp. the references in Josephus and 2 Baruch given above.

41. *they resolved to . . . go to a distant land never yet inhabited by man:* this is meant to explain why the ten tribes were not to be found in any known land.

43. *the narrow passages of the Euphrates:* possibly a tributary of the Euphrates is meant, but where exactly is not clear.

44. *stopping up the channels of the river until they had crossed over:* a deliberate parallel seems to be intended with the miraculous crossings of the Red Sea (Exod. 14: 21–31) and of the Jordan (Josh. 3: 14–17), but the fact that a miracle was needed also serves to explain the inaccessibility of the area occupied by the ten tribes.

45. *Their journey through that region, which is called Arzareth, . . . took a year and a half:* a further indication of the remoteness of the land in which the ten tribes were supposed to dwell.

Arzareth: generally interpreted as a corruption of a Hebrew expression *'erets 'ahareth,* 'another land', which occurs in Deut. 29: 28, part of a passage which explains why the Jews were taken into exile, 'The LORD uprooted them from their soil in anger, in wrath and great fury, and banished them to another land, where they are to this day.' Deut. 29: 28 was used in the rabbinic debate mentioned in the note on verses 39–50, and it seems likely that the author of 2 Esdras 3–14 was also alluding to this passage (cp. also verse 40 where the N.E.B. 'a strange country' might also be translated 'another land').

46. *Now they are on their way back:* perhaps better translated 'Now they are about to come back.'

47. *once more the Most High will stop the channels of the river:* the crossing of the Euphrates will again be miraculous (see the comment on verse 44), and implicitly the return of the ten tribes is presented as a new exodus. Cp. Isa. 11: 15–16:

> 'The LORD will divide the tongue of the Egyptian sea
>   and wave his hand over the River
>   to bring a scorching wind;
>   he shall split it into seven channels
>   and let men go across dry-shod.
> So there shall be a causeway for the remnant of his people,
>   for the remnant rescued from Assyria,
> as there was for Israel when they came up out of Egypt.'

48. *the survivors of your own people:* i.e. those who have survived the destruction of the nations and the woes which will occur at the end of this age; cp. 7: 27–8; 9: 7–8. But the text of this verse is uncertain. The N.E.B. gives a possible interpretation of the Latin text which assumes that these survivors are to be distinguished from the ten tribes. However, the Syriac reads 'But those who survive of your people, who are found inside my sacred borders, will be saved', and thus does not make the same distinction. The other versions differ, and it is not clear what the original text was. *all who are found inside my sacred boundary:* the messianic kingdom will be based on the land of Israel; see the comments on 9: 8 and 12: 34.

49–50. A summary of the meaning of the vision. *his people*

who are left: presumably all Israel is meant, both the Jews
already in Palestine and the ten tribes. No mention is made
in the interpretation of the many other Jews who lived outside
Palestine, nor of gentile converts (cp. verse 13), but possibly
the ten tribes are intended in a symbolic way to include both
these groups. *and show them many prodigies:* the miracles that
will be experienced during the reign of the Messiah.

51–2. Further elucidation of a detail of the vision. *explain
to me why the man that I saw rose up out of the depths of the sea:*
cp. verses 1–3. *no one on earth can see my son and his company
until the appointed day:* the Messiah is already in existence (cp.
12: 32; 13: 25–6), but is kept hidden by God until the time
comes for his activity. See the comment on 12: 31–3 and the
passages from 1 Enoch quoted there which refer to the pre-
existence and the concealment of the Son of Man. *his company:* there is no mention in the vision of anyone accompanying the man from the sea, nor has there so far been any
mention of companions in the interpretation. But see 7: 28
and the comment on that passage. Presumably again either
angels or immortal men such as Enoch or Elijah (cp. 6: 26)
are meant. ✳

THE CONCLUSION OF THE VISION

The revelation has been given to you, and to you
54 alone, because you have given up your own affairs, and
devoted yourself entirely to mine, and to the study of my
55 law. You have taken wisdom as your guide in everything,
56 and called understanding your mother. That is why I
have given this revelation to you; there is a reward in
store for you with the Most High. In three days' time
I will speak with you again, and tell you some momen-
tous and wonderful things.'

57 So I went away to the field, giving worship and praise

to the Most High for the wonders he performed from
time to time and for his providential control of the 58
passing ages and what happens in them. There I remained
for three days.

* *53b–56a. The revelation has been given to you, and to you
alone:* Ezra's unique position, here attributed to his devotion
to the law and to wisdom, is again stressed, see the comments
on 6: 32–3 and 12: 36. As has already been suggested, statements such as this no doubt give an indication of how the
author regarded his own status. *You have taken wisdom as your
guide in everything, and called understanding your mother:* cp.
Prov. 7: 4:

> 'Call Wisdom your sister,
>   greet Understanding as a familiar friend'

there is a reward in store for you with the Most High: i.e. the
reward of life in the age to come; cp. 7: [77]; 8: 33.

56b. In three days' time I will speak with you again: the
pattern of a week's interval between each revelation is broken
for a second time; see the comment on 10: 58–9. Why this
should be so is not clear, although it is unlikely that it is to be
explained, as was at one time suggested, in terms of the use
within 2 Esdras 3–14 of different sources. Perhaps the shorter
interval is an external indication that the cycle of revelations
is about to reach its climax.

57–8. Transition to the seventh section. *So I went away to
the field:* so the Latin version (literally 'So I set out and went
to the field'), but since Ezra is already in the field (cp. 9: 26;
12: 51), we should perhaps follow the reading of the Syriac
and Ethiopic: 'So I set out and walked through the field.'
*and for his providential control of the passing ages and what
happens in them:* the determinism characteristic of many apocalyptic writings is again stressed; cp. the comment on
4: 37. *

The writing of the sacred books

✵ The last section of 2 Esdras 3–14 differs completely from
the previous six. It consists of a legend which describes how
Ezra, warned of the approaching end of his life, asked to be
given the inspiration to restore the scriptures (both the books
of the Old Testament and the apocalyptic books), and how
he subsequently did this. The purpose of this legend is to
explain how the scriptures, and more particularly the apocalyptic writings (see pp. 105–8), survived the fall of Jerusalem
in 587 B.C. and were thus available at the time at which
2 Esdras 3–14 was written, i.e. the end of the first century A.D.
It represents, in other words, an attempt to give authority
to the apocalypses by presenting them as genuinely ancient
writings. The apocalyptic literature was ultimately rejected
by the Jews, and 2 Esdras 14 reflects a situation in which the
authority of this literature was already being questioned. The
legend builds upon the Old Testament tradition that Ezra
established the law as the basis of the life of the community
after the exile (Neh. 8), but it differs considerably from this
tradition. ✵

EZRA IS TOLD TO PREPARE FOR THE END OF HIS LIFE

14 ON THE THIRD DAY I was sitting under an oak-tree,
when a voice came to me from a bush, saying,
2 'Ezra, Ezra!' 'Here I am, Lord', I answered, and rose to
3 my feet. The voice went on: 'I revealed myself in the
bush, and spoke to Moses, when my people Israel was in
4 slavery in Egypt, and sent him to lead my people out of
Egypt. I brought him up on to Mount Sinai, and kept
5 him with me for many days. I told him of many won-

ders, showing him the secrets of the ages and the end of time, and instructed him what to make known and what [6] to conceal. So too I now give this order to you: commit [7, 8] to memory the signs I have shown you, the visions you have seen, and the explanations you have been given. You yourself are about to be taken away from the world [9] of men, and thereafter you will remain with my son and with those like you, until the end of time. The world has [10] lost its youth, and time is growing old. For the whole of [11] time is in twelve divisions; nine[a] divisions and half the tenth have already passed, and only two and a half still [12] remain. Set your house in order, therefore; give warnings [13] to your nation, and comfort to those in need of it; and take your leave of mortal life. Put away your earthly [14] cares, and lay down your human burdens; strip off your weak nature, set aside the anxieties that vex you, and be [15] ready to depart quickly from this life. However great [16] the evils you have witnessed, there are worse to come. As this ageing world grows weaker and weaker, so will [17] evils increase for its inhabitants. Truth will move farther [18] away, and falsehood come nearer. The eagle that you saw in your vision is already on the wing.'

✻ 1. *On the third day:* cp. 13: 56, 58. *a voice came to me from a bush, saying, 'Ezra, Ezra!':* cp. Exod. 3: 4, 'When the LORD saw that Moses had turned aside to look, he called to him out of the bush, "Moses, Moses."' In accordance with his role as the restorer of the scriptures Ezra is presented as a second Moses. This is indicated in verse 1 by the fact that God speaks to Ezra from a bush, and by the repetition of Ezra's name, and

[a] *Probable reading; Lat.* ten.

is made explicit in verses 3–8 by the parallel that is drawn between Moses and Ezra.

2. '*Here I am, Lord*', *I answered:* cp. Exod. 3: 4, 'And Moses answered, "Yes, I am here."'

3–4a. A summary of Exod. 3: 1–12.

4b. *I brought him up on to Mount Sinai, and kept him with me for many days:* cp. Exod. 24: 18 (with its sequel in 31: 18); 34: 28.

5. *I told him of many wonders, showing him the secrets of the ages and the end of time:* this is hardly a summary of the legislation in the Pentateuch given at Mount Sinai; rather it presents Moses as the recipient of apocalyptic visions. There are a number of works associated with the name of Moses which were composed in the Christian era, and of these we know of at least one that is apocalyptic in character, namely the Assumption of Moses (see p. 108 and R. H. Charles, *Apocrypha and Pseudepigrapha*, vol. 2, pp. 407–24; the Assumption dates from the beginning of the first century A.D.). The author of 2 Esdras 3–14 no doubt had in mind such works as the Assumption of Moses in his statement in verse 5, but his words also seem intended to claim the authority of Moses for apocalyptic literature generally.

6. *and instructed him what to make known and what to conceal:* the laws contained in the Pentateuch and the apocalyptic writings. The concealment of the latter is part of the apocalyptic fiction which is intended to explain how these supposedly ancient writings only became known long after they were composed; cp. verses 26, 46 and the comment on 12: 37.

8. *commit to memory:* perhaps better 'keep in your mind'. But in any case the implication is that, like Moses, he is not to make public the secret revelations he has received. *the signs . . . the visions . . . the explanations:* i.e. what is contained in chs. 3–13.

9. *You yourself are about to be taken away from the world of men:* Ezra's life is about to end, not through death, but

through his being 'translated' to heaven. The Old Testament records that two particularly pious men were 'carried away to another life without passing through death' (Heb. 11: 5), namely Enoch (Gen. 5: 24) and Elijah (2 Kings 2: 11), and the same fate is here attributed to Ezra. The actual 'translation' is described in the oriental versions at the end of the chapter, but the passage is not present in the Latin version, and so is not given in the N.E.B. *my son:* the pre-existent Messiah; cp. 7: 28; 13: 32. *those like you:* those already translated to heaven. *until the end of time:* i.e. until the end of the present age.

10–12. The thought of the end of this age leads to a comment that the end will not be all that long delayed. *The world has lost its youth, and time is growing old:* cp. 5: 50–5 and the comment on that passage. *For the whole of time is in twelve divisions:* the division of history into a set number of ages is a common characteristic of apocalyptic writings; cp. the idea, found in Dan. 7 and carried over into 2 Esdras 11–12 (e.g. 11: 39; 12: 11), that there were to be four empires between the exile and the end of this world. *nine divisions and half the tenth have already passed, and only two and a half still remain:* the text is uncertain at this point. The N.E.B. follows the Latin, but with one plausible correction (see the footnote); other versions either omit verses 11–12, or are rather different. The essential point is that the world is nearer its end than its beginning (cp. 4: 48–50).

13. *Set your house in order, therefore:* in view of his impending 'translation' to heaven Ezra is to give his last instructions; cp. verses 27–36. This motif is traditional; it is recorded of several great men in the Old and New Testaments that, shortly before the end of their lives, they gave a last speech or testament; cp. e.g. the speech of Paul to the Ephesian elders in Acts 20: 18–35. *your house:* the house of Israel, *your nation.*

14–15. As further preparation for the end of his life Ezra is to put on one side all the troubles which oppress him.

16–18. Because he is to be taken away from this world,

Ezra will escape the evils which will occur as this age approaches its end. *However great the evils you have witnessed:* the events of the Jewish war of A.D. 66–73 were no doubt primarily in the author's mind. *there are worse to come:* i.e. what are elsewhere described as the 'signs' of the end; cp. 5: 1–12; 6: 18b–28; 9: 1–13. *As this ageing world grows weaker and weaker:* cp. verse 10. *Truth will move farther away, and falsehood come nearer:* cp. 5: 9b–11 and contrast 6: 27–8 which describes the conditions which will apply in the new age. *The eagle that you saw in your vision is already on the wing:* i.e. the Roman Empire already holds power, a sign that the end of this age is near (cp. chs. 11–12). This statement does not, of course, relate to the time of Ezra, but to the time in which the author of 2 Esdras 3–14 lived. ✻

EZRA'S CONCERN TO RESTORE THE SCRIPTURES

19, 20 'May I speak[a] in your presence, Lord?' I replied. 'I am to depart, by your command, after giving warning to those of my people who are now alive. But who will give warning to those born hereafter? The world is shrouded in darkness, and its inhabitants are without
21 light. For your law was destroyed in the fire, and so no one can know about the deeds you have done or intend
22 to do. If I have won your favour, fill me with your holy spirit, so that I may write down the whole story of the world from the very beginning, everything that is contained in your law; then men will have the chance to find the right path, and, if they choose, gain life in the last days.'
23 'Go,' he replied, 'call the people together, and tell
24 them not to look for you for forty days. Have a large

[a] May I speak: *so other Vss.; Lat. omits.*

number of writing-tablets ready, and take with you
Seraiah and Dibri, Shelemiah, Ethan, and Asiel, five men
all trained to write quickly. Then return here, and I will 25
light a lamp of understanding in your mind, which will
not go out until you have finished all that you are to
write. When your work is complete, some of it you must 26
make public; the rest you must give to wise men to keep
secret. Tomorrow at this time you shall begin to write.'

✶ 19–22. Ezra acknowledges his responsibility to speak to
those who were then alive, but is concerned as to what will
happen in the future. The scriptures had been destroyed, and
he asks to be given the inspiration to restore them.

20. *after giving warning to those of my people who are now
alive:* cp. the command to do this in verse 13 and the speech
in verses 27–36. *The world is shrouded in darkness, and its
inhabitants are without light:* because the illumination provided
by God's law no longer exists – the reason for this is made
clear in the following verse. For the idea of the law as a light
cp. Ps. 19: 8*b*:

> 'The commandment of the LORD shines clear
>   and gives light to the eyes.'

21. *For your law was destroyed in the fire:* the author assumes
that the law was lost in the fire which destroyed the temple
and the rest of Jerusalem in 587 B.C.; cp. 2 Kings 25: 8–9,
'Nebuzaradan, captain of the king's bodyguard, came to
Jerusalem and set fire to the house of the LORD.' *and so no one
can know about the deeds you have done or intend to do:* an
allusion to the narrative and prophetic portions of the Old
Testament. In this chapter 'law' is used in a loose sense to
refer to the Old Testament scriptures generally (for a similar
use cp. John 15: 25; 1 Cor. 14: 21).

22. *If I have won your favour:* see the comment on 5: 56.
the whole story of the world from the very beginning, everything

that is contained in your law: here it is quite clear that 'law' is being used in a very general sense.

23–6. Ezra is given instructions to restore the scriptures.

23. *and tell them not to look for you for forty days:* Ezra is again presented as a second Moses (see the comment on verse 1). Just as Moses spent forty days on Mount Sinai when he received the law (cp. Exod. 24: 18; 34: 28; Deut. 9: 9), so Ezra is to spend forty days in the restoration of the scriptures.

24. *Seraiah and Dibri, Shelemiah, Ethan, and Asiel, five men:* the names can all be found in the Old Testament, but not as a group belonging to the time of Ezra. There may be some significance in the fact that *five men* are mentioned inasmuch as it is possible that there is an allusion here to the five famous disciples of Rabban Joḥanan ben Zakkai, the man largely responsible for the survival of Judaism in the period after the fall of Jerusalem in A.D. 70. The five disciples are mentioned in the Mishnah, Aboth 2: 8; see H. Danby, *The Mishnah*, p. 448, or R. H. Charles, Aboth 2: 10 in *Apocrypha and Pseudepigrapha of the Old Testament*, vol. 2, p. 696.

25. *Then return here:* i.e. to the field; cp. 13: 57.

26. *some of it you must make public:* the books of the Old Testament. *the rest you must give to wise men to keep secret:* the apocalyptic writings; see verse 6 and the comment on 12: 37. *wise men:* as we have already observed, the apocalyptic books are only for the learned, not the general public; cp. verses 46–7 and the comment on 8: 62. ✳

EZRA'S LAST WORDS TO THE PEOPLE

27 I went as I was ordered and summoned all the people,
28, 29 and said: 'Israel, listen to what I say. Our ancestors lived originally in Egypt as foreigners. They were rescued from
30 that land, and were given the law which offers life. But they disobeyed it, and you have followed their example.
31 Then you were given a land of your own, the land of

Zion; but you, like your ancestors, sinned and abandoned
the way laid down for you by the Most High. Because 32
he is a just judge he took away from you in due time
what he had given. And so you are now here in exile, 33
and your fellow-countrymen are still farther away. If 34
then you will direct your understanding and instruct your
minds, you shall be kept safe in life and meet with mercy
after you die. For after death will come the judgement; 35
we shall be restored to life, and then the names of the just
will be known and the deeds of the godless exposed.
From this moment no one must come to talk to me, nor 36
look for me for the next forty days.'

* As commanded, Ezra summons the people and tells them
not to seek him for forty days (verses 27, 36; cp. verse 23).
But the speech also provides the opportunity for Ezra to give
his last instructions (verses 28–35; cp. verse 13), and in this
respect it has a significant place in the structure of 2 Esdras
3–14. The speech consists of a summary of the main events of
Israel's history from the time in Egypt to the exile, and as
such it seems intended to provide a deliberate contrast to the
summary given in the prayer with which 2 Esdras 3–14 begins.
In ch. 3 Ezra blamed God for the situation in which Israel
found herself, but here the exile is accepted as being the fully
merited punishment for Israel's sin, and God is called a 'just
judge' (verses 29–33). Furthermore, whereas ch. 3 ended on
a note of despair, this speech ends on a note of hope (verses
34–5).

Ezra's words refer ostensibly to the situation which existed
after 587 B.C., but what is really in mind is the situation after
A.D. 70. The contrast between the opening and closing sections
of 2 Esdras 3–14 is a clear indication of the way in which the
attitude of the author has changed (see above pp. 219); he now

acknowledges the reality and the justice of the disaster of A.D. 70, but holds out to his readers hope for the future.

27. Cp. verse 23.

30. *and were given the law which offers life:* cp. 3: 17–22; 5: 27; 9: 30–1. The gift of the law was intended to provide the means of salvation (participation in the life of the age to come), but Israel failed to observe it. For the law as the source of life cp. Ecclus. 17: 11; 45: 5.

31. *Then you were given a land of your own:* the people are addressed as if they were the generation which received the gift of the land of Palestine.

32. *Because he is a just judge:* contrast the complaints uttered in 3: 28–36.

33. *And so you are now here in exile:* i.e. in Babylon, the place in which the book is supposedly set (cp. 3: 1). *and your fellow-countrymen are still farther away:* the ten northern tribes; cp. 13: 40–7.

34–5. *If then you will direct your understanding and instruct your minds:* despite the difficulties of the situation, if the people discipline their lives, there is still hope. *you shall be kept safe in life:* the Latin text could also be translated 'you shall be kept alive'; in this case the reference would be to life in the age to come. *and meet with mercy after you die:* i.e. at the judgement. *For after death will come the judgement; we shall be restored to life:* for the resurrection and the judgement see 7: 31–[44]. *and the deeds of the godless exposed:* cp. 7: 35.

36. Cp. verse 23. ✻

THE RESTORATION OF THE SCRIPTURES

37 I took with me the five men as I had been told, and we
38 went away to the field, and there we stayed. On the next day I heard a voice calling me, which said: 'Ezra, open
39 your mouth and drink what I give you.' So I opened my mouth, and was handed a cup full of what seemed like

water, except that its colour was the colour of fire. I took 40
it and drank, and as soon as I had done so my mind began
to pour forth a flood of understanding, and wisdom grew
greater and greater within me, for I retained my memory
unimpaired. I opened my mouth to speak, and I con- 41
tinued to speak unceasingly. The Most High gave under- 42
standing to the five men, who took turns at writing down
what was said, using characters[a] which they had not
known before. They remained at work through the forty
days, writing all day, and taking food only at night. But 43
as for me, I spoke all through the day; even at night I was
not silent. In the forty days, ninety-four[b] books were 44
written. At the end of the forty days the Most High 45
spoke to me. 'Make public the books you wrote first,'
he said, 'to be read by good and bad alike. But the last 46
seventy books are to be kept back, and given to none
but the wise among your people. They contain a stream 47
of understanding, a fountain of wisdom, a flood of knowledge.' And I did so. 48

✶ Ezra carries out the instructions which had been given to
him and, under divine inspiration, miraculously restores the
scriptures.

37. *I took with me the five men as I had been told:* cp. verse 24.
and we went away to the field: i.e. Ardat (9: 26); cp. verse 25.

38–41. Ezra had prayed for inspiration, and this is now
granted to him (cp. verses 22, 25). He is told to drink a cup of
liquid which fills him with understanding and wisdom and
enables him to dictate the scriptures.

39. *a cup full of what seemed like water:* the description of the
means of inspiration is unique, but may perhaps be compared

[a] *Probable reading, based on other Vss.; Lat. corrupt.*
[b] *So other Vss.; Lat. corrupt.*

with Ezek. 2: 8 – 3: 3 (Ezekiel is inspired to prophesy by eating a scroll) and Rev. 10: 8–11. *except that its colour was the colour of fire:* the fire is possibly intended to symbolize the spirit; cp. verse 22 and Acts 2: 3–4, 'And there appeared to them tongues like flames of fire ... And they were all filled with the Holy Spirit.'

42. The five men are also given inspiration which enables them to copy out the scriptures at Ezra's dictation. *using characters which they had not known before:* an allusion to the Jewish tradition that Ezra was the inventor of the square Hebrew letters which are still in use today. *the forty days:* cp. verse 23.

43. *even at night I was not silent:* in order to complete the work within the forty-day period.

44–7. Ninety-four books are copied at Ezra's dictation, but of these only the first twenty-four are to be made public; cp. verse 26.

45. *Make public the books you wrote first:* the books of the Old Testament. Their number (twenty-four – the Syriac version actually gives this figure, but the number is in any case clear from the context; see verse 46) reflects the arrangement of the Hebrew Bible, namely the five books of the Pentateuch, the eight books of the Prophets (Joshua, Judges, Samuel, Kings, Isaiah, Jeremiah, Ezekiel, the Twelve Minor Prophets [counted as one]) and the eleven books of the Writings (Psalms, Job, Proverbs, Ruth, the Song of Songs, Ecclesiastes, Lamentations, Esther, Daniel, Ezra–Nehemiah [counted as one], Chronicles); see in this series, *The Making of the Old Testament*, pp. 105–32.

46. *But the last seventy books are to be kept back, and given to none but the wise among your people:* the apocalyptic writings; see verses 6 and 26 and the comments on both passages.

47. *They contain a stream of understanding, a fountain of wisdom, a flood of knowledge:* these words are important inasmuch as they give some indication of the way in which the author

regarded the apocalyptic writings; for him they were in some sense a form of wisdom.

48. *And I did so:* after these words the Syriac version adds

'in the seventh year, in the sixth week, after five thousand years of creation and three months and twelve days. And at that time Ezra was carried away and taken to the place of those who are like him, after he had written all these things. He was called the scribe of the knowledge of the Most High for ever and ever.'

A similar ending is found in all but one of the other oriental versions of 2 Esdras 3–14, and it is likely that the ending was omitted from the Latin version when chs. 15 and 16 were added to 2 Esdras 3–14. For the 'translation' of Ezra to heaven see the comment on verse 9.   ✻

2 ESDRAS 15–16

Prophecies of doom

✻   We have already seen that chs. 15 and 16, often referred to in modern writings as 6 Ezra, do not belong with chs. 3–14, but are a quite separate work (see pp. 76–7). The origin of these chapters is, however, not entirely clear. They seem to have been deliberately composed as an appendix to 2 Esdras 3–14, although there is some evidence to suggest that they also circulated independently. But it would appear not un-likely that the author of this appendix took over and adapted for his purposes traditions that were already in existence. In form these chapters consist of a series of prophecies which are only loosely strung together and in which there is no attempt to develop a sustained argument. The prophecies imitate the style of, and draw their inspiration from, Old

Testament prophecy. As in the case of chs. 1 and 2, chs. 15 and 16 have survived in their entirety only in Latin. The indications are, however, that these chapters were composed in Greek, and were written as an appendix to chs. 3–14 when the latter had already been translated into Greek. A papyrus fragment containing a Greek text of 15: 57–9 has been found.

The background to 2 Esdras 15–16 is a period of persecution; the author threatens judgement to the oppressors and attempts to comfort and encourage those who are being persecuted. These latter are apparently Christians, and the work is apparently a Christian composition, but although there are a number of parallels with the New Testament, the Christian colouring is not very marked. However, in its present form it does seem likely that 2 Esdras 15–16 is a Christian work, and its character is perhaps to be explained – as was hinted above – by the assumption that the Christian author made use of already existing Jewish traditions; but if this is correct, neither the date nor the place of composition of 2 Esdras 15–16 is very clear. Christians were subjected to persecution at various times throughout the second and third centuries, and a date at any time within this period is theoretically possible. But allusions have been detected, particularly in 15: 28–33, which make it seem likely that they were composed in the latter part of the third century. The place of composition is more difficult to determine. References to events in the east suggest the eastern part of the Roman Empire; it is not possible to be more precise. ✳

GOD'S VENGEANCE ON THE WICKED

15 PROCLAIM TO MY PEOPLE the words of prophecy
2 which I give you to speak, says the Lord; and have
them written down, because they are trustworthy and
3 true. Have no fear of plots against you, and do not be
4 troubled by the unbelief of those who oppose you. For

everyone who does not believe will die because of his unbelief.[a]

Beware, says the Lord, I am letting loose terrible evils 5 on the world, sword and famine, death and destruction, because wickedness has spread over the whole earth and 6 there is no room for further deeds of violence. Therefore 7 the Lord says, I will not keep silence about their godless 8 sins; I will not tolerate their wicked deeds. See how the blood of innocent victims cries to me for vengeance, and the souls of the just never cease to plead with me! I will 9 most surely avenge them, says the Lord, and will hear the plea of all the innocent blood that has been shed. My people are being led to the slaughter like sheep. I will 10 no longer allow them to remain in Egypt, but will use 11 all my power to rescue them; I will strike the Egyptians with plagues, as I did before, and destroy their whole land. How Egypt will mourn, shaken to its very founda- 12 tions, when it is scourged and chastised by the Lord! How 13 the tillers of the soil will mourn, when the seed fails to grow, and when their trees are devastated by blight and hail and terrible storm![b] Alas for the world and its inhabi- 14 tants! The sword that will destroy them is not far away. 15 Nation will draw sword against nation and go to war. Stable government will be at an end; one faction will 16 prevail over another, caring nothing in their day of power for king or leading man of rank. A man may want 17 to visit a city, but will not be able to do so; for ambition 18 and rivalry will have reduced cities to chaos, destroyed houses, and filled men with panic. A man will violently 19 assault his neighbour's house and plunder his goods; no

[a] Or *in his unbelief.*   [b] *Probable meaning; Lat. obscure.*

pity will restrain him, when he is in the grip of famine and grinding misery.

20 See how I summon before me all the kings of the earth, says God, from sunrise and south wind, from east and south,[a] to turn back and repay what they have been
21 given. I will do to them as they are doing to my chosen people even to this day; I will pay them back in their own coin.

22 These are the words of the Lord God: I will show sinners no pity; the sword will not spare those murderers
23 who stain the ground with innocent blood. The Lord's anger has overflowed in fire to scorch the earth to its foundations and consume sinners like burning straw.
24 Alas for sinners who flout my commands! says the Lord;
25 I will show them no mercy. Away from me, you rebels!
26 Do not bring your pollution near my holiness. The Lord well knows all who sin against him, and has consigned
27 them to death and destruction. Already disaster has fallen upon the world, and you will never escape it; God will refuse to rescue you, because you have sinned against him

✶ 1–4. The person addressed is instructed to announce the prophetic message which God gives to him.

1. *Proclaim to my people the words of prophecy:* the person addressed is commissioned as a prophet; cp. 1: 1; 12: 42, and see p. 77. *which I give to you to speak:* literally 'which I will place in your mouth'; cp. Jer. 1: 9.

2. *and have them written down:* the command to have the prophecies written down appears to build on the theme of ch. 14 and was perhaps intended to provide a link between chs. 15–16 and chs. 3–14. *because they are trustworthy and true:* cp. Rev. 21: 5.

3. *Have no fear of plots against you:* cp. Jer. 1: 7–8.

[a] south: *probable reading; Lat.* Lebanon.

5–19. God is about to take vengeance on the wicked because of their persecution of the innocent; in consequence the world will be overwhelmed by chaos and destruction.

8. *See how the blood of innocent victims cries to me for vengeance:* cp. Gen. 4: 10, 'The LORD said, "What have you done? Hark! your brother's blood that has been shed is crying out to me from the ground"'; cp. also Rev. 6: 10.

10*a*. *My people are being led to the slaughter like sheep:* cp. Ps. 44: 22; Isa. 53: 7.

10*b*–13. God will deliver his people from Egypt and once more afflict the land *with plagues.* It is often thought that the immediate occasion for the prophecy contained in these verses was the occurrence in Alexandria of a devastating plague which followed shortly after a period of war and famine. These events took place during the reign of the Emperor Gallienus (260–8) and are mentioned in Eusebius, *Ecclesiastical History*, VII.21.22 (see H. J. Lawlor and J. E. L. Oulton, *Eusebius. The Ecclesiastical History* (London, 1927–8), vol. 1, pp. 232–4). However, the deliverance from Egypt and the plagues are presented as a repetition of God's action on behalf of his people at the time of the exodus. *but will use all my power to rescue them:* literally 'but will bring them out with a strong hand and an outstretched arm'; in the Old Testament the expression 'with a strong hand and an outstretched arm' is used several times in reference to God's deliverance of his people from Egypt; cp. e.g. Deut. 4: 34.

14–19. The reference to judgement on Egypt leads into a description of the chaos that will overtake the earth as the end approaches. This passage, in common with other passages in chs. 15 and 16, is similar to the descriptions of the signs of the end in the gospels (cp. Mark 13 and parallels) and in 2 Esdras 3–14 itself (cp. e.g. 5: 1–12).

15. *Nation will draw sword against nation and go to war:* cp. 13: 31; Matt. 24: 7.

18. *for ambition and rivalry will have ... filled men with panic:* cp. 13: 30; Luke 21: 26.

19. Cp. 6: 24.

20–7. The theme of judgement is continued. Verses 20–1 are directed specifically at 'the kings of the earth' who persecute God's chosen people; they are to be repaid in kind for their deeds. Verses 22–7 refer to two groups: the sinners who shed innocent blood (verses 22–3, cp. verses 7–10) and apostates (verses 24–7).

25. *rebels:* literally 'apostate sons' – it is presumably Christian apostates who are meant. ✴

A HORRIBLE VISION

28 How terrible the sight of what is coming from the
29 east! Hordes of dragons from Arabia will sally forth with countless chariots, and from the first day of their advance their hissing will spread across the land, to fill all who hear
30 them with fear and consternation. The Carmanians, mad with rage, will rush like wild boars out of the forest, advancing in full force to join battle with them, and will
31 devastate whole tracts of Assyria with their tusks. But then the dragons will summon up their native fury, and will prove the stronger. They will rally and join forces,
32 and fall on them with overwhelming might until they are routed, until their power is silenced, and every one
33 of them turns to flight. Then their way will be blocked by a lurking enemy from Assyria, who will destroy one of them. Fear and panic will spread in their army, and wavering among their kings.

✴ This section of 2 Esdras 15–16 has often been thought to allude, in a cryptic style similar to that of Dan. 11, to specific events of the third century (and thereby to provide an approximate date for the composition of these two chapters). Under the Sassanid king Shapur I (240–73) the Persians made a series of attacks on the Roman province of Syria, and in 260 they again overran the area; Shapur conquered Antioch for a third time and was able to pursue his campaign into Asia Minor. However, Shapur was not completely successful and on his return he was defeated in battle by the forces of the city of Palmyra under the leadership of Odenathus. For this and for other services Odenathus was given various honours by the Emperor Gallienus and was placed in overall control of Roman forces in the east. But he was murdered by a relative in 267, and his wife Zenobia effectively assumed power.

29. *Hordes of dragons from Arabia:* the Palmyrene forces under Odenathus. It is a little surprising that these are mentioned first, since the attack of Odenathus came after Shapur's campaign (verse 30). The dragon symbolism was possibly suggested by the idea that the wilderness was the home of snakes and serpents; cp. Deut. 8: 15; Isa. 30: 6.

30. *The Carmanians:* the Persian forces under Shapur I. Carmania (Kirman) was the name of the southern province of the Parthian Empire, the region from which the Sassanid dynasty came. *Assyria:* here a symbolic name for Syria.

31–2. The defeat of Shapur by the forces of Odenathus.

33. *Then their way will be blocked by a lurking enemy from Assyria, who will destroy one of them:* apparently an allusion to the murder of Odenathus.   *

JUDGEMENT ON BABYLON

See the clouds stretching from east and north to south! 34
Their appearance is hideous, full of fury and tempest.
They will clash together, they will pour over the land a 35
vast storm;[a] blood, shed by the sword, will reach as high
as a horse's belly, a man's thigh, or a camel's hock. Terror 36, 37
and trembling will cover the earth; all who see the raging
fury will shudder and be stricken with panic. Then vast 38

[a] storm: *probable meaning; Lat. obscure.*

storm-clouds will approach from north and south, and
39 others from the west. But the winds from the east will
be stronger still, and will hold in check the raging cloud
and its leader; and the storm[a] which was bent on destruction will be fiercely driven back to the south and west
40 by the winds from the east. Huge mighty clouds, full of
fury, will mount up and ravage the whole land and its
inhabitants; a terrible storm[a] will sweep over the great
41 and the powerful, with fire and hail and flying swords;
and a deluge of water will flood all the fields and rivers.
42 They will flatten to the ground cities and walls, mountains and hills, trees in the woods and crops in the fields.
43 They will advance all the way to Babylon, and blot it
44 out. When they reach it, they will surround it, and let
loose a storm[a] in all its fury. The dust and smoke will
reach the sky, and all her neighbours will mourn for
45 Babylon. Any of her survivors will be enslaved by her
destroyers.

✻ Shapur's attacks on the Roman provinces in the east
coincided with attacks on the borders of the Roman Empire
in Europe by various groups of peoples, of which the Goths
represented the most serious danger, and for a time the
empire, which had been seriously weakened internally, must
have seemed to be on the point of collapse. It was against this
background that the prophecy in 2 Esdras 15: 34–45 appears
to have been composed. Using the image of storm-clouds the
author depicts the nations overwhelming the Roman Empire
and carrying their attack as far as Rome itself (verses 44–5).
In 2 Esdras 15–16, as in Revelation, Babylon is a symbol for
Rome (cp. Rev. 14: 8). It may be that specific historical

[a] storm: *probable meaning; Lat. obscure.*

events underlie some of the statements in this prophecy (e.g. in verses 38–9), but if so, it is not possible to identify these events precisely. It is, however, equally likely that the whole thing is to be read as a prophecy of the future; inspired by the events of his day, the author believed the end of the Roman Empire to be near at hand, and in symbolic language he described the way in which this would come about.

35. *as high as a horse's belly:* cp. Rev. 14: 20.
43. *Babylon:* i.e. Rome. ✳

JUDGEMENT ON ASIA

And you, Asia, who have shared the beauty and the 46 splendour of Babylon, alas for you, poor wretch! Like 47 her you have dressed up your daughters as whores, to attract and catch your lovers who have always lusted for you. You have copied all the schemes and practices of 48 that vile harlot. Therefore God says, I will bring upon 49 you terrible evils: widowhood and poverty, famine, sword, and plague, bringing ruin to your homes, bringing violence and death. Your strength and splendour will 50 wither like a flower, when that scorching heat bears down upon you. Then you will be a poor weak woman, 51 bruised, beaten, and wounded, unable to receive your wealthy lovers any more. Should I be so fierce with you, 52 says the Lord, if you had not killed my chosen ones 53 continually, gloating over the blows you struck them, and hurling your drunken taunts at their corpses?

Paint your face; make yourself beautiful! The harlot's 54, 55 pay shall be yours; you will get what you have earned. What you do to my chosen people, God will do to you, 56 says the Lord; he will consign you to a terrible fate. Your 57

children will die of hunger; you will fall by the sword, your cities will be blotted out, and all your people will
58 fall on the field of battle. Those who are up on the mountains will be dying of hunger, and their hunger and thirst will force them to gnaw their own flesh and drink
59 their own blood. You will be foremost in misery, and
60 still there will be more to come. As the victors go past on their way home from the sack of Babylon, they will smash your peaceful city, destroy a great part of your territory, and bring much of your splendour to an end.
61 They will destroy you – you will be stubble, and they
62 the fire. They will completely devour you and your cities, your land and your mountains, and will burn all
63 your forests and your fruit-trees. They will make your children prisoners and plunder your property; and not a trace will be left of your splendid beauty.

✳ The announcement of judgement on Babylon (Rome) is followed by the announcement of judgement on Asia; God will hand her over 'to a terrible fate' (verse 56) because of her persecution of his chosen people. In this passage 'Asia' has sometimes been thought to represent Palmyra under Odenathus and Zenobia, and it has been held that there are allusions here to the fate of this city which for a short time enjoyed considerable importance. We have already seen that after his defeat of Shapur I in 260 Odenathus, as an ally of Rome, achieved a position of power and influence in the east. He was murdered in 267, and his widow, Zenobia, took effective control of Palmyra. Her ambition eventually led her to attack Asia Minor and Egypt, but she was defeated by the forces of the Emperor Aurelian (270–5), and Palmyra was besieged and captured. It is possible that these events are alluded to here, and in particular that the fall of Palmyra

is referred to in verses 60–3. However, these verses make
better sense if they are read as a prophecy of a future judgement, and not as a cryptic account of past events. It is, furthermore, also possible that in this passage (15: 46–63) 'Asia' is
used to refer to the Roman Empire in the east, just as in 16: 1
Babylon, Asia, Egypt and Syria are used together to refer
to the totality of the Roman Empire. This passage can then
be understood as a prophecy of judgement on the provinces
in the east which follows not unnaturally on the prophecy of
judgement on Rome itself (15: 34–45).

47–8. Apparently inspired by Rev. 17: 4–5:

> 'The woman was clothed in purple and scarlet and be-
> dizened with gold and jewels and pearls. In her hand she
> held a gold cup, full of obscenities, and the foulness of her
> fornication; and written on her forehead was a name with a
> secret meaning: "Babylon the great, the mother of whores
> and of every obscenity on earth."'

Cp. also Rev. 14: 8; 18: 2–3.

49. Cp. Rev. 18: 7–8.

55. *The harlot's pay shall be yours:* possibly intended ironic-
ally – in the Old Testament death is the punishment for a
woman who became a prostitute; see Gen. 38: 24; Lev. 21: 9;
Deut. 22: 21.

56. Cp. verse 21.

60. *As the victors go past on their way home from the sack of
Babylon:* cp. verses 43–4. ✻

THE IRREVERSIBLE JUDGEMENT

Alas for you, Babylon and Asia! Alas for you, Egypt **16**
and Syria! Put on sackcloth and hair-shirt, and raise a 2
howl of lamentation for your sons; your doom is close
at hand. The sword is let loose against you, and who will 3
turn it aside? Fire is let loose upon you, and who will put 4

5 it out? Calamities have been let loose against you, and
6 who is there to stop them? Can any man stop a hungry
lion in a forest, or put out a fire among the stubble once
7 it has begun to blaze? Can any man stop an arrow shot
8 by a strong archer? When the Lord God sends calamities,
9 who can stop them? When his anger overflows in fire,
10 who can put it out? When the lightning flashes, who will
not tremble? When it thunders, who will not shake with
11 dread? When it is the Lord who utters his threats, is there
any man who will not be crushed to the ground at his
12 approach? The earth is shaken to its very foundations,
and the sea is churned up from its depths; the waves and
all the fish with them are in turmoil before the presence
13 of the Lord and the majesty of his strength. For strong is
his arm which bends the bow, and sharp the arrows which
he shoots; once they are on their way, they will not stop
14 before they reach the ends of the earth. Calamities are let
loose, and will not turn back before they strike the earth.
15 The fire is alight and will not be put out until it has burnt
16 up earth's foundations. An arrow shot by a powerful
archer does not turn back; no more will the calamities be
recalled which are let loose against the earth.

* The dominant theme of this passage is that the judgement
of God, which is seen already to have begun in various
disasters which are taking place, cannot be stopped, but must
run its course. The passage is addressed to Babylon, Asia,
Egypt and Syria, and these four serve here to represent the
entire Roman Empire. The disasters are described in such
vague terms that they cannot be related to a specific historical
situation. But it seems likely that this passage was written
against the general background of the period of internal

instability and external danger which overwhelmed the Roman Empire from the death of Alexander Severus (235) to the accession of Diocletian (284), and that it belongs to more or less the same time as the prophecies of judgement in ch. 15.

2. *Put on sackcloth and hair-shirt:* conventional signs of mourning; cp. e.g. 2 Sam. 3: 31.

6. *Can any man stop a hungry lion in a forest?:* cp. Amos 3: 8, 'The lion has roared; who is not terrified?' The chain of rhetorical questions in verses 3–11 is to some extent reminiscent of the chain of questions in Amos 3: 3–8.

12. Cp. 2 Sam. 22: 8, 16, and the parallel Ps. 18: 7, 15.

14. Cp. Jer. 30: 24.

15. Reflected here is the belief that at the judgement the earth will be consumed in fire; cp. e.g. 2 Pet. 3: 7, 10; the Hymns from Qumran, III.29–31:

> 'The torrents of Satan shall reach
>   to all sides of the world.
> In all their channels
>   a consuming fire shall destroy
>   every tree, green and barren, on their banks;
> unto the end of their courses
>   it shall scourge with flames of fire,
> and shall consume the foundations of the earth
>   and the expanse of dry land.
> The bases of the mountains shall blaze
>   and the roots of the rocks shall turn
>   to torrents of pitch;
> it shall devour as far as the great Abyss.'

(Translation from G. Vermes, *The Dead Sea Scrolls in English*, 2nd ed. (Harmondsworth, 1975), pp. 159–60) ✳

THE HORRORS OF THE LAST DAYS

17 Alas, alas for me! Who will rescue me on that day?
18 When troubles come, many will groan; when famine strikes, many will die; when wars break out, empires will tremble; when the calamities come, all will be filled with terror. What will men do then, in the face of calamity?
19 Famine and plague, suffering and hardship, are scourges
20 sent to teach men better ways. But even so they will not abandon their crimes, nor keep in mind their scourging.
21 A time will come when food grows cheap, so cheap that they will imagine they have been sent peace and prosperity. But at that very moment the earth will become
22 a hotbed of disasters – sword, famine, and anarchy. Most of its inhabitants will die in the famine; and those who
23 survive the famine will be destroyed by the sword. The dead will be tossed out like dung, and there will be no one to offer any comfort. For the earth will be left
24 empty, and its cities a ruin. None will be left to till the
25 ground and sow it. The trees will bear their fruits, but
26 who will pick them? The grapes will ripen, but who will tread them? There will be vast desolation everywhere.
27 A man will long to see a human face or hear a human
28 voice. For out of a whole city, only ten will survive; in the country-side, only two will be left, hiding in the
29 forest or in holes in the rocks. Just as in an olive-grove
30 three or four olives might be left on each tree, or as a few grapes in a vineyard might be overlooked by the
31 sharp-eyed pickers, so also in those days three or four will be overlooked by those who search the houses to
32 kill. The earth will be left a desert, and the fields will be

overrun with briers; thorns will grow over all the roads
and paths, because there will be no sheep to tread them.
Girls will live in mourning with none to marry them, 33
women will mourn because they have no husbands, their
daughters will mourn because they have no one to support them. The young men who should have married 34
them will be killed in the war, and the husbands wiped
out by the famine.

* The thought of judgement leads once again into a description of the horrors that will occur as the end approaches; see
the comment on 15: 14–19. The passage employs a number
of traditional motifs which are familiar from the Old and
New Testaments.

18b–20. *What will men do then, in the face of calamity?:* at
the moment of crisis men will not know how to respond.

19. *Famine and plague, suffering and hardship, are scourges sent
to teach men better ways:* the thought underlying such passages
as Amos 4: 6–12.

20. Cp. Hag. 2: 17.

21. A brief time of plenty just before the end will give men
a false sense of security; cp. Luke 12: 16–21.

22. For the thought cp. Isa. 24: 17–18a.

23. *The dead will be tossed out like dung:* cp. Jer. 9: 22.

28. *For out of a whole city, only ten will survive:* cp. Amos
5: 3. *in the country-side, only two will be left:* cp. Matt. 24: 40–1;
Luke 17: 34–5.

29–31. Apparently inspired by Isa. 17: 4–6:

'On that day Jacob's weight shall dwindle
　　and the fat of his limbs waste away,...
　　　　as when one beats an olive-tree
　　and only gleanings are left on it,
two or three berries on the top of a branch,
　　four or five on the boughs of the fruiting tree.'

32. Cp. Isa. 7: 23.

33–4. Cp. Jer. 7: 34; Rev. 18: 23.   ✷

ADVICE TO THE LORD'S SERVANTS
AS THE END APPROACHES

35 But listen to me, you who are the Lord's servants, and
36 take my words to heart. This is the word of the Lord.
37 Receive it, and do not disbelieve what he says. Calamities
38 are here, close at hand, and will not delay. When a pregnant woman is in the ninth month, and the moment of
her child's birth is drawing near, there will be two or
three hours in which her womb will suffer pangs of
agony, and then the child will come from the womb
39 without a moment's delay; in the same way calamities
will come on the earth without delay, and the world will
groan under the pangs that grip it.

40   Listen to my words, my people; get ready for battle,
and when the calamities surround you, be as though you
41 were strangers on earth. The seller must expect to have
42 to run for his life, the buyer to lose what he buys; the
merchant must expect to make no profit, the builder
43 never to live in the house he builds. The sower must not
44 expect to reap, nor the pruner to gather his grapes. Those
who marry must expect no children; the unmarried must
45 think of themselves as widowed. For all labour is labour
46 in vain. Their fruits will be gathered by foreigners, who
will plunder their goods, pull down their houses, and
take their children captive. If they have children, they
47 will have been bred only for captivity and famine; any
who make money do so only to have it plundered. The
more care they lavish on their cities, houses, and property,

298

and on their own persons, the fiercer will be my indig- 48
nation against their sins, says the Lord. Like the indig- 49
nation of a virtuous woman towards a prostitute, so will 50
be the indignation of justice towards wickedness with all
her finery; she will accuse her to her face, when the
champion arrives to expose all sin upon earth. Do not 51
imitate wickedness, therefore, and her actions. For in a 52
very short time she will be swept from the earth, and
the reign of justice over us will begin.

✳ 35-9. The Lord's servants are warned that the evils which
will precede the end of this age and the judgement of God are
about to take place, and that nothing will delay their occurrence.

37. *Calamities:* of the kind described in 15: 14-19; 16:
17-34.

38. The illustration from child-birth is a reminder that in
the New Testament the signs that precede the end are called
'the birth-pangs of the new age' (Matt. 24: 8; Mark 13: 8).
Cp. 4: 40; 1 Thess. 5: 3.

40-52. When the moment of crisis comes, God's people
must be prepared to act as though they 'were strangers on
earth' (verse 40), to dissociate themselves completely, that is,
from all the concerns of human life (verses 41-4). The reason
for this is that at that moment all labour will prove to be
worthless. The things for which men work will be taken from
them, and God's anger will be particularly roused against the
sins of those who lavish care on themselves and their property
(verses 45-8). The judgement will mark the end of wickedness
and the beginning of the reign of justice, and God's people
are warned not to 'imitate wickedness' (verses 49-52).

41-4. The thought resembles that of 1 Cor. 7: 29-31.
must expect to have to run for his life: 'must be ready to run for
his life' would better convey the sense (and similarly in the
following examples).

46. *Their fruits will be gathered by foreigners:* cp. Lev. 26: 16; Deut. 28: 33, 51.

50. *when the champion arrives to expose all sin upon earth:* literally 'when he comes who will vindicate him who exposes all sin upon earth' – a reference to the coming of God at the judgement. Both God and his agent (in the context we are no doubt meant to see an allusion to Jesus) will be involved in this. ✳

FURTHER ADVICE: SIN CANNOT BE HIDDEN FROM GOD

53 The sinner must not deny that he has sinned; he will only bring burning coals on to his own head if he says, 'I
54 have committed no sin against the majesty of God.' For the Lord knows all that men do; he knows their plans,
55 their schemes, and their inmost thoughts. He said, 'Let the earth be made', and it was made; and 'Let the heavens
56 be made', and they were made. It was by the Lord's word that the stars were fixed in their places; the number
57 of the stars is known to him. He looks into the depths with their treasures; he has measured the sea and every-
58 thing it contains. By his word he confined the sea within the bounds of the waters, and above the water he sus-
59 pended the land. He spread out the sky like a vault, and
60 made it secure upon the waters. He provided springs in the desert, and pools on the mountain-tops as the source
61 of rivers flowing down to water the earth. He created man, and placed a heart in the middle of his body; he
62 gave him spirit, life, and understanding, the very breath of Almighty God who created the whole world and
63 searches out secret things in secret places. He knows well
64 your plans and all your inward thoughts. Alas for sinners

who try to hide their sins! The Lord will scrutinize all
their deeds; he will call you all to account. You will be 65
covered with confusion, when your sins are brought
into the open, and your wicked deeds stand up to accuse
you on that day. What can you do? How can you hide 66
your sins from God and his angels? God is your judge:
fear him! Abandon your sins, and have done with your 67
wicked deeds for ever! Then God will set you free from
all distress.

* Sinners are advised not to attempt to deny that they have
sinned because nothing can be kept hidden from God, the
creator of the world. On the day of judgement all sins will be
exposed, and those who have tried to hide their sins will be
overcome with shame. The best policy is to abandon sin; the
man who does this will be kept safe by God.

53. *The sinner must not deny that he has sinned:* cp. 1 John 1: 8.
he will only bring burning coals on to his own head: a reinterpretation of Prov. 25: 22; cp. Rom. 12: 20.

54–63. God's omniscience is shown by the fact that he is
the creator of the world. The passage is very loosely based on
Gen. 1, but there are reminiscences of other Old Testament
passages as well.

54. *For the Lord knows all that men do:* cp. Ecclus. 15: 18–19;
39: 19.

55. *He said, 'Let the earth be made',* ... *'Let the heavens be
made':* not exact quotations, but cp. Gen. 1: 6–10.

56. *It was by the Lord's word that the stars were fixed in their
places:* cp. Gen. 1: 14–19. *the number of the stars is known to
him:* cp. Ps. 147: 4.

57. Cp. Job 38: 16.

58. *By his word he confined the sea within the bounds of the
waters:* cp. Gen. 1: 9; Job 38: 10–11; Prov. 8: 29. *and above
the water he suspended the land:* cp. Pss. 24: 1–2; 136: 6.

301

59. *He spread out the sky like a vault, and made it secure upon the waters:* cp. Gen. 1: 6–8. The idea that God 'stretched out the skies' occurs in a number of places in the Old Testament; cp. e.g. Isa. 44: 24.

60. *He provided springs in the desert:* cp. Ps. 107: 35.

61–2. *He created man:* cp. Gen. 1: 26–7. *he gave him spirit, life, and understanding, the very breath of Almighty God:* cp. Gen. 2: 7.

63. *He knows well your plans and all your inward thoughts:* an idea that finds frequent expression, in various different ways, in both the Old and the New Testaments; cp. e.g. Ps. 44: 21; Heb. 4: 12–13.

64–5. God will judge the sinners, and *on that day* of judgement there will be no possibility of hiding sin. ✶

ENCOURAGEMENT FOR THOSE WHO FACE PERSECUTION

68 Fierce flames are being kindled to burn you. A great horde will descend on you; they will seize some of you 69 and make you eat pagan sacrifices. Those who give in to 70 them will be derided, taunted, and trampled on. In place after place*a* and in all the neighbourhood there will be 71 a violent attack on those who fear the Lord. Their enemies will be like madmen, plundering and destroying 72 without mercy all who still fear the Lord. They will destroy and plunder their property, and throw them out 73 of their homes. Then it will be seen that my chosen people have stood the test like gold in the assayer's fire. 74 Listen, you whom I have chosen, says the Lord; the days of harsh suffering are close at hand, but I will rescue 75 you from them. Away with your fears and doubts! For

[a] In place after place: *possible meaning; Lat. obscure.*

God is your leader. You who follow my commandments 76
and instructions, says the Lord God, must not let your
sins weigh you down, nor your wicked deeds get the
better of you. Alas for those who are entangled in their 77
sins, and overrun with their wicked deeds! They are like
a field overrun by bushes, with brambles across the path
and no way through, completely shut off and doomed to 78
destruction by fire.

* As 2 Esdras 15–16 began with threats of judgement on
those who were persecuting God's people, so it ends with
encouragement for those who faced persecution.

68–73. The author warns that 'there will be a violent
attack on those who fear the Lord' (verse 70). Some will be
compelled to eat food that had been used in sacrifices, others
will be driven from their homes. The only consolation is that
the persecution will show the true quality of those who remain
faithful. It has sometimes been thought that these verses were
written in the light of events that had already occurred, and
they certainly give that impression. More specifically, it has
been suggested that it was the persecution of Decius in the
year 250 that was in the mind of the author, but the evidence
is insufficient to determine whether this is so or not.

68. *pagan sacrifices:* literally 'that which has been sacrificed
to idols'. The eating of food that had been used in pagan
sacrifices posed a problem at various times to both Jews and
Christians; cp. e.g. 2 Macc. 6: 7–9, 21; Acts 15: 20; 1 Cor. 8.
In the persecution of Decius Christians were commanded to
take part in pagan sacrifices.

73. *my chosen people have stood the test like gold in the
assayer's fire:* cp. Isa. 48: 10; Zech. 13: 9; 1 Pet. 1: 7.

74–8. A final exhortation. Persecution is imminent, but
God will rescue those whom he has chosen. They should

have courage, and not allow themselves to be overcome by the deadly effects of sin.   ✵

✵   ✵   ✵   ✵   ✵   ✵   ✵   ✵   ✵   ✵   ✵   ✵   ✵

POSTSCRIPT

2 Esdras is a composite work which reflects the circumstances of three quite different periods. The largest and most important component within it, i.e. chs. 3–14, was written in response to the crisis of faith which overwhelmed Judaism in the years following the unsuccessful outcome of the revolt of A.D. 66–73. By the very nature of things its response to that crisis was expressed in the thought-forms and ideas of its own day, and thus it speaks of such topics as God, sin, or life after death in terms that may seem alien in the twentieth century. It also contains some specific prophecies about the end of this world order; the author believed that the end of this age would follow shortly after the death of the Emperor Domitian, and the fact that his prophecies, in common with many comparable biblical prophecies, were unfulfilled may likewise make his work seem strange or irrelevant. Despite this, there are two reasons why 2 Esdras 3–14 is still a work of considerable interest and importance; it represents a very serious attempt, at a specific point in time, to grapple with the difficulties of belief in God, and it provides a valuable picture of the kind of theological ideas which were current in some Jewish circles at more or less the same time as that at which many New Testament writings were composed.

Although 2 Esdras 3–14 is a Jewish work, it seems, like other apocalyptic writings, to have fallen out of favour amongst the Jews, and it owes its survival to the fact that it was taken over by the Christian Church. Within the Christian Church 2 Esdras 3–14 was held in high regard, and it was because of this that, in a time of persecution in the latter part of the third century A.D., a Christian author added chs. 15 and

16. Despite some uncertainties, it seems reasonably clear that these two additional chapters were composed from the outset as an appendix to chs. 3–14, the purpose of which was to make the earlier work refer more directly to a new situation. The author of this appendix urges his readers to stand firm in the face of persecution. The fact that he should have made this addition is an indication that, nearly two centuries after it was originally composed and in rather different circumstances, 2 Esdras 3–14 was still thought to have a relevant message to convey.

2 Esdras 1–2, a Christian work dating in all probability from the mid-second century A.D., is quite distinct from the remainder of 2 Esdras. The author takes up the question of the relationship of the Church to Judaism. His answer, that Israel has been completely rejected, and that the Church has taken her place, is no longer satisfying, but the question he raises is one of fundamental importance to practising Christians and Jews.

A NOTE ON FURTHER READING

A number of other commentaries on 2 Esdras are available. Those by W. O. E. Oesterley, Westminster Commentaries (London, 1933) and by J. M. Myers, Anchor Bible (Garden City, New York, 1974) cover the whole of 2 Esdras and are somewhat more detailed than the present volume. The commentary by G. H. Box, *The Ezra Apocalpyse* (London, 1912), is even more detailed, but deals only with chs. 3–14; it provides a mass of helpful information, but needs to be used with very great caution. Box reproduced the substance of this commentary in his contribution to the second volume of R. H. Charles, *The Apocrypha and Pseudepigrapha of the Old Testament* (see below).

The events which form the immediate background to 2 Esdras 3–14 are vividly described by Josephus in the *Jewish War*; the wider background, the history of the Roman Empire in the first century A.D. (and particularly in the troubled period which followed the death of Nero). is described in equally vivid terms by Suetonius (*The Lives of the Caesars*) and Tacitus (*The Histories*). English translations of all three works are available as Penguin Classics, or, together with the text, in the series The Loeb Classical Library. For a concise modern treatment of Jewish history in this period see M. Noth, *A History of Israel*, 2nd ed. (London, 1960); for Roman history see M. Cary and H. H. Scullard, *A History of Rome down to the Reign of Constantine*, 3rd ed. (London, 1975).

English translations of most of the apocalyptic and

related writings mentioned in this commentary (including 2 Esdras 3–14 itself) are available in vol. 2 of R. H. Charles, *The Apocrypha and Pseudepigrapha of the Old Testament in English* (Oxford, 1913; reprinted 1963), but for the Apocalypse of Abraham see the translation edited by G. H. Box (London, 1918). For 1 Enoch see also M. A. Knibb, in consultation with E. Ullendorff, *The Ethiopic Book of Enoch* (Oxford, 1978) (from which the translations in this commentary have been taken). K. Koch, *The Rediscovery of Apocalyptic* (London, 1972) provides a very lively and helpful account of the character of the apocalyptic writings.

A number of other Jewish and Christian writings have been mentioned or quoted in this volume, and for convenience a list of readily available English translations is given below:

The Dead Sea Scrolls: G. Vermes, *The Dead Sea Scrolls in English*, 2nd ed. (Harmondsworth, 1975).

The Mishnah: H. Danby, *The Mishnah* (Oxford, 1933).

Philo: F. H. Colson, G. H. Whitaker and R. Marcus, The Loeb Classical Library edition of the works of Philo.

The Shepherd of Hermas: Kirsopp Lake, The Loeb Classical Library edition of the Apostolic Fathers, vol. 2.

Eusebius, *Ecclesiastical History*: H. J. Lawlor and J. E. L. Oulton, *Eusebius. The Ecclesiastical History* (2 vols., London, 1927–8).

INDEX TO 1 ESDRAS

INDEX TO 2 ESDRAS